PRAISE FOR *MARKE*

'Will provide you with the approach, understanding and framework to create and execute a considered business marketing strategy that is primed for success. If you are new to marketing then this book could easily form the foundation of your marketing career. For experienced marketers, there is still plenty to learn.'
Ade Lewis, Partnerships Director, Mailchimp

'Jenna Tiffany adds to the body of knowledge on how to make an email marketing programme more effective and more profitable! The chapter on common pitfalls is particularly good as it addresses the most common issues head-on. If you're looking to start or improve an email marketing programme, this is a book that will help.'
Jeanne Jennings, CEO, Email Optimization Shop, General Manager, Only Influencers and Programming Chair, Email Innovations Summit

'Our research shows that many businesses don't have a digital marketing strategy, although they're actively using digital marketing. Even more lamentable, many don't have a marketing strategy to align with their digital strategy. If your business doesn't have a coherent marketing strategy, this book will provide you with a practical handbook that combines both classic marketing and brand strategy concepts with advice on tactics and execution, including digital channels, which are missing from many books on marketing strategy. You can use the many frameworks to guide your thinking, as well as interviews and examples from many practitioners to help inform your strategy.'
Dave Chaffey, Co-founder, SmartInsights.com (marketing training platform) and co-author of *Digital Marketing Strategy: Implementation and Practice*

'Jenna Tiffany is one of those marketing practitioners who manages to be an experienced *and* skilled tactician, as well as extremely adept at communicating strategic thinking and planning in the most clear and concise way.'
Nichola Stott, Managing Director, Erudite

'The modern marketer must truly understand what their strategy is to stand a chance of competing domestically, let alone in the global marketing place. My advice: stand on the shoulders of the marketing giants featured in this book and reap the rewards.'
James Delves, Head of PR and External Engagement, CIM (Chartered Institute of Marketing)

'A testament to Jenna Tiffany's unique approach to working; whether it's building from scratch or re-evaluating a current strategy, it's all about generating results. The interviews with real-life marketers add a unique layer and sprinkles added flavour, colour and relevance to an already insightful and practical read – a must for anyone looking to challenge or reaffirm what they're already doing.'
Gavin Laugenie, Head of Strategy and Insight, dotdigital

'A must-have for marketing strategy professionals and students alike. Its unwavering focus on the application of marketing theory using practical templates and insightful case studies shows you how to put theory into practice to create effective marketing strategies.'
Alicia Farrell, university marketing lecturer

'Simple, practical steps on how to break out from endless, frustrating, tactical marketing. This book belongs on every marketer's shelf.'
Tim Watson, professional EOS implementer

'A superbly practical, up-to-date and comprehensive marketing textbook that includes relevant updates on classic frameworks, insightful interviews and useful case studies. This easy-to-read guide to the art of marketing is a must for students and marketers alike, offering guidance not just on what to do and why, but also what not to do.'
Joolz Joseph FCIM, marketing mentor, trainer and university lecturer

'If I were to reference a credible source and a marketing practitioner, then Jenna Tiffany's contribution to our community of practice would be top of the list.'
William Ang'awa, Senior Lecturer in Marketing and Enterprise, Faculty of Business, Law and Tourism, University of Sunderland

Marketing Strategy

Overcome common pitfalls and create effective marketing

Jenna Tiffany

KoganPage

First published in Great Britain and the United States in 2021 by Kogan Page Limited

Apart from any fair dealing for the purposes of research or private study, or criticism or review, as permitted under the Copyright, Designs and Patents Act 1988, this publication may only be reproduced, stored or transmitted, in any form or by any means, with the prior permission in writing of the publishers, or in the case of reprographic reproduction in accordance with the terms and licences issued by the CLA. Enquiries concerning reproduction outside these terms should be sent to the publishers at the undermentioned addresses:

2nd Floor, 45 Gee Street	122 W 27th St, 10th Floor	4737/23 Ansari Road
London	New York, NY 10001	Daryaganj
EC1V 3RS	USA	New Delhi 110002
United Kingdom		India
www.koganpage.com		

Kogan Page books are printed on paper from sustainable forests.

© Jenna Tiffany, 2021

The right of Jenna Tiffany to be identified as the author of this work has been asserted by her in accordance with the Copyright, Designs and Patents Act 1988.

ISBNs

Hardback	978 1 78966 743 1
Paperback	978 1 78966 741 7
Ebook	978 1 78966 742 4

British Library Cataloguing-in-Publication Data

A CIP record for this book is available from the British Library.

Library of Congress Cataloging-in-Publication Data

Names: Tiffany, Jenna, author.
Title: Marketing strategy : overcome pitfalls and create effective
    marketing / Jenna Tiffany.
Description: 1 Edition. | New York : Kogan Page Inc, 2021. | Includes
    bibliographical references and index.
Identifiers: LCCN 2021007275 (print) | LCCN 2021007276 (ebook) | ISBN
    9781789667417 (paperback) | ISBN 9781789667431 (hardback) | ISBN
    9781789667424 (ebook)
Subjects: LCSH: Marketing. | Strategic planning.
Classification: LCC HF5415 .T5564 2021 (print) | LCC HF5415 (ebook) | DDC
    658.8/02–dc23
LC record available at https://lccn.loc.gov/2021007275
LC ebook record available at https://lccn.loc.gov/2021007276

Typeset by Integra Software Services, Pondicherry
Print production managed by Jellyfish
Printed and bound by CPI Group (UK) Ltd, Croydon, CR0 4YY

CONTENTS

LIST OF FIGURES AND TABLES

TABLES

ABOUT THE AUTHOR

 Jenna Tiffany, award-winning marketer, has been recognized as one of the top 50 marketers to follow in the world. She is the Founder and Strategy Director at marketing agency Let'sTalk Strategy, providing strategic consultancy services across the digital marketing mix. She is a Chartered Marketer and awarded Fellow of the Institute of Data & Marketing (IDM) with over ten years' marketing experience, and has consulted on marketing strategy with brands such as Shell, Hilton and World Duty Free.

Jenna is a keynote speaker, having spoken at hundreds of marketing events worldwide, and is an elected member of the prestigious DMA UK Email Marketing Council. Jenna is also a qualified teacher regularly teaching marketing at universities. She is frequently interviewed for her thoughts on marketing strategy and the latest trends.

Twitter: twitter.com/jennatiffany

LinkedIn: www.linkedin.com/in/jennatiffany/

Website: letstalkstrategy.co.uk/

FOREWORD

On a train journey a couple of years ago, that ended up being delayed by seven hours, I got talking to the man opposite. He was a consultant, from Brussels, but with a much kinder manner and a dozen times more energy than you'd expect from that mental picture. At one point in the conversation he mentioned a particular author.

'Ah, I think I've read something by him,' I said, mentioning the name of the book.

'I can't believe you've read that!' he said. 'He was my tutor! That's such a good book!'

It turned out he'd recently finished a triple MBA, taking up a couple of years of his life, and costing almost $200,000. I'd enjoyed the book, and found it hugely useful, so I asked him various questions about the author, and about the course, and what he'd learned. After a while I asked, 'Do you think it was worth the time and the cost?'

He thought for a moment and clarified: 'Worth it in general, or are you asking if it would be worth it for you?'

'Either…'.

He thought for a moment more and replied, 'Well, to be honest, if you've read that book you probably wouldn't learn a huge amount from the course.'

I'm sure it was an exaggeration, but perhaps not by a huge amount. A great book can literally perform magic. The right book, at the right moment in your life, can change the entire path of your future. An excellent book, by a skilled writer, with the right knowledge, can provide you with all of the concepts of the most expensive, or most in-depth course on Earth, in a fraction of the time, at a fraction of the cost. And the book you hold in front of you, whether digitally or in paper copy, is a niche deeper within that.

Jenna Tiffany is a Fellow of the Institute of Data & Marketing, a Chartered Marketer, has been recognized as one of the world's top 50 marketers to follow, and works to define and shape strategy for companies all over the world. Jenna has all the knowledge you could wish for on the two concepts that have changed the world more than almost any other over the last hundred years, and will shape it for at least the next hundred ahead of us.

Firstly, this book relates to marketing, the concept that defines almost everything around us today. Marketing is why the world's biggest companies are where they are. It is why Google and Apple are household names, and why Nokia is no longer. It is why the current President of the United States is the current President of the United States. It is why the food in your fridge is from the brands that you chose, and why you use the phone that you do, and why this book caught your eye in the first place.

Secondly, this book relates to strategy: 'The General's Wisdom', as the originating word loosely means, and a concept today much broader than military, and with a practicality beyond the modern definition of wisdom. Strategy is why some countries saved trillions of dollars, and thousands of lives, in the recent pandemic. Strategy is why Amazon is the business it is today, made up of more than a million people, in a wide variety of roles, and no longer – as it once was – a bookstore run from a garage, by a man who used a recycled door as a desk. Strategy is why your next business, or your next project, or your next product, may crawl forward in one direction, or why it will succeed beyond any expectation in another.

We are in the Golden Age of marketing strategy. An age where the tools and means of achieving huge marketing success are within reach of almost everyone on the planet. What separates the best from the others is firstly the will, and secondly the knowledge and ability to plan and execute better than their competitors. In picking up this book, it is apparent that you have the will; and in writing this book, Jenna has provided you with the history, and the knowledge, and the case studies, and the examples to allow you to create and shape and execute a winning marketing strategy.

Dan Barker
e-commerce consultant to more than 100 companies worldwide
@danbarker

Introduction

We are in a brand new era of marketing dominated by social media, reams of data, automation and the widely debated data privacy concerns.

Did you know that we have seven seconds to make a first impression when meeting someone new, face-to-face (Petrone, 2019)? Well, that mentality also applies to marketing. If you don't grab their attention immediately, the information-saturated consumer will delete, ignore or simply filter out your message. Research from Thinkbox (2018) revealed that 70 per cent of consumers are multi-screening each week. Even when watching TV (and particularly during the ad breaks) they're likely to be tuned into multiple other devices – surfing the web on their tablet or browsing social media on their phone. Where is their attention truly focused at one given time?

The tactically driven short-term approach to marketing has manifested itself into being discount driven. Black Friday now lasts a full month. Boxing Day sales start before Christmas Day is even over and summer sales get earlier each year. Is there ever a time when products are listed at full price for more than two weeks?

Strategy is often misunderstood, but its role is vital when producing marketing campaigns which win hearts, minds, accolades and conversions. In this straightforward and engaging book, I will draw on my years of experience as a world-renowned strategy expert to teach you all the skills you need to become a successful strategic marketer.

We will together cover everything you need to know about marketing strategy, from definitions to implementation, analysis and even history. With an easy-to-follow breakdown to create marketing strategies that include all elements, this book leaves no stone unturned.

Brand examples and workshop exercises will help you to apply the book's lessons to real marketing life simply and intuitively.

This book provides practical, real-life aid for its readers. It will give you the tools, the techniques and the structures you'll need to create a marketing strategy for every business.

So, if you're seeking a comprehensive and engaging guide to marketing strategy, written by an expert in the field, then let's get started!

The biggest error most marketers make when they develop a strategy is to not have one. I know that sounds basic but I see it time and time again. Marketers mistake tactics for strategy and fail miserably as a result. There are three phases to all marketing work. First, we diagnose the situation of the brand via consumer research and understand just what is going on. Secondly, we use that diagnosis to build a clear and simple marketing strategy. Finally, with that strategy in place, we select the appropriate tactics to deliver the strategy and win the day.

Strategy is a very complicated thing to work out but should be a very simple thing to eventually explain. In our world of marketing it comes down to being able to answer three basic questions and answer them long before we have started spending money on VR headsets and the latest Facebook ads. Who am I targeting? What is my position to that target? What are my strategic objectives for that target market? My current estimate is that around 20 per cent of brands could adequately or semi-adequately pass this test, and the rest have not the faintest clue how to even approach these questions. So the big error in my experience when it comes to marketing strategy is that most marketers don't have one.

Mark Ritson, 2020

Who is this book for?

I have written this book to help marketers, business owners, employers and students who are studying, interested in or working in marketing.

As a marketer myself, I spent years searching for that single book which would clearly explain the formula for creating a successful marketing strategy. But I never found it.

So, I finally decided to write it myself.

My aim is for readers to finish this book with a true understanding of what a marketing strategy is. I want to teach you how to recognize and avoid the common pitfalls facing marketers. I want you to learn the fundamentals of creating a winning strategy. I want to provide you with the context you'll need to adapt and innovate in a strategic way. And I want to do all of this in an easy-to-understand, practical way with my new frameworks to help guide you every step of the way.

My experience as a marketing consultant resonates with Mark Ritson's: that many brands simply do not have a marketing strategy.

Sure, they may have some bits and pieces here and there – but they don't have a complete strategy. Often, this is because they've let a focus on tactics overshadow the other equally (if not more) important elements of a successful strategy.

It's understandable. I refer to tactics as the 'shiny shiny' part of marketing. Tactics are what we, as marketers get excited about. They're the fun part. It's for tactics that we create and choose the imagery, design, content, message, marketing channels and so on.

Thing is: tactics are not the be-all and end-all. For a strategy to work as it should, it needs a lot more than a bunch of shiny tactics.

I am also increasingly concerned and frustrated by the lack of understanding regarding the elements contained in a marketing strategy, as well as strategy's often overlooked importance, and an industry-wide over-emphasis on tactics.

All of those vital elements you need to create a successful marketing strategy are what I'm going to teach you and share examples of in this book.

Why read this book?

You may already know what you want to do with your marketing. You may have some great ideas about how to do it. So, what's the point in reading this book?

Well, I'll go into this in more detail in Chapter 1, but, for starters:

1 *It will give your business direction.* A strategy is a roadmap to success. Without one, you're driving blind. As Mark Ritson says, 'Who are you targeting? What is your position relative to that target?' Without a strategy, you will lack even this most basic element of direction.

2 *It will make your tactics successful.* Ah, my bugbear – the constant confusion between 'strategy' and 'tactics'. I'll be covering this a lot in the following chapters. But let's set the tone by pointing out that a collection of independent tactics is nothing without the backbone of a solid strategy. My hope is that this book will convince you not to rush into a new campaign idea or project until you have set out a clear strategy. You must clearly determine what you are setting out to achieve before diving into shiny tactics.

3 *It will help you to gather the right data.* Data is virtual gold, but without a strategy, you'll be blindly panning data streams, sifting through dust and rocks but never hitting the valuable pieces.

4 *It will build trust with your audience.* A strategy will help you to get to know your audience, to build a relationship with them, and to gain their trust. Trust is crucial in our era of data-savvy and privacy-concerned consumerism.

5 *It will improve your performance.* All of the above (plus more – read on!) add up to massive performance gains, huge ROI and KPIs smashed through the roof. Sound good? It is! And it's not as complicated as it sounds. This book will help you to achieve all of the above in the simplest and most straightforward way possible.

The structure of this book

These chapters follow the stages involved in creating a marketing strategy from start to finish. To do this I have turned the word STRATEGY into an acronym which provides you with a checklist to ensure no element is left out. Inside each chapter are tasks to complete along with my examples detailing the strategy I created to launch this book. The book concludes with 10 of the most common pitfalls facing marketers and tips on how to avoid and overcome each one.

The chapters are as follows:

Chapter 1. What is strategy? This chapter covers the definition and importance of marketing strategy, as well as running through its history and evolution.

Chapter 2. Scenario: Establishing the current situation. This chapter includes various models and frameworks to analyse the marketing environment and how this affects an organization. It also looks at segmentation, targeting and the positioning of your audience, as well as how to determine a company's competitive advantage and how to work out whether or not you are attracting the right kind of customer.

Chapter 3. Targets: Setting objectives. Determining objectives is a crucial aspect of any strategy. This step will steer the rest of your strategy's development. In this chapter I will share a new acronym which will help you to SCALE your objectives.

Chapter 4. Reach: Researching your customers. Here we'll go into the most important element of any strategy: the customer. This chapter will cover how to identify, understand, segment, target and build relationships with your audiences.

Chapter 5. Awareness: Planning your marketing campaign. This chapter looks at how you can turn your strategy into a successful marketing campaign.

Chapter 6. Tactics: Selecting the right channels. This chapter will provide insight into how to pick the right channels and tactics for your strategy. We'll also cover how to weave tactics into a campaign so that they complement the strategy and drive conversion.

Chapter 7. Execution: Implementing your marketing strategy. This is the bit you've been waiting for! Time to let your strategy and campaign loose on your audience. In this chapter, I'll cover how you can do this most effectively.

Chapter 8. Generate: Tracking the results. The ability to measure the success of a marketing strategy is key to business budgeting decisions. In this chapter, I will outline an effective action plan, how to choose the right marketing KPIs for your business, and how to control success.

Chapter 9. Yield: Analysing your strategy's success. A full post-mortem analysis should be conducted to determine what went well, what underperformed and (most importantly) to critically assess why. How to do this will be covered in this chapter.

Chapter 10. Common pitfalls in marketing strategy. Ten of the most common pitfalls facing marketers are featured in this chapter. I include examples and tips from my extensive marketing experience on how to avoid and overcome these pitfalls if you ever find yourself facing any one of them.

References

Petrone, P (2019) You have 7 seconds to make a good first impression [Online], LinkedIn Learning Blog, available at: www.linkedin.com/business/learning/blog/productivity-tips/body-language-to-make-a-good-impression (archived at https://perma.cc/3Q68-VFHP)

Ritson, M (2020) Marketing Thought Leader [Interview] 13 October 2020

Thinkbox (2020) Multi-screening [Online], Thinkbox, available at: www.thinkbox.tv/research/nickable-charts/vod-and-devices/multi-screening/ (archived at https://perma.cc/H9GJ-GY5X)

01

What is strategy?

This chapter covers:

- The definition of strategy.
- The difference between strategy and tactics.
- The history of marketing and it's evolution.

Definitions

Simply put:

Strategy is the map which takes you to your destination.

Tactics are the vehicles you use to get there.

Tactics are the 'how'.

Strategy is the 'who, what, where, when and why'.

Let's dig a little deeper.

Sun Tzu is one of the greatest strategists of them all. More than two millennia ago, he defined strategy in ways which are still relevant today:

> Strategy without tactics is the slowest route to victory. Tactics without strategy is the noise before defeat.
>
> Sun Tzu, *The Art of War*

Strategy and tactics work together, hand-in-hand. Neither will be as effective as they could be on their own. Unfortunately, many marketing campaigns today tend to be 'noise before defeat' – throwing tactics around without much strategy. Remember General Motors? The car company that famously went out of business in 2009 for their reluctance to keep up with changing times? For decades, their 'strategy' was little more than a fixed deck of tactics. Later in this chapter we'll uncover the damage this did to the brand.

Most modern marketers are well versed in the execution – the tactical 'how' – of a marketing plan. However, not many have been taught, have learned or experienced the 'who', 'what' and 'when' of strategy. This is where this book will take your marketing efforts to a strategic level.

To recap:

Strategy = the who, what, where, why and when

Tactics = the how

For example, when planning this book, my strategy involved:

- *Who* – identifying my audience (that's you, readers! marketing students, managers, business owners) to then be able to establish what my audience would find most useful to read about.
- *Where* – working out where I'd distribute the book to reach that audience (online and in appropriate retailers).
- *What* – considering how I could adapt and utilize my skills and resources to best suit the needs of my customers. For example, I can bring my years of experience to the fore – but this is my first book. However, I can employ proofreaders, editors and publishing industry experts to mitigate lack of author experience.
- *When* – setting out a timescale for completion and publication.

The next step is 'how', which is the tactical part. For this book that involves, for example, speaking at events and taking part in interviews (more detail on this in Chapter 6). As you can see, the strategic element always comes first. Tactics come into play afterwards to implement the strategy.

In this book I will guide you through the S-T-R-A-T-E-G-Y framework. As an example below, the tactics are defined after S-T-R-A when the following questions are answered:

S: *Scenario* – Where is the business now?

T: *Targets* – What are the objectives?

R: *Reach* – Who is your customer?

A: *Awareness* – How will you drive awareness to the target market?

Only after we've answered these questions do we bring tactics into the picture.

Using this framework I've created, it is easier to identify the different stages of creating a strategy and ensuring they follow this sequence. It's useful both when building a brand new strategy and when identifying potential gaps in an existing one.

Five reasons why you need a marketing strategy

For those who need a reminder, here are the five major reasons why you need a marketing strategy:

1 It will give your business direction.

2 It will make your tactics successful.

3 It will help you to gather the right data.

4 It will build trust with your audience.

5 It will improve your performance.

Let's unpack those five points below.

1. It will give your business direction

As Kevin Dunckley, Chief Digital & Innovation Officer from HH Global puts it: 'Without a plan you are planning to fail and marketing is no different. How can you hit your target if you don't know where it is?' (Dunckley, 2020).

I am sure that your business is heading in a particular direction, aiming to achieve specific goals and objectives. But, as Dunckley (2020) highlights, how is your marketing going to help this process without a plan? Well, it won't.

There is a place for ad hoc tactical activity when something changes last minute, or when a new product becomes available. But having 90 per cent of your marketing operate on an ad hoc basis means that you'll struggle to understand what you're trying to achieve from one minute to the next, let alone to communicate clearly with your audience. As for managing your marketing budget and securing your bottom line – you can forget about that when operating without a clear plan.

A strategy will give you a clear roadmap towards your goals and objectives. Your strategy will define the who, where and when of your message. Who needs to hear your message? When? Where can you reach them?

2. It will make your tactics successful

From working with and talking to many marketers, I understand that tactics have increasingly become the main focus of activity in a lot of cases. That's understandable. Tactics are fun! Many of us are creative 'ideas' people, and may not get as excited about long-term planning.

However, you really do need that long-term strategic planning if your tactics are going to work out. If you haven't got a long-term goal in place, data analytics informing your decisions or even market research, how do you know that your tactics are appropriate? How do you even know what they are? Putting tactics into play without an overarching strategy is like buying all of the ingredients to bake a cake without knowing which type of cake you're baking. A recipe for disaster, as Steve Kemish, Managing Partner & IDM Trainer at Junction Agency explains:

> … it's critical an organization has a marketing strategy. Without this, it is very hard to ensure your marketing effort – resource, budget and time – are all used effectively and in a way that delivers commercial value for the organization. A marketing approach that isn't aligned to the key goals and aims of the overall organization, is destined to struggle and fail.

Short-term tactics have a place, but not for 90 per cent of your marketing activity. As Steve explains, this will reduce the effectiveness of your marketing strategy. With consumers increasingly busy and distracted, now is the time to have an 80 per cent strategically focused and 20 per cent ad hoc marketing plan.

3. It will help you to gather the right data

Data is like virtual gold, giving unprecedented insights into consumer wants and needs. However, the issue of data collection and analytics is not as simple as it used to be. The General Data Protection Regulation 2018 (GDPR) has enshrined data protection in European law, and not a moment too soon so far as the public is concerned.

Events like the Cambridge Analytica scandal have eroded a lot of public trust in data-gathering practices. The GDPR is helping to restore that trust, but there's a long way to go.

Gathering data is not impossible – but you should never do it without the customer's full knowledge and permission. You must demonstrate to the customer that providing their data will be of benefit to them – and, legally, they must provide informed consent before you can extract, store or use their data.

Without data collection and analysis woven into your strategic plan, you'll struggle to gather any data at all – let alone relevant data which can provide you with those all-important insights.

4. It will build trust with your audience

Trust is crucial for successful marketing. Building faith between brand and customer involves creating 1:1 communications which are useful and relevant for the recipient. This can't be done without a good strategy.

Your strategy (supported by data insights and research) will inform the direction you take. It will help you to identify consumer needs, preferences and ideals. It will flag up problems, warn of weaknesses and help you to give your customers consistent value. It will ensure that you are talking to an audience which you know and with whom you've developed a relationship, rather than shooting into the dark.

Beyond individual campaigns, strategizing will give you a greater understanding of how customers engage with your product or service. This is very helpful for improving your offering as a brand.

All of this will create a closer relationship with your audience, and close relationships foster trust. Trust is what customer loyalty is made of – and as James Delves from the Chartered Institute of Marketing (CIM) rightly highlights in the interview at the end of this chapter 'trust can take years to secure and just moments to lose' (Delves, 2020).

5. It will improve your performance

A planned approach to your marketing will enable you to quickly and easily identify areas of your activity which are performing well, as well as those areas which aren't.

Knowing what you're doing well and what you're struggling with is crucial to refining and improving your activity. If you want to seriously up your performance, a good strategy is essential!

The modern strategic challenge

If we're to face up to this rapidly changing world, strategy is more than just important: it's essential. Modern marketing is confronted with some unprecedented challenges, which only strategizing can overcome.

It wasn't so long ago (about 50 years ago) that you could walk into your local store and the shop owner would have known your entire life story. From memory, they'd have known your size, your preferences, your typical purchases. Technology wasn't part of everyday life back then; the virtual conversation didn't even exist.

Fast forward to today. Technology has pushed a surge of social media and messaging platforms. Modern devices have changed how we communicate. We can now have multiple conversations all at the same time on multiple social platforms without even leaving our beds! It's become a crucial part of everyday life – 17 per cent of Americans check their email as soon as they wake up! (Sleep Advisor, 2020). What's more, according to Ofcom (2020) the amount of time we spend online each day is growing exponentially – particularly since Covid-19 forced us to rely on digital communications for pretty much everything.

All of this new technology has led to the rise of the mobile, 'always-on' consumer. People are constantly on the go. Purchasing paths have changed drastically and mobile technology has transformed the public's expectations of real-time, relevant messaging. This all has a bearing on how a brand's message is perceived – if it's even received at all.

One consequence of all this is message overload. The competition for consumer attention is real, and it's fierce. As a marketer, you now have much less time in which to make your move.

Consumer patience is a thing of the past. This is in part due to the rise of disruptive brands such as Uber, who have conditioned customers to wait a maximum of three minutes for a taxi. If the taxi isn't nearby, it will lose its potential customer. This has a huge impact on how people receive brand messages.

To see what I mean, go onto any crowdfunding website where brand new, innovative products are launched every day and observe how appalled many people are by the idea of waiting for any given process or product.

In a world of one-click shopping, consumers expect an immediate email confirmation and delivery in days, no matter the item. Failure to do so can cause a lot of anger.

In 2016, for example, Apple had to delay the release of their new AirPods because they did not yet work properly. However, the world was not impressed. Engadget (2016) called the delay 'an unusual and humbling let-down', and popular podcaster Rush Limbaugh (2016) ran a show entitled 'Is Apple losing its edge?' More recently, online grocery company Ocado experienced a massive drop in ratings (*Financial Times*, 2020) as they struggled to maintain their normal delivery standards during the huge demands of the Covid-19 lockdown. It seems that not even a global pandemic mitigates people's need for immediate service – or their anger when it's not provided.

It's also worth noting that budgets are tighter than ever before – particularly since Covid-19 dealt a blow to many bank accounts. Marketing really has to prove its worth and ensure that your campaigns aren't wasting any of your precious budget. You can't just wing it – every penny spent must be justified by a comprehensive strategy.

What does this mean for marketing?

It may sound like a lot of doom and gloom but, in fact, it means that things just got a whole lot more interesting.

You can't 'grab' the attention of a 'captive' audience any more. Tactics-based marketing just won't cut it. If you want people to focus on your message, your campaign needs to be targeted, punchy, timely and on-message – something only a good strategy can ensure.

To explain what I mean, let's take a look at a common issue with modern marketing: the strategy-free strategy.

The strategy-free strategy

As I mentioned earlier, a lot of marketers mistake tactics for strategy. Apart from the fact that tactics are fun and creative while 'strategy' sounds way more serious (it's not – but I know it gives that impression), there's a good reason for this. And that reason exemplifies one of the problems with promotion-based marketing.

Many marketers have, for some time, been tasked with promoting constant sales messaging, with discounts, offers, etc. Discounts and offers are tactics. They are not strategies. But a lot of marketing over the past few decades has focused solely on these kinds of tactics nonetheless. The result is a generation of marketers who've learned to view tactics as strategy.

It goes a bit like this: A managing director or sales director of a business will tell marketing, 'We need to drive more sales in June' and – hey presto – a 10 per cent off promotional offer is born.

Great! Money-off promotions can be a great tactic… IF they're informed by a good strategy.

Here's the big problem with strategy-free sales drives: everyone has the same idea at the same time. We're all using the same methods to draw in customers and sell our stuff:

> Strategy is essentially about prioritizing down to a very few hard choices. This gives rise to challenges when colleagues believe that wider audiences, wider offers, and more customer choice will lead to growth instead of recognizing that leads to bland customer experiences and weak differentiation. Less is always more.
> Robert Hancock, Managing Director at Marketing Know-How, 2020

Think of the retail industry. With the exception of higher-end verticals like luxury clothing and fragrances, the retail marketing calendar is typically filled with price-cut events and seasonal sales. So much so that things like the DFS sale are a running joke and have been 'ending soon' for over 18 years (Comedy Central, 2020).

And it's not as if these sales drive profits. All they do is shift revenue around the calendar. High sales in January draw from a slump in July, and so on. Where is the long-term vision in a constant reel of sales and slumps? Does this lack of foresight not have a worrying tinge of the traditional retail collapse about it?

The internet has altered consumer behaviour and expectations forever. But many retailers haven't changed to meet those expectations. They're focusing solely on sales tactics; they're not looking at the bigger strategic picture. And the high-street shopping experience is suffering as a result.

Walk into a clothing store now and you'll be greeted with the same kind of bland layout that you'd have seen 10 or even 20 years ago. The products may be new, but the basic experience is the same. In my opinion, there's a huge lack of energy and soul in high-street shopping – what exactly is different about this shop to any other retailer?

But this can all be changed with the right strategy.

A few years ago, I was in Paris visiting clients, and I will never forget the experience of entering a Hollister store for the first time.

While their brand and products are targeted for a much younger age group than me, the entire experience of shopping in Hollister is unique. All three senses of sight, sound and smell are engaged at the door (where you're greeted by a model wearing the latest swimwear all year round!) The inside of the store has no resemblance to any other shop I could name. It has the relaxed vibe that you get when walking into a friend's house. The scent that can be smelt throughout the store is from the brand's signature perfume. The staff match their target demographic in terms of age. They are friendly, relaxed, not overly pushy, and they don't follow you around the store.

This, for me, is an example of a brand that really understands how important strategy is. They've not got tactics tunnel-vision. They're working from a bigger strategic picture. And it shows in the immersive nature of their shopping experience.

Hollister hasn't just created their business and marketing strategy on paper; they live by and believe it. They have a clear identity, of which their stores are an excellent example. As their website states, 'The Hollister brand epitomizes the liberating and carefree spirit of the endless California summer for the teen market' (Abercrombie & Fitch, 2020). Hollister has built this strategic vision into the very fabric of their stores – and it's working well for them. Right now, retail chains are dropping like flies. High streets are emptying out. But at the time of writing Hollister is still going strong.

It is clear to me that failing retail chains are suffering from a lack of strategy. Without the insights and direction provided by a strategy, they can't adapt to the changing times. Unlike Hollister, they're struggling to identify and engage with the evolving needs of their target customer. The end result of this approach is an increasing need to use short-term promotions and discounts, which repeatedly erodes the value and profits of the company. Consequently, there is less available to invest in the long-term success of the brand, and customers are trained to expect (and will only engage when there are) discounted price promotions.

We'll take a closer look at how to analyse the marketing environment successfully in Chapter 2 but, for now, let's focus on how we can get modern marketing back on track.

What can be done?

This sales tactics vs overall strategy issue is a hard one for grassroots marketers to overcome. After beating the drum that this short-sighted sale cycle isn't going to be the best solution long term, we often find that our message is not heard. So, we give up and cave in to the constant sales and push messaging. Unmotivating, isn't it?

But you're in the right place to change everything.

By focusing on strategy first rather than focusing on tactics, the bigger picture suddenly becomes a lot clearer for everyone – marketers and the brand bosses included. At last, everyone is on the same page!

Which brings me, finally, to what a strategy actually is in detail.

What a strategy is

A strategy is an overarching plan by which you hope to achieve your vision.

A good strategy should be **well researched,** have strongly defined **goals** and act as a **roadmap** towards achieving **clear objectives.**

FIGURE 1.1 The STRATEGY framework

S • **SCENARIO** Where is the business now? What situation is it in, what could impact the organization and what's changing externally?

T • **TARGET** What is the desired destination, ambition? What are your objectives?

R • **REACH** What is the appropriate route to take to attract and engage your customer?

A • **AWARENESS** How will you raise awareness with your target customers?

T • **TACTICS** What tactics are you going to use and how they are going to be used?

E • **EXECUTE** How will the strategy be executed, and what resources, skills and tools do you need?

G • **GENERATE** How are you going to track marketing performance, measure results and response?

Y • **YIELD** What KPIs will you use? What learnings will you take to improve or inform the next marketing campaign?

To identify the key stages in strategy building, I created an acronym from the word STRATEGY (Figure 1.1). Each letter represents, in order, the steps to take when creating a strategy and is the flow of this book.

To get a bit deeper into what we mean, let's take a closer look at the marketing scene over the past few decades.

How did we get here? A quick history of marketing

> Marketing is the management process responsible for **identifying, anticipating** and **satisfying** customer requirements profitably.
>
> CIM official definition, 1976 (CIM, 2020)

I've highlighted the key terms to take away from this quote: our role, as marketers, has always been to **identify, anticipate** and **satisfy** customer needs. It's worth reminding ourselves of this when we're wrestling with things like sales targets.

Figure 1.2 illustrates the various stages, or 'eras', in the development of marketing.

SIMPLE TRADE ERA

Before the Industrial Revolution, every product was made or harvested by hand. As such, supply was limited. Once something had sold out, it took a lot of effort to replenish the stock.

The way we purchased goods was very different from the methods we use now. Exchanges were made with whatever the purchaser had available, and commodities ruled the day.

PRODUCTION ERA: 1860S TO 1920S

New production methods expanded the marketplace throughout this era, and manufacturing brands thrived on new, faster, cheaper ways to make their products.

FIGURE 1.2   The history of marketing

After approximately 60 years, however, a new issue began to arise — too much stock, and saturated demand. Brands needed to find a way to reignite that demand and shift their stock. Which leads us to...

SALES ERA: 1920S TO 1940S

By this point, businesses could no longer easily sell everything they produced. So, brands began to seek new ways to differentiate their own products from those of competitors.

Enter the salesman (and nearly all of them at this time were men). The salesman's job was to convince customers that their brand's product was the very best in the market. This is where billboards and sales teams were first introduced, and it was a significant shift in culture to what had gone before. And then along came World War II.

Following World War II, many soldiers left the forces and created their own businesses. They brought wartime experiences to the fore, and the organizations they founded owed much to military structuring, methodology and operations.

The post-war business revolution led to...

MARKETING DEPARTMENT ERA: 1940S TO 1960S

Following the war 'marketing departments' began to emerge as part of the squad- (or team-) based military model that a lot of post-war businesses used. These departments were essentially platoons for marketing, with a top-down hierarchical structure.

As the era progressed, manufacturing firms began to realize that the sales-oriented approach of the previous era was no longer resonating with their consumers. People were growing increasingly affluent, which gave them greater power. In response, marketing departments started to focus heavily on the customer.

MARKETING COMPANY ERA: 1960S TO 1990S

In this era a new marketing concept became widely accepted. The idea was that every business exists to address customer needs and that the customer should be the focus of all business endeavours. The customer became King. Consequently, marketing assumed prominence across all aspects of a business. In the classic theory of marketing evolution, this is the final phase and is still in play today.

RELATIONSHIP MARKETING ERA: 1990s–2010s

The next significant shift in marketing occurred when services entered the mix.

Services have some differences to products and need a slightly different marketing strategy approach because of the complex nature of service models. So, a different approach was developed which led to several new theories – most notably the transformation of 'The 4Ps' to 'The 7Ps' in order to add service marketing.

SOCIAL MOBILE MARKETING ERA: 2010s–2020s

This, along with the 'marketing company era' and the 'relationship marketing era', is one of the most relevant for marketing today.

The social mobile marketing era is about communicating with the 'always-on' mobile consumer. The development of social media, artificial intelligence (AI), and other digital innovations presents both great opportunities and complex challenges for marketers.

Are you stuck in the post-war era?

The world has changed a lot, but many brands haven't changed with it.

A lot of companies are suffering because they are still using the same (or lack of) strategies from the post-war era. While these approaches certainly helped to win the war, modern business has very different needs to a 1930s military unit.

A modern business needs to be able to adapt swiftly and creatively to new challenges. It must be agile in order to respond to the unforeseen. A military-style operation just isn't capable of this. With endless protocols to follow and permissions to be sought, the post-war mode of business is simply too rigid.

Let me illustrate what I mean by taking you through the General Motors problem.

The General Motors problem

When modernizing his corporation in the 1930s and 40s, Alfred Sloan of General Motors introduced a rigid, military-style hierarchy. Rank determined responsibility. All orders flowed downwards. Under Sloan, little to no feedback could work its way back up the chain of command. Thick books appeared, filled with reams of marketing intelligence, tactics and procedures. To anyone who has ever worked for or with the military, this will all seem very familiar.

And it worked. For the world in which Sloan was operating, this kind of rigid formalization of procedure was right. General Motors was able to emerge from the fog of post-war confusion and market itself as a stable, reliable manufacturer (*Automotive News*, 2008).

But the modern world is very different from the one in which Alfred Sloan was operating. Things these days are much more fluid; scrutiny is more intense, and change is a whole lot faster. It's not enough to be stable – in fact, those rigid foundations may well prove a bit too heavy for a company to pull ahead in the modern world.

General Motors did not transition well into modernity. The company was dogged with problems; in the late 20th and early 21st century, it had to recall faulty vehicles several times. These vehicles would never, in a more communicative, more adaptable and less militaristic company, have made it off the factory floor.

As a consequence, falling profits and a loss of consumer trust saw General Motors liquidated in 2009. Its successor – General Motors Company LLC – inherited much of the old organization's structure and found itself confronted with the same problems.

Commentators on the General Motors saga have been quick to call out a business structure which does not allow for feedback, thus preventing 'lower ranks' (the factory-floor engineers and vehicle testers) from alerting senior management to problems (Guilford, 2018). This non-adaptive, non-listening culture permeated the organization so deeply that it even began to extend to customer feedback, leaving General Motors blind to its worsening problems until things were too late.

GM vs Ford

By contrast, General Motors' major rival, Ford, reformed their structure to allow communication both down and up the chain of command. Those who reported risks and issues within both the company's products and the company's culture were rewarded rather than penalized for 'backtalk'. Senior management made themselves more accessible to the rest of the workforce and the company's structure as a whole became more fluid – allowing for effective communication at all levels.

The company was rewarded with a flourishing of creativity, hugely improved products, and a significant increase in customer satisfaction.

So what's all this got to do with marketing strategy? Everything! A company's structure reflects its vision (more on that in a moment), which impacts every aspect of the company's operation. Thinking about how your company is structured and the problems that may arise as a result of this structure is an excellent way of identifying where (and why) you may be having issues within your marketing strategy.

A marketing strategy must complement the overall business strategy and contribute towards its achievement. If an organization has not clearly defined its business strategy, then the marketing strategy may also lack focus (and vice versa).

There are times when situational research (covered in Chapter 2) throws up new information which is relevant to a pre-existing business strategy. The ideal scenario in this case would be that the organization has a clearly defined business strategy that the marketing strategy can draw upon to influence things like the direction of the plan and the business objectives. However, this isn't always the case.

In those instances where the organization doesn't have a defined business strategy, marketing strategy can start to drive the need for one.

As marketers, we can bring a lot of information, insights, tools, techniques and experience to a business. Marketers can, if conducting regular analysis and research, become the voice of the customer in an organization.

Modern commerce is evolving into a form which replaces certainties with probabilities. Modern strategists need to accept that these probabilities will alter rapidly and in real time. Businesses which can't adapt to this pace and these modes of thought will never evolve into the digital world and will swiftly find themselves becoming irrelevant to the modern market.

Both businesses as a whole and marketers in particular can survive and thrive in this fast-changing world through strategy.

Where should you start? I suggest with a Vision.

Vision

A vision is the cornerstone of any decent strategy.

Steve Jobs had a clear vision. His vision was to develop technology for everyone (Fell and Sun, 2020). This vision, alongside his core principles and values, is what drove Apple to success, rising from a 1976 garage side-project to a company now valued at a trillion dollars (Stone, 2018). Jobs never deviated from his vision. Not even when times were tough for the business and when pressure mounted to sell more products. He stuck to his core principles and his vision – and it paid off.

Jobs' actions in maintaining his vision even when sales suffered were unusual. Most retail organizations today cave into the pressure to sell, sell, sell. Hitting sales targets becomes the core goal of the business, whatever the cost. In doing so, these organizations often sacrifice their brand, their values and – in the long term – their vision.

This loss of vision (or transformation of 'vision' into 'sales targets') can be devastating for a brand and company culture. Visions are incredibly important. They are what bring everyone within an organization together to achieve a common goal. They are the soul of the company and will give vitality to your strategy.

Without a real vision, the objectives of the business and the direction in which it is heading will become blurred and unfocused.

EXAMPLE 'VISION' STATEMENTS

Amazon: 'We aim to be earth's most customer centric company' (Amazon, 2020).

Ikea: 'Our vision is to create a better everyday life for the many people – for customers, but also for our co-workers and the people who work at our suppliers' (Ikea, 2020).

WWF: 'Our vision is to build a future in which people live in harmony with nature' (WWF, 2018).

Remember — people follow people, not concepts. Your business leaders need to promote your vision if it's going to be the driving force that it needs to be. If they follow the vision, your other employees will take their lead. But they'll also follow if business leaders turn away from the vision. Refer back to the vision frequently. Remind people what they're aiming for, and why. Make the vision a part of your team's culture, and it will become easier for everyone to understand and implement it.

There are many challenges when communicating the roll-out of a new vision (or refreshing an established vision). One common problem occurs when the teams which create the vision are fixed in their way of thinking and/or have a closed team culture. In cases like these, communicating the vision outside those teams will be difficult, as employees on the 'outside' will find it hard to understand the thinking behind the vision. This is one of the reasons why the structure of the whole business is so important for a successful marketing strategy.

There can also be a lack of connection between the vision and the direction of the organization. This can be caused by several factors. In my experience, most ultimately come back to the CEO not clearly communicating the direction of the company. If the desired direction isn't clearly outlined at the start the vision won't match. A great example of this is Ryanair.

Ryanair's CEO Michael O'Leary has a clearly defined vision: 'To offer low fares that generate increased passenger traffic while maintaining a continuous focus on cost containment and efficiency operation' (Ryanair, 2020).

Everyone, employees and customers alike, know what they are buying into: low-cost air travel which is stripped back to the bare basics. If you want to add more to the basic service, each additional extra (eg baggage, a specific seat, food, early check-in) is chargeable. This is how the company can provide flights at a cheaper price than competitors. Even the aircrafts are stripped back to the bare essentials – Ryanair travel isn't luxurious because that isn't their vision.

For visions that are already in place, a very common issue is employees forgetting what it is or dismissing it entirely as one of those 'marketing things'.

TIPS

1 The vision needs to be easy to remember, succinct and written in the language used throughout the company. If the language is overly complex and does not fit with the organizational culture, it won't be remembered. If the vision is overly wordy and trying to say too many things without a clear point then, again, it will be difficult to remember. I once worked for a company which was creating a new vision. The goal was to define the direction of the company. However, when the vision statement was created, it was more than four lines of text, using overly complicated words and (worst of all), the senior leadership team struggled to remember it! This

meant that each team had a different take of the vision based on what the senior leading director could remember. Reciting the new vision from memory even became a quiz question at the company's monthly quiz! So do try to make the statement as succinct as possible. The shorter the better.

2   Encourage employees from each department to participate in the creation of the vision. If they are part of the process, they will feel invested and advocate for the vision company-wide. Without a selection of employees involved in the process, employees in general will be less likely to engage with it.

3   Regular check-ups on how the vision is being implemented in each department are also important. Tip 2 is a good way to start this, but do also ensure that the senior management team is involved. This will demonstrate that the vision is a company-wide initiative, and will be checked upon. The senior leaders of the company can also help support the roll-out across the business. Checks could be conducted each month and could be included on the wall of each meeting room (or in the main room of the office) to be a constant reminder.

4   Rewarding employees and/or departments that are actively engaging with the new vision is an effective way to bring the vision to life. A reward system will help everyone to understand the vision beyond its words. It also encourages others to follow suit. There is a balance, though, as *over-rewarding* could cause resentment amongst other teams or employees, and therefore a negative relationship with the vision, so rewards do need to be treated with caution. A small reward with a clear explanation as to why it has been won and how that relates to the new vision would be ideal. Rewards don't have to be monetary: a reward could be something like an additional annual leave day.

5   Choose the person who delivers the vision statement to the company carefully. For many organizations, the obvious person to deliver the new vision would be the CEO or managing director. But, if that person is not a good public speaker, isn't energetic or doesn't portray positivity, then nominate another person. From experience, if the person presenting the vision isn't enthusiastic about doing so or doesn't communicate it clearly, then all the time and effort spent on establishing a vision will be wasted.

6   In the same vein, ensure that the representative is well briefed on any answers to give to potential questions. This is important. The vision may be communicated effectively and then fall flat on its face because an employee asks a question to which the representative doesn't have an answer. Admittedly it will be difficult to prepare for all potential questions, but you can at least establish a clear response if a question asked needs more time to respond to. Confidence will be lost if, at any stage, the vision appears not to have been thoroughly thought through. Also, be sure to have a way for employees to raise any questions after the 'launch'.

7   Most of all, make the vision's delivery fun. This is an exciting milestone! The communication and roll-out don't need to be stiff; you can even use a party format with games and quizzes.

From vision to strategy

Once you've established a vision, you should find that you have a much clearer idea of your brand's direction, values and so on. You're now fully equipped to get beyond the theory and into the fine detail of strategizing.

The process of creating a strategic marketing plan should start like this:

1   Conduct market research (find out the 'who').

2   Define your marketing objectives and goals (I'll go into the difference between objectives and goals in Chapter 3).

3   Segment the audience to target them effectively.

These foundation steps should be taken long before you even start thinking about tactics.

These should be first and foremost, front and centre when you're working out your strategy. Without identifying marketing objectives and goals your focus will be unclear. You won't know where to concentrate your efforts and how to measure your performance.

Often, however, marketing campaigns aren't planned this way. The biggest challenge when I'm consulting with brands on strategic marketing is that they'll have already predetermined the execution (the tactical 'how') element of the plan. Things like the channel that is going to be used and even the ad copy are decided long before the key goals (if they ever get decided at all). When I ask these same companies 'what are the objectives, goals and target markets of each activity?', I'm faced with confusion (see why 'tactics before strategy' is a bugbear of mine). They know the answer to the objectives and goals question, but they don't understand why it's essential to establish these things.

The point is that creating any activity without clear objectives and goals inevitably ends in confusion. Being unclear in what you're trying to achieve will make it difficult to determine if you've reached a good result.

A strategy is there to help you: the marketer establishes a plan to achieve set goals and objectives. A strategy should always define the 'why' before the 'how'. This links back to the 'vision' aspect we mentioned earlier in this chapter. At all points, the overarching goals and objectives of each strategy should be working towards the brand's vision as a whole. We will go through how to create marketing objectives in Chapter 3.

But first – a bit of housekeeping, some hints and a word or two of caution!

WHERE DOES STRATEGY COME IN?

We've covered some of the most vital reasons why strategy is important. It gives your campaign direction, it clarifies your objectives, it's essential for campaign success. But, as the length of this book should suggest, there's a bit more to it than that.

There are many more specific (and more individualized) reasons why a strategy is important to a given brand (and I've suggested five to present to your team, manager or co-worker at the end of this section). These reasons have a lot to do with the number of challenges to overcome before our message gets through, such as diminishing attention spans of audiences, dual screening where attention is distracted and disruptive new competitors entering existing markets. Let's look at these in more detail below.

Let's take disruptive competition as an example, as it's this factor which is driving the changing relationship with content and technology (at least, from a marketing point of view). 'Disruptive companies' include famous names like Airbnb, Amazon, Netflix, Uber. Genuinely disruptive companies have changed the landscape of their industries forever and, with that, they have changed customers' expectations.

Disruptive technological changes such as the IoT (Internet of Things), voice technology, AI and machine learning have a massive influence on consumer behaviour in terms of on-demand, 24/7, at the press of a button expectations. Information availability and interconnectivity between devices (and between the consumer and brand) are now anticipated as standard.

What's this got to do with strategy? Well, it raises expectations from your company towards you as a marketer to provide the customer with what they want (instantly) and, what's more, to know what that is without the customer telling you. That's hard enough as it is but, without a good strategy, it's impossible.

If you're still playing the short-term, week-by-week tactical game without focusing on the long-term strategic plan, you're at huge risk of being left behind and failing to meet those customer requirements which, if we remember back to the CIM quote at the beginning of this chapter ('Marketing is the management process responsible for *identifying*, *anticipating* and *satisfying* customer requirements profitably'), is our sole role as marketers to fulfil. Ultimately, data and technology have changed the game – and strategy is essential to staying ahead in this new world.

Using data to shape your strategy

Now, data is a big topic, so I'll start with a bit of background into why it's important.

Planning has started to fall behind the hectic pace of modern business, with its technological change and ever-fluctuating consumer expectations. Information now comes at us in real time; we no longer have the option to spend days analysing, forming a consensus and then acting.

Many marketers see this as an impossible obstacle to thorough strategizing, but I recommend looking at this another way.

If your customers are engaging with you and have willingly shared their data with you, then you'll have access to a wealth of real-time data. There may be 'anonymous' data within the mix where the individual person cannot be identified which can come from sources such as web traffic, advert clicks and impressions, which are very useful. This data when analysed will provide valuable insight into your customers and their needs.

Engaging with data is crucial to the development of an effective marketing strategy. With the emergence of AI, marketers' interaction with data is going to become increasingly sophisticated. Which is good, because well-conducted data insight and analysis can reveal the top areas of focus or concern that should be informing our decisions. While data doesn't have all the answers, those things you can learn from data may play a big part in guiding your future direction. Turning a blind eye to data insights, or not tapping into the right knowledge when you need to, will leave your business open to failure.

A note at this point: data needs to be gathered and used ethically. I'll be going into this in a lot more detail later but, for now, let's note that trust is crucial in any relationship – including the customer/brand relationship. Data is sensitive, and dodgy data dealings in the past have left consumers wary of sharing their precious data. To gather and use data correctly, you need to position the customers' needs in the centre of your data practices. There is also a need to ensure you obtain reliable and credible data, as Catherine Loftus, Head of Marketing at Inshur explains:

> Without reliable data, strategy can be a shot in the dark and dangerous
> assumptions can be made. From identifying trends in certain markets to
> understanding seasonality and anticipating challenges, data gives a solid
> foundation for success.

Technology: it's great, but be careful!

When we speak of 'utilizing technology', most peoples' minds jump immediately to shiny new tech. Data analysis is much less sexy, but it's by far the best way of getting to grips with the latest trends and the prevailing mood. That's not to say that you shouldn't play with shiny new technology too, but be sure to know what you're dealing with before you take the plunge!

CASE STUDY
Burger King

Technology is a valuable tool, and it's vital to keep up to date. But shiny new tech shouldn't blind us to the fundamentals of what we're doing.

Examples of marketers forgetting the basics of marketing are evident every day. A great example is Burger King's ad featuring what was then the latest shiny addition to the market: Google Home.

Burger King, like all fast-food chains, has been plagued with rumours that their products do not contain the ingredients they say they do. The brand wanted to challenge these rumours head-on, so they devised what they thought was a clever, cutting-edge advert utilizing the Google Home technology.

The idea was that a voice-over in the advert would use the words 'OK Google' to trigger (or hijack) all Google Home devices within 'listening range' of the advert. The advert continued by asking Google Home to recite the ingredients of Burger King's most iconic product – The Whopper.

What Burger King did not foresee was that the primary source of Google Home's information is Wikipedia – the biggest free online encyclopaedia in the world, which can be edited by anyone. Predictably, the general public cottoned on to the trolling potential of this pretty quickly and edited the Whopper's Wiki page to include things like 'rat' and 'toenail clippings' in the Whopper's ingredients list. This meant that every time the ad was played, Google Home innocently trotted out whatever ingredients the public had edited into the Whopper's Wikipedia page!

Funny as it may seem, it was a complete disaster for both Burger King and Google. Google – which wasn't involved in creating the campaign – pulled the ad within three hours of going live and prevented all Google Home devices from responding to it. The whole exercise generated a ton of press coverage, but the objective (to eradicate rumours of unpleasant ingredients used within their burgers) failed – and phenomenally so. If anything, the campaign fuelled those rumours.

SOURCE The Verge, 2017

The key questions and lessons from this example are: how can such an oversight happen? Did no one involved in this campaign highlight this as a potential issue? Where was the due diligence? And how could the source of information, the most significant factor, not be vetted? A coherent strategy rather than an innate reliance upon the next shiny piece of tech could have nipped this dangerous tactic in the bud.

Marketing, when conducted correctly, is an intelligent and sophisticated art. Many marketers study for years to learn the disciplines that create effective campaigns, and that learning never really ends. Yet, with advancements in technology, we're becoming increasingly obsessed with jumping upon the next shiny thing to raise the profile of a campaign without worrying about the finer details of how this can be done effectively. Our obsession with basic performance metrics of likes, shares, followers and opens comes at the detriment of creating high-quality campaigns with longevity.

Always think 'customer first'

Your campaign's audience needs to be a constant touchpoint throughout your strategizing. It's not about starting with the channels or media that

TABLE 1.1 Breakdown of the key questions and detail of each stage of the STRATEGY framework

	Stage	Key questions	Detail
S	SCENARIO	Where is the business now? What is your current scenario? What are the environments internally and externally? What's happening inside your organization that could limit or amplify success?	This first stage is focused on discovering the positioning of the business today. What is happening inside and outside of the organization (also known as the micro and macro environments)? There are two fundamental models to use to analyse both of these environments: SWOT – focused on analysing the internal/micro environment. And PESTLE – concentrated on analysing the external/macro environment. We'll cover these in detail in Chapter 2. The overall aim of the first 'S' stage is to understand what may limit or amplify success. For example, are there any particular strengths the organization has which its competitors doesn't have?
T	TARGET	What is the desired destination, ambition? What are your objectives?	Determining objectives is a crucial aspect of all strategies. If an objective isn't clear and specific, it will be difficult to measure success or failure. The key model to use when creating objectives is to implement SCALE. This will be covered in more detail in Chapter 3.
R	REACH	Who are your customers? What are you customers seeking to gain from the product or service you are offering? What is the key benefit to them?	It's easy to focus on the company and lose sight of the target audience. This is why customers have their own section in the STRATEGY framework. Focusing on the customer is an essential part of marketing successfully. Organizations that spend time researching, identifying and sympathizing with their target audiences will be able to successfully align their product/service to the needs of their customers. They'll be rewarded with conversions. It may be that your product or service appeals to many people, but there will be segments (smaller groups within a large group) that have unique characteristics. We will explore this is in more depth in Chapter 4.

(continued)

TABLE 1.1 (Continued)

	Stage	Key questions	Detail
A	AWARENESS	How do you drive a response? What's your strategic approach to reaching your audience? How are you planning to target and position your messaging so that the right people see it?	Every marketing strategy is aiming to stimulate a reaction of some sort. It could be to drive more sales, more website traffic and/or more in-store customers. How can you drive the reaction that you want? We will cover this in Chapter 5.
T	TACTICS	Based on what you discovered in the 'A' stage of this framework, what tactics are most appropriate to reach the target audience?	I've witnessed many brands focus heavily on identifying tactics before turning to the scenario and the specific needs of the customer. In doing so the marketers have created a recipe for disaster, because the chosen tactics haven't been validated with the audience. Inevitably, the messaging will not connect with what each segment values the most. We'll cover tactics in more detail in Chapter 6.
E	EXECUTION	Who will implement the strategy? What will be implemented? When will activity take place?	The who, what and when of implementing your strategy. The execution stage is where the timing, resources, budget and approach to measuring KPIs throughout the strategy's activity is planned. The budget can be set for the entire marketing campaign or can be split by individual tactics or channels. It's vital to ensure that these elements reflect the objectives created in the 'Target' section because, if there is a mismatch in which the appropriate resources or skills to implement the strategy aren't available, then it is likely to underperform against the target set. This will be covered in more detail in Chapter 7.

(continued)

TABLE 1.1 (Continued)

	Stage	Key questions	Detail
G	GENERATE	Are you on track to achieve the goals set?	Generate feedback, results and response. This element focuses on measuring the desired response you're gaining based on the objectives set. For example, if your objective is to increase sales of a particular product from a specific customer segment, you would measure your success by focusing on revenue and number of sales compared against the target set. Doing this on an ongoing basis will tell you whether or not you're on track. Monitoring and measuring performance should be a regular task, as it will provide the marketing team with the opportunity to adjust if there appears to be an issue. Chapter 8 covers the Generate element of strategy.
Y	YIELD	Were the objectives achieved? How do the Year-on-Year (YOY) results compare if this is a multi-annual marketing strategy? Was the target audience reached and engaged?	This section is focused on analysing the success of your strategy: KPIs, YOY results. A full post-mortem analysis should be conducted to determine what went well, what underperformed and (most importantly) to critically assess why. We will cover this in more detail in Chapter 9.

you're going to use (Facebook, TikTok, Snapchat or email); it's about ensuring that, no matter the media, your message will benefit your customer and enhance their experience with your brand. After all, it's the customer who wants to hear your company's story, and it's the customer you need to convince that you're the brand to choose.

A strategy is the first point of call, yet many marketers delve straight into the shiny, sexy part of marketing – creating lavish campaigns and creative content – without stopping to analyse and assess their customers' needs and wants. It's also important to ensure that the product lives up to the marketing message, otherwise there is a danger of overselling which will lead to disappointed consumers.

To ensure your strategy has the right components, I have created the STRATEGY framework. Table 1.1 breaks this down into stages.

Interview: James Delves

James Delves is Head of PR and Engagement at CIM (Chartered Institute of Marketing). Here he discusses the key ingredients to include when creating a successful strategy, concepts he recommends, thoughts on the future of marketing and much more.

JT: *What do you think are the key ingredients that should be included in a marketing strategy?*

JD: Start with a business objective, this is critical, because if your marketing strategy is not aligned to the rest of the business then it can't deliver value. Understand the market, customers, competitors and budgets.

JT: *Describe what a marketing strategy is in one sentence.*

JD: CIM describes a marketing strategy as: 'The set of objectives which an organization allocates to its marketing function in order to support the overall corporate strategy, together with the broad methods chosen to achieve these objectives.'

Put simply, it's about defining what is important to your company, what you want to achieve, and how you are going to get there.

JT: *From your experience, what do you think are the key challenges to implementing a marketing strategy?*

JD: Start with the objectives of the business and then work back. It's almost impossible to deliver value for any marketing campaign unless it is aligned with the business as a whole.

Communication – clearly articulating and effectively communicating the strategy across the key stakeholders in the organization in order to receive support and buy-in, as well as across all functions to ensure everyone is working towards the same goals, and people see how the marketing strategy aligns with what they are doing.

Resource – a common challenge is ensuring the right structure and resource to effectively implement and take the strategy forward. And in a fast-paced profession such as marketing, skills gaps can be an issue. Failure to keep up to date can seriously hinder a marketer's ability to deliver against a brief. If you can't take advantage of the latest social channels or digital marketing techniques, you may well be unable to effectively reach certain audience segments.

JT: *What common pitfalls do you see marketers falling into when they are creating a marketing strategy?*

JD: When developing your marketing strategy, it can be tempting to look at how to create some quick wins to prove your approach is working. Marketers can also fall into a trap of:

- not understanding their audience and the channels they engage with;
- not doing enough research to support planned marketing activities effectively;
- not engaging outside of the marketing department to get buy-in from across the business.

JT: *Do you think marketing can be effective without a strategy?*

JD: In short, no. Without a strategy, execution of activities and their impact is impossible. A strategy amongst other things allows focus to enable marketing to deliver against the priorities.

JT: *Are there any stand-out marketing strategies that you have seen? What made that particular marketing strategy stand out?*

JD: Being true to your heritage and consumers is key. Nike has a clear strategy that has succeeded for 55 years. Forging partnerships that create strong connections with consumers is also key. Nike's third-party relationships are treated as an extension of the brand which has made it one of the biggest sports brands on the planet, from the million-pound deals with Liverpool Football Club to individual sponsorship deals with athletes at the Olympics. It means Nike can charge a premium for its products.

The brand more recently has used its global following to disrupt the leisure market, from Women's Hijab to using Colin Kaepernick as the face of its 'Dream Crazy' campaign. The brand might take short-term criticism and alienate a small percentage of their consumer base, but in the long run the brand looks to grow even stronger and be more successful.

Wetherspoon is another brand which has a great marketing strategy. The brand's relentless commitment to its customers and putting customers at the very heart of its marketing strategy has enabled it to continue to prosper and retain loyalty where more established rivals have failed. From attractive pricing and locations easily accessible to consumers, to removing plastic straws, the brand responds to customer habits quickly. It's not just in the real world, the popularity of its app is unparalleled and provides a meaningful new brand experience rather than just being a gimmick.

John Lewis is always held up as a stalwart of great branding and it's hard to argue [with that]. Its respected heritage sets it apart from other retail competitors allowing the brand to build unrivalled customer loyalty. The joint rebrand with Waitrose has only strengthened this position, while other brands on the high street falter.

Another campaign that stood out for me was the 'distressed' campaign from the Highways Agency, that won 'Best Content Marketing Campaign' award at the CIM Marketing Excellence Awards 2019. The campaign set out to help bikers realize what could happen if they ride in the wrong clothing. The campaign featured a pop-up shop in East London, with the 'distressed' clothing range which, instead of showing the cost of the clothing, showed a range of serious injuries a biker could suffer if they are not wearing the right gear.

Customers' reactions were captured when they realized what the price labels referred to. The content was then used to drive an awareness campaign. A survey after the campaign showed an increase of more than three-quarters in the number of young riders who said they were more likely to wear protective clothing. The campaign is a great example of how a marketing strategy doesn't have to be complex to trigger a change in consumer behaviour.

JT: *Are there any key marketing models, theories or concepts that you'd recommend marketers utilize when creating a marketing strategy?*

JD: There are many. PR Smith's SOSTAC, SWOT, Segmentation, Targeting and Positioning (STP) and the 7Ps of the Marketing Mix to name a few.

Not so much a theory or concept but something marketers need to be mindful of in all stages of their strategic planning and execution is a clear understanding of legislation such as GDPR.

Data is one of the most valuable assets organizations have access to, and used in the right way it can be very useful in informing strategy. As consumers, we all leave digital footprints as we go about our daily lives via countless internet searches, the myriad apps and the online services we use such as shopping, banking and social media activity. The data generated through our digital actions is seen, recorded and analysed every day – with the aim of providing us with a better level of service. Marketers must remember that trust can take years to secure and just moments to lose. And it is a fact that consumers don't trust businesses with their data. (Research undertaken a year after GDPR showed that 42 per cent of consumers had received communications from businesses they had not given permission to contact them).

Only a quarter of people (24 per cent) believe that businesses treat people's personal data in an honest and transparent way, only slightly higher than the 18 per cent when GDPR took effect.

JT: *Do you think artificial intelligence has a role in a marketing strategy?*

JD: A lot has been written about IoT, big data, cloud computing, automation – but AI is the tech to rule them all and is set to change the face of both marketing and PR for good. Hyper-individualized campaigns, interactive AI-powered ads, ultra-analytics and AI-driven newsroom technologies are set to change how we consume information, build marketing strategies and manage the customer buying journey forever.

In almost 20 years of PR and marketing I've never been quite so excited and wary of the impact AI could have on our lives. In a survey, McKinsey found that 47 per cent of respondents said that their company had embedded at least one AI capability in business processes – compared with 20 per cent of respondents in 2017 (McKinsey, 2019). For our division the figure is even higher, with 52 per cent of retail respondents stating that they were using AI in some form for marketing and sales. It's clear AI and machine learning are already redefining marketing both within companies and in the agency world – and we've only just started understanding its potential.

A key activity [when] building a marketing strategy is listening to customer needs and then map[ping] them against products and services, which AI can do in spades – enabling marketing teams to give customers what they want at the right time, reducing guesswork and cost.

If I were to offer one piece of advice to marketers considering AI, my advice would be to accept that the robots are here, get ahead of the competition and start learning what AI can do for you because the chance is your competitors already have.

JT: *Do you have any tips to share on creating a successful marketing strategy?*

JD: Use the data you have available to you and take the time to understand it; do your research; know what your competitors are doing; and get the buy-in of your key stakeholders.

JT: *What do you think the future of marketing holds?*

JD: Marketing will continue to evolve at pace, driven by ongoing advancements in technology. By the end of this year [2020] more people around the world will have mobile phones than running water or electricity in their homes. This proliferation of mobile or smartphones has driven the social and digital revolution we now live in, which in turn has fuelled the rise [of] AI.

With the pace only getting faster, the need to stay up to date has never been so important. Marketers need to ensure they are taking their development seriously both in the technical skills and the 'soft' skill areas such as communication and relationship building skills.

The value of data has passed the point of being more valuable than oil and is now regarded as [being as] valuable as gold for many marketers. New data collection methods and analytical tools enable marketers to understand, and even predict consumer habits in far greater detail than ever before. The key is the mix between human and machine. Yes, AI is becoming more advanced, but it still requires marketers who have the skill sets to interpret the data correctly and then the ability to build it into a marketing strategy which will stand out from their peers.

Conscious consumerism continues to grow, people are increasingly more aware of their data rights and are choosing authenticity and brands that match their own values. GDPR has cleared up a lot of bad practice across all areas of business. Consumers now expect organizations to demonstrate a professional approach to data collection and use it ethically. Brands need to demonstrate that data collection is providing value to the consumer by using it to tailor their customer experience.

Summary

In this chapter we have:

- Defined the meaning of strategy.
- Identified the difference between strategy and tactics.
- Explored the history of marketing and its evolution.
- Highlighted the importance of gaining trust from customers.

References

Abercrombie & Fitch (2020) Company history [Online], available at: corporate. abercrombie.com/our-company/about-us/company-history (archived at https://perma.cc/5Z8R-4E2Z)

Amazon (2020) Our mission [Online], Amazon in the UK, available at: www.aboutamazon.co.uk/uk-investment/our-mission (archived at https://perma.cc/PGA2-BTB5)

CIM (2020) Our history [Online], Chartered Institute of Marketing, available at: www.cim.co.uk/about-cim/our-history/ (archived at https://perma.cc/FYX2-JGXT)

Comedy Central (2020) Someone worked out just how long the DFS sale has been going off for [Online], Comedy Central, available at: www.comedycentral.co.uk/news/someone-worked-out-just-how-long-the-dfs-sale-has-been-going-on-for (archived at https://perma.cc/7CDX-BVAV)

Delves, J (2020) Head of PR and Engagement at the Chartered Institute of Marketing [Interview] 31 January 2020

Dunckley, K (2020) Chief Digital & Innovation Officer at HH Global [Interview] 28 July 2020

Engadget (2016) Apple's AirPods won't be ready for the holidays [Online], Engadget, available at: www.engadget.com/2016-12-09-apples-airpods-wont-be-ready-for-the-holidays.html (archived at https://perma.cc/QUB3-973M)

Fell, J and Sun, C (2020) Steve Jobs: An extraordinary career [Online], *Entrepreneur Europe*, available at: www.entrepreneur.com/article/197538#:~:te xt=Co%2Dfounder%20of%20Apple%20Computer%20Inc.&text=Steve%20 Jobs'%20vision%20of%20a,the%20company%20he%20helped%20found (archived at https://perma.cc/5MLB-LCR8)

Financial Times (2020) Online grocers fail to shine during biggest test yet [Online], *The Financial Times*, available at: www.ft.com/content/6c9c2378-5904-4cad-9c52-304157465cb8 (archived at https://perma.cc/L85X-SWJA)

Guilford, G (2018) GM's decline truly began with its quest to turn people into machines [Online], Quartz, available at: qz.com/1510405/gms-layoffs-can-be-traced-to-its-quest-to-turn-people-into-machines/ (archived at https://perma.cc/K8PB-H7P8)

Hancock, R (2020) Managing Director at Marketing Know-How [Interview] 20 October 2020

IKEA (2020) Vision & Business idea [Online], Ikea, available at: www.ikea.com/gb/en/this-is-ikea/about-us/vision-and-business-idea-pub9cd02291 (archived at https://perma.cc/RE38-UHK3)

Kastrenakes, J (2017) Burger King's new ad forces Google Home to advertise the Whopper [Online], The Verge, available at: www.theverge.com/2017/4/12/15259400/burger-king-google-home-ad-wikipedia (archived at https://perma.cc/2PM9-B3KT)

Kemish, S (2020) Founder at Junction Agency & IDM trainer [Interview] 28 July 2020

LaReau, J (2008) After the frenetic Durant era, Sloan brought order from chaos [Online], *Automotive News*, available at: www.autonews.com/article/20080914/OEM02/309149952/after-the-frenetic-durant-era-sloan-brought-order-from-chaos (archived at https://perma.cc/DZ92-BLSF)

Limbaugh, R (2016) Is Apple losing its edge? [Online], The Rush Limbaugh Show, available at: www.rushlimbaugh.com/daily/2016/12/09/is_apple_losing_its_edge_/ (archived at https://perma.cc/K6X6-RBKE)

Loftus, C (2020) Head of Marketing at Inshu [Interview] 28 July 2020

McKinsey (2019) Global AI Survey: AI proves its worth, but few scale impact [Online], McKinsey & Company, available at: www.mckinsey.com/featured-insights/artificial-intelligence/global-ai-survey-ai-proves-its-worth-but-few-scale-impact (archived at https://perma.cc/7N79-EK3Z)

Ofcom (2020) Online Nation 2020 report [Online], Ofcom, available at: www.ofcom.org.uk/research-and-data/internet-and-on-demand-research/online-nation (archived at https://perma.cc/FG8A-WPP9)

Ryanair (2020) Ryanair's mission statement 2020 [Online], Ryanair, available at: mission-statement.com/ryanair-mission/ (archived at https://perma.cc/FC5Y-NFY3)

Sleep Advisor (2020) More than half of Americans start their day by checking their emails [Online], Sleep Advisor, available at: www.sleepadvisor.org/email-before-work-survey/#:~:text=Our%20findings%20show%20that%20a,ever%20going%20in%20to%20work (archived at https://perma.cc/2Q7Y-HDCN)

Stone, B (2018) Apple's trillion dollar world [Online], Bloomberg, available at: www.bloomberg.com/features/2018-apple-trillion-dollar-world/ (archived at https://perma.cc/SG3J-Q3PB)

Sun-Tzu and Griffith, SB (1964) *The Art Of War,* Clarendon Press, Oxford

WWF (2018) WWF's Mission & Vision [Online], WWF, available at: help. worldwildlife.org/hc/en-us/articles/360007905494-WWF-s-Mission-Vision#:~:text=The%20mission%20of%20World%20Wildlife,planet%2C%20a%20world%20of%20life (archived at https://perma.cc/77K6-F5PM)

02

Scenario

Establishing the current situation

In this chapter we are going to:

- Analyse your organization's internal marketing environment by utilizing a SWOT.
- Analyse your organization's external marketing environment with a PESTLE.
- Focus on company-specific strengths in existing capabilities, assess limitations and what can be leveraged with the SWOTELL.
- Analyse your competitors with a COMPETE framework.
- Assess the organization's resources and capabilities to implement the strategy with the VRIO framework.

There are exercises included from this chapter onwards for you to complete, so have a pen or pencil handy!

The combination of analyses created by using these frameworks is an important step in building your marketing strategy. These analyses provide context regarding where the business and the market are now, the opportunities and threats (both internally and externally) you face, and the strengths which will help you gain a competitive advantage. More detail on this further into this chapter.

What do I mean by 'competitive advantage'? Well, simply put, a competitive advantage is something which helps you to win custom over your competitors. Examples include:

- lower production costs (increasing ROI);
- unique access to resources like tech or patented production methods;

- stellar team members who do a much better job than competitor teams;
- a totally unique product which nobody else can offer.

And excellent strategic analysis of your business environment.

Where is the business now?

Our first step in creating a marketing strategy with the STRATEGY framework begins with S – Scenario. This involves analysing the context of your organization by assessing the internal (micro) and external (macro) factors which could be affecting it. This is known as analysing the situational environment.

Micro factors have a direct influence on the firm's marketing operations, some of which are controllable (eg resourcing). Macro factors have an indirect influence – mostly uncontrollable. These factors make up the typical PESTLE forces (Political, Economic, Social, Technological, Legal, Environmental) which will be explored in more detail further along in this chapter.

Micro environment

WHAT IS IT?
The micro marketing environment consists of the factors which affect an organization internally, and the resources which help it to respond to these factors. Team skills, patents, financial stability, reputation or supplier relationships, for example.

WHY ANALYSE IT?
Well, for example, the structure of your organization is a micro factor. Perhaps this structure might prevent it from adapting quickly to change – as in the General Motors example discussed in Chapter 1.

Then there's the resources factor. An organization could have a limited pool of internal skills, and adding new skills could be costly. This will make a difference to what the company can realistically achieve in the way of marketing. Meanwhile, another organization which already has the skills and experience could consider these things a strength.

Macro environment

WHAT IS IT?

The macro, external environment consists of all the outside forces and influences that could affect the organization. The economy, for example, or current events.

WHY IS IT IMPORTANT?

If, for example, sterling suddenly dropped in value, this could dramatically reduce the profits of an organization. That's a macro factor, and it could make a huge impact on profit. That impact could vary again depending on the nature of the business. If the company operates on a global scale, a drop in the value of the pound would make doing business abroad more expensive, thus having a direct impact upon the profit margin. More domestic-focused businesses, meanwhile, would not experience the downturn in such a direct way.

The best way to remember the difference between micro and macro is that 'internal' is the 'i' in micro. Micro = internal and Macro = external.

The benefits of analysing the marketing environment

It is vital for marketers to understand the environment in which their business is operating. Analysing the marketing environment helps marketers to understand customer needs and wants, as well as how well equipped their own business is to fulfil these.

Business strengths and weaknesses can also be compared with those of the competition, which gives crucial insight into how the business shapes up against others when it comes to meeting customer needs and holding a place in the wider market context.

Organizations that regularly and systematically conduct such analyses often spot trends before others, thus gaining a competitive advantage.

Without monitoring and analysing the market, marketers are simply guessing. The marketing environment represents the total sum of factors and variables impacting upon the firm. The very survival of an organization depends on understanding it. If the marketing environment is not monitored closely, the firm is at risk of being caught out by market changes that have the potential to impact corporate survival. The business environment is an open system, and many elements of that system are unpredictable.

Models to analyse the two environments

There are two key models that can be used to analyse both the micro and macro environments. For the micro environment there is the SWOT (Figure 2.1).

FIGURE 2.1 The SWOT framework

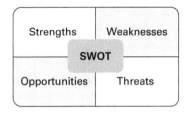

SWOT analysis

HOW IT WORKS

SWOT is a simple but useful framework for analysing your organization's **strengths** and **weaknesses,** as well as the **opportunities** and **threats** that you face. It helps you focus on your strengths, minimize threats and take the greatest possible advantage of opportunities available to you.

WHY IS IT USEFUL?

An organization that has awareness of its weaknesses as well as its strengths has a lot of power. A self-aware organization is one that can utilize its self-knowledge throughout the business, ensuring that the ambitions and goals of the organization match its capabilities – whether by adapting, changing and expanding where weaknesses lie, or by playing to existing strengths.

HOW TO USE IT

You may find some crossover in your SWOT findings. For example, the weaknesses identified may also be opportunities for the organization. The most important thing to ensure with a SWOT is that it is internally focused. SWOT is about assessing the organization's capabilities. Wider things are at play, sure – and we'll get onto analysing those in a moment. Keep your SWOT as internally focused in the analysis and findings as you can.

Table 2.1 provides an example of a SWOT I created as the author of this book. Although this is focused on me as a person, the same applies when applying the SWOT to an organization.

TABLE 2.1 An example of SWOT for the launch of this book

STRENGTHS	WEAKNESSES
1. Over 10 years' experience and expertise to share. 2. Client case studies – industry quotes/ perspectives. 3. Easy to digest – actionable blueprint taking experience from communicating complex issues in an easy-to-understand way. 4. Passion for the topic.	1. First book – unknown as an author. 2. As a result of no 1, it could be difficult to get reviews. 3. Lots of marketing strategy books readily available which are already established as core course text books. 4. Long-established existing concepts could make adoption of new approaches challenging.
OPPORTUNITIES	THREATS
1. To engage my network into my book. 2. To establish the book as a core text for marketing and strategy courses. 3. For the book to showcase expertise and agency services. 4. Self-publishing has low barrier to entry and publishers regularly seeking new commissions.	1. Idea/format could be copied. 2. There's only me writing the book – sole author. 3. Other projects for business may get in the way. 4. Numerous books on the market about similar topic.

You'll see from Table 2.1 that the micro environment of this book endeavour is – at the outset – pretty evenly balanced between strengths, weaknesses, threats and opportunities. Having identified these factors, I can capitalize on the positives and work to combat the negatives. For example, by taking on proofreaders and getting second opinions from industry experts, I can mitigate the solo and first-time-author issues. By identifying the threats I can create actionable defensive strategies, eg by having a very clear USP: that my book is clearer and more practical than others out there, shows me how I need to position and communicate it for success.

TASK

Now over to you. Create your SWOT by using the template in Table 2.2 to analyse the organization you're working for or an organization of your choice. List four key findings per factor (16 findings in total).

TABLE 2.2 Your SWOT template

STRENGTHS	WEAKNESSES
1.	1. ....
2.	2. ....
3.	3. ....
4.	4. ....
OPPORTUNITIES	THREATS
1.	1. ....
2.	2. ....
3.	3. ....
4.	4. ....

PESTLE analysis

HOW IT WORKS

To analyse the macro, external environment influencing an organization, we have the PESTLE framework.

PESTLE is an analytical framework used for understanding the external factors that could impact an organization. It stands for Political, Economic, Social, Technological, Legal and Environmental.

WHY USE IT?

It helps marketers to understand all of the factors that could impact a brand from outside the organization.

HOW TO USE IT

The important part here is to not simply list the changes in the external environment but to apply how those findings directly impact the organization.

EXAMPLES: THE MACRO ENVIRONMENT

Famously, Nike adopted controversial American footballer Colin Kaepernick as their US figurehead in 2018 (Abad-Santos, 2018). Kaepernick had become an outcast player when, in 2016, he refused to stand during the national anthem. After first sitting in protest, he then knelt in a protesting effort against the police killings of African–Americans and other injustices. Despite the initial boycott of Nike by some retailers and members of the public, the campaign was a huge success, undoubtedly because the marketing team had done a thorough PESTLE analysis beforehand. They were able to bring a sensitive, profound and valuable message (which, yes, was also attached to a marketing campaign) out of a politically tumultuous time.

Compare this with the infamous Kendall Jenner Pepsi ad that had to be pulled after receiving backlash (Batchelor, 2017). It attempted something similar but without the deep understanding of the social and political environment into which the campaign would be released. PESTLE analysis would have helped Pepsi to predict societal reactions to their campaign before launching.

Let's run through each element of PESTLE, illustrated in Figure 2.2.

FIGURE 2.2   Breakdown of each stage of the PESTLE framework

P
- **POLITICAL** This factor is focused on any changes in government legislation. Things like tax laws, import or export regulation, and environmental legislation can all have an impact on an organization.

E
- **ECONOMIC** Employment rates, wages, stock market trends, inflation and exchange rates, the interest rate, fiscal and monetary policy. All of these economic factors can impact an organization.

S
- **SOCIAL** Social factors are focused on buyer behaviour, trends, and changes to society over time.

T
- **TECHNOLOGICAL** Businesses performing PESTLE analyses on a regular basis are able to keep themselves equipped and to adapt to new technology rather than falling behind.

L
- **LEGAL** This area is focused on legal factors with which the company will need to comply. This applies to both existing and impending regulation and legislation.

E
- **ENVIRONMENTAL** This concerns an organization's impact on the environment, as well as any changes in legislation within this area that may impact the organization's operations.

Remember, even though a PESTLE is focused on wider, external factors, it should still be unique to the organization. The idea is to identify factors which will impact the specific organization, and how that impact may occur. If there are generalizations – if the analysis is not organization-specific enough – it will provide little actionable insight.

As you can see in Table 2.3, it may not be possible to combat all of these potential factors, but by conducting this analysis you can start to prioritize the ones that may have the most impact.

TABLE 2.3 An example of the PESTLE framework analysing the external environment before developing this book

		Analysis findings	Risk of impact
P	POLITICAL	Brexit could impact launching the book in European markets due to potential new tariffs (Informi, 2020). This may limit the number of countries where the book can be sold, ultimately reducing potential sales.	High
E	ECONOMIC	Fluctuations in the exchange rate between sterling, euro and dollar could impact the royalties I receive from each book sale.	Medium
S	SOCIAL	It is forecast that the e-book market will be worth over $17m in 2021 (Statista, 2020). This provides an opportunity to expand the readership and sales of the book to global markets as an e-book.	High (positive)
T	TECHNOLOGICAL	Changing all of the time – new adoption of tools, ie TikTok. E-book vs print format. Channels for book sales. Digital marketing spend is estimated to reach £14bn in the UK by the end of 2020 (Statista, 2020). This growth in the use of technology in marketing will require a need for marketing strategists which this book supports.	High (positive)
L	LEGAL	Throughout the development of the book's content, it was important to ensure that it abides by UK Copyright Law (UKCCS, 2020). Any inclusion of third-party material must have been granted permission for reproductive use. Changes in the UK and EU trade agreement could mean that there are new laws to comply with when selling, promoting and distributing my book to the EU (at the time of writing it was to still be agreed).	Medium High
E	ENVIRONMENTAL	Printing in greyscale and not full colour reduces the impacts to the environment which is how this book has been printed (Pacific Office, 2018).	Low

TASK

Now it's your turn. Complete a PESTLE focusing on the external environment that is affecting your organization or the one you work for below. Analyse the same company that you SWOT-analysed before, using the PESTLE model.

Fill in the template in Table 2.4, including at least two findings per section. Remember that each finding needs to be analysed with reference to how it will directly affect the specific organization.

TABLE 2.4 Your PESTLE framework template

		Analysis findings	Risk of impact
P	POLITICAL		
E	ECONOMIC		
S	SOCIAL		
T	TECHNOLOGICAL		
L	LEGAL		
E	ENVIRONMENTAL		

Once you've conducted your SWOT and PESTLE analyses, summarize your key findings. You can do this in whatever form works for you (bullet points are popular!), but it's important that you can use your analysis to draw conclusions which will form the basis of the marketing strategy.

SWOT and PESTLE provide useful actionable insights which can inform not only marketing's direction but also an organization's direction. For example, if a company were considering launching a new product in a specific country but discovered through PESTLE analysis that this same country was set to dramatically increase import rates, this would decrease the organization's potential profit. The company could sidestep this difficulty and aim instead for a country with a friendlier import rate, or increase their prices to absorb the extra costs.

If an organization doesn't conduct any analysis of the micro and macro marketing environment, it risks going into a market blind, without the full awareness or knowledge needed to compete successfully.

SWOTELL

To advance your SWOT analysis even further, I've added ELL to the original SWOT.

This model will take your analysis conducted in the SWOT to another level by analysing and adding a further three elements (Table 2.5).

This model is useful for adding further actionable areas when assessing where the business needs to make strategic preparations. The ELL are purely marketing focused and remain aligned to the specific organization but also incorporate external perception, such as engagement, to determine what's currently effective, the limitations you face, and what is available to leverage and enhance further.

WHY IS IT USEFUL?

The SWOTELL adds the marketing-specific focus to the SWOT. While the SWOT focuses on the situation as it is in the present, when combined with the SWOTELL the focus is more action-based.

TABLE 2.5   The ELL additions to a SWOT analysis creating the SWOTELL framework

		Analysis findings
E	EXISTING	What does your existing marketing activity consist of? What channels is the organization actively using? Are they achieving the KPIs set? Do they engage the target audience? What's working and not working?
L	LIMITATIONS	What's holding your marketing back? What's the structure of the marketing team? Are there skill gaps or is this an experienced team? Is there an adequate marketing budget available when considering the competitive landscape? (Covered in more detail later in this chapter).
L	LEVERAGE	What's already successful that can be leveraged? Are there agencies in place, for example? Is this an experienced and capable team? Which of your tactics are working, and why?

EXAMPLE: SWOTELL

TABLE 2.6 SWOTELL applied to the development and promotion of this book

		Analysis findings
S	STRENGTHS	Over 10 years' experience and expertise to share. Client case studies – industry quotes/ perspectives. Easy to digest – actionable blueprint taking experience from communicating complex issues in an easy-to-understand way. Passion for the topic.
W	WEAKNESSES	First book – unknown as an author. As a result of no 1, it could be difficult to get reviews. Lots of marketing strategy books readily available which are already established as core course text books. Long-established existing concepts could make adoption of new approaches challenging.
O	OPPORTUNITIES	To engage my network into my book. To establish the book as a core text for marketing and strategy courses. For the book to showcase expertise and agency services. Self-publishing has low barrier to entry and publishers regularly seeking new commissions.
T	THREATS	Idea/format could be copied. There's only me writing the book – sole author. Other projects for business may get in the way. Numerous books on the market about similar topic.
E	EXISTING	Current marketing activity consists of speaking at events, authoring whitepapers, blogs and articles, training, teaching and promoting across social media, with partners and on company website.
L	LIMITATIONS	Limited resources that are focused on consulting with clients. Heavy dependence of the book's promotion on the author to be available. Excellent skills and experience available for the marketing activity of the book with the publishing team.
L	LEVERAGE	Leverage the experience and existing processes of the publishing team. Experts that have contributed to the book. Author's own profile and network.

TASK

Now over to you: add to your SWOT analysis by adding ELL. Using the template in Table 2.7, analyse the organization you're working for or an organization of your choice. List three key findings per factor.

TABLE 2.7 Your ELL of a SWOTELL framework template

		Analysis findings
S	STRENGTHS	
W	WEAKNESSES	
O	OPPORTUNITIES	
T	THREATS	
E	EXISTING	
L	LIMITATIONS	
L	LEVERAGE	

Analysing the competition

Your competition is a vital part of your marketing environment. It's important that you know as much as possible about your competitors if you are to build and maintain your competitive advantage.

So, now that we have analysed the micro and macro marketing environments, the next area to research and analyse is the competition. The framework I have created to do this is called COMPETE.

COMPETE

WHAT IS IT?

When analysing competitors there are key areas to focus on. COMPETE provides a structure that ensures all the bases are covered. Figure 2.3 provides a breakdown of each stage.

FIGURE 2.3 The COMPETE framework

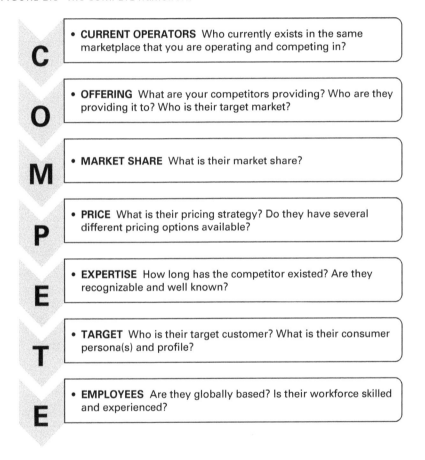

HOW DO I USE IT?

Here is a breakdown of each stage, including key focus areas and questions to ask.

C – Current operators   Who currently exists in the same marketplace that you are operating and competing in? What are they called (including their website URL)? It is useful to document your analysis and enable other members of the team to do the same. Key questions to ask:

- Are the current companies in the market easy to imitate? (There is a model which adds further depth to this analysis called the VRIO, which I'll run through in more detail below).

- Are there any start-ups entering the marketplace or is the marketplace dominated by established organizations (ie organizations that have been operating in that market for eight years or more)?:

  o How strictly is the market regulated?

  o What are the costs to enter?

  o How long would it take for a new company to enter the market?

- Are there any barriers to entry? Think about things like patents, technology, high start-up costs/operating costs, etc.

- How many competitors are there?

- Which competitors are your biggest? What makes them our biggest?

If the barrier to entry is low (ie it is easy for a new competitor to enter the market even with little money, resources and effort), the strategy needs to be adapted to compete with any new potential rivals.

O – Offering   What are your competitors providing? Who are they providing it to? Who is their target market? Are there different tiers or packages available? Include as much information here about their offering as possible. The key questions to ask when assessing the offering of competitors are:

- What makes your product/service different from that of your competitors?

- Why would a customer buy your offering instead of a competitor version? And vice versa?

- How many similar products to yours are available in the market?

- Is there a cost or disadvantage to the consumer if switching to a competitor's product?

- Is it easy or difficult to switch?

M – Market share   Market share refers to the amount of available custom that your competitor is taking. If you picture the market as a literal market square, a company with a large market share would be taking up a lot of space, and customers would be crowding around them.

Key questions to ask when assessing your competitor's market share include:

- What is their market share? Are they a dominator of the market, a market leader, the go-to company for that product/service?

- Does the market appear to be growing or contracting?
- What's your prediction for the future of the marketplace?

All of this is important to know in order to build a full picture of your market. This picture can inform your strategic direction. Without any assessment or knowledge of the make-up of the industry you are competing in, your strategy may steer your company in completely the wrong direction.

P – Price   Pricing strategies are important to understand, as they tell you a lot about supply and demand in the market, and how your competitors are responding to those forces. Key questions to ask when assessing this include:

- What is your competitor's pricing strategy?
- Do they have several different pricing options available?
- What criteria are their different pricing options based upon?
- Is there a range of suppliers available to help you produce your product or service?
- Do you rely on one, a handful or lots of suppliers?
- Would it be easy to switch to another supplier?
- Are there alternative suppliers available?
- How do the prices of your existing supplier compare to alternatives?
- Would it be costly to switch from one supplier to another?

These last ones might not seem directly related to your competitors, but they are very important for understanding the market as a whole. Think of it this way: if the supplier increased its prices by 100 per cent, would there be many alternative suppliers to switch to? If there aren't any alternatives, the supplier will likely know this. They therefore have a lot of power when bargaining for the renewed contract, and they may increase prices with relative impunity.

It is dangerous for a supplier to hold a lot of power over an organization. It could result in the organization being trapped into a poor, financially unstable contract with a supplier.

E – Expertise   Expertise counts for a lot in any industry! Key questions to ask when assessing your competitors' expertise include:

- How long has the competitor existed?
- Are they recognizable and well known? For example, did they exist for five years but weren't well known in the industry until the sixth year?

- What are they known for? Is it something in particular, such as their service?
- Are they accredited/certified or have they won awards?

T – Target   Here, you're looking to understand if your organization is also targeting the same customer. If you are and the product/service is similar, then what makes your organization different? Why would the same customer choose your organization over the competition?

Key questions to ask here:

- Who is their target customer?
- What is their consumer persona(s) and profile?
- How easy is it for your buyers to switch suppliers?
    - In switching, would the price remain the same?
    - Does the buyer have many alternatives available to them, or is there little choice? If the market is at the micro level and incredibly small, then that target market holds a lot of power, and an organization will be keen to seal the deal – thus fulfilling demands made by the buyer.

E – Employees   An organization's employees are its best asset. It's vital to understand the human resources your customers are working with. Key questions to ask include:

- Are they globally based?
- Is their workforce skilled and experienced?
- What do their team, departments and structure look like?
- Are they efficient or are they slow to react to changes in the marketplace?

WHY USE THE COMPETE FRAMEWORK?

The analysis included in COMPETE provides a complete overview of your competitors and the marketplace that you're competing in. By analysing your competitors' offering and the marketplace you'll be more aware of your organization's challenges, the opportunities in the marketplace and competitors to keep a close eye on.

If your COMPETE analysis findings are then actioned to adapt, improve or stop something in your organization, this can all lead to the development of developing a competitive advantage as explained earlier in this chapter.

TASK

Over to you. Analyse your competitors using the COMPETE framework in Table 2.8.

TABLE 2.8 Your COMPETE framework template

		Key findings	Competitor 1	Competitor 2	Competitor 3	Competitor 4	Competitor 5
C	CURRENT OPERATORS						
O	OFFERING						
M	MARKET SHARE						
P	PRICE						
E	EXPERTISE						
T	TARGET CUSTOMER						
E	EMPLOYEES						

Now, compare your SWOT, SWOTELL and PESTLE with the outcomes from your COMPETE analysis to inform your marketing strategy. By this point, you should be starting to see how wider strategic analysis can get you the best starting point for your campaign by highlighting solid and actionable insights.

VRIO: Resources and capabilities

The most critical aspect of a strategy is the execution. Many organizations create a strategy which can't be implemented in the organization. This happens for a number of reasons. A model that helps to ensure that the strategy you have created actually can be implemented is the VRIO framework (Figure 2.4). VRIO stands for: Value, Rarity, Imitability and Organization (Barney, 2007).

HOW DO I USE IT?

By going through each area in the form of a decision tree, an organization is able to understand its sustained competitive advantage. Alternatively, the same analysis could be conducted on competitors.

Competitive advantage can be broken down into: being comparable and being differential.

FIGURE 2.4 The VRIO framework

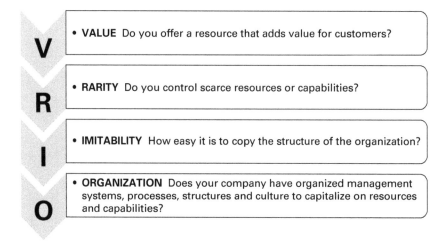

- **VALUE** Do you offer a resource that adds value for customers?

- **RARITY** Do you control scarce resources or capabilities?

- **IMITABILITY** How easy it is to copy the structure of the organization?

- **ORGANIZATION** Does your company have organized management systems, processes, structures and culture to capitalize on resources and capabilities?

FIGURE 2.5 The key questions and levels of competitive advantage at each stage of the VRIO framework

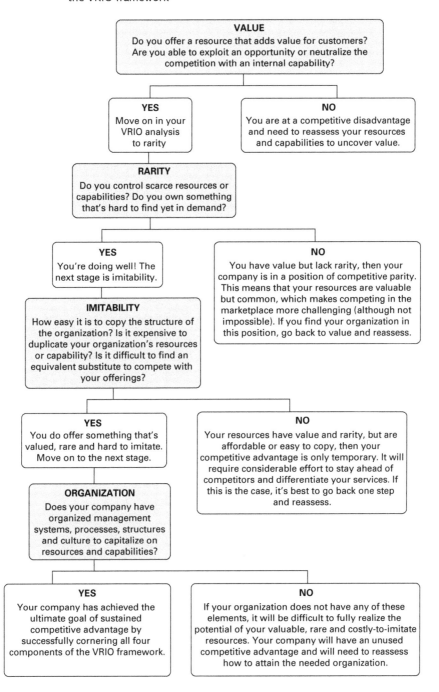

A *comparative advantage* happens when the item or service being produced is the same as the competitors, but the organization with the advantage can do so more efficiently and therefore achieves a higher profit margin.

A *differential advantage* is when the products or services are unique to competitors, for example, they are of a higher quality.

WHY DO I USE IT?

By analysing your resources (or those of your competitors), you will learn more about your competitive advantage.

Competitive advantages provide organizations with an edge over the competition, adding value to the company. It becomes increasingly difficult for competitors to match a competitive advantage, the more sustainable it is. If it is difficult for the organization to retain the advantage, then the competition will eventually match it, or the company will struggle to maintain it.

A prime example of a company with a differential advantage is Apple, who are famous for creating innovative products. For several years competitors were unable to match Apple. But, as you can also see, a differential advantage's lifetime isn't indefinite. In Apple's case, competitors have caught up with what was once innovative technology and – whilst their competitive advantage of perceived premium quality still remains – competitors such as Samsung and Huawei are coming close to matching it.

So let's review the model in more detail below with the key questions to ask at each stage (Figure 2.5).

The VRIO framework can be applied across the organization or to individual departments. It provides a solid perspective on each area of the business and how it should position itself in the marketplace. Capabilities and resources change over time, so the framework should be used regularly (and competitors also adapt).

TASK

Over to you! Analyse your organization, or one of your choice, using the VRIO framework template in Table 2.9. Insert answers to the questions at each stage and describe its level of competitive advantage.

TABLE 2.9 Your VRIO framework template

	VRIO stage	Key questions to ask	Levels of competitive advantage
V	VALUE		
R	RARITY		
I	IMITABILITY		
O	ORGANIZATION		

Summary

Congratulations, you have successfully analysed your organization's marketing environment both internally and externally!

- We've identified a clear view of what is happening inside and outside of the organization.
- We've analysed the organization's ability to respond to those potential challenges.
- We've identified company-specific strengths, opportunities, weaknesses and threats.
- We've identified the existing marketing challenges, where we can leverage current capabilities and how to lift performance with the SWOTELL framework.
- We analysed competitors with the COMPETE framework.
- We assessed the organization's resources and capabilities using the VRIO framework.

Bring this analysis with you as we progress into Chapter 3, where your analysis findings are translated into objectives.

References

Abad-Santos, A (2018) Nike's Colin Kaepernick ad sparked a boycott – and earned $6 billion for Nike [Online], Vox, available at: www.vox.com/2018/9/24/17895704/nike-colin-kaepernick-boycott-6-billion (archived at https://perma.cc/8JAC-Y5KW)

Barney, J (2007) *Gaining and Sustaining Competitive Advantage*, 3rd edn, Pearson Prentice Hall, Upper Saddle River, NJ

Batchelor, T (2017) Pepsi advert with Kendall Jenner pulled after huge backlash [Online], *Independent*, available at: www.independent.co.uk/arts-entertainment/tv/news/pepsi-advert-pulled-kendall-jenner-protest-video-cancelled-removed-a7668986.html (archived at https://perma.cc/AR4Q-4PUS)

ICO (2020) Guide to the General Data Protection Regulation [Online], Information Commissioner's Office, available at: ico.org.uk/for-organisations/guide-to-data-protection/guide-to-the-general-data-protection-regulation-gdpr/ (archived at https://perma.cc/CNP3-NXHV)

Informi (2020) Selling to EU countries – what could change post-Brexit transition? [Online], available at: informi.co.uk/legal/selling-to-eu-countries-what-could-change-post-brexit-transition (archived at https://perma.cc/9WFQ-TMFX)

Pacific Office (2018) Go Grey for Earth Day? [Online], Pacific Office Automation, available at: www.pacificoffice.com/about/blog/post/go-gray-for-earth-day-how-industries-can-save-money-and-resources-by-printi (archived at https://perma.cc/KA3M-UEXQ)

Statista (2020) Advertising in the United Kingdom – statistics & facts [Online], Statista, available at: www.statista.com/topics/1747/advertising-in-the-united-kingdom/#dossierSummary__chapter1 (archived at https://perma.cc/JJ5Z-R6S8)

Statista (2020) eBooks Worldwide [Online], Statista, available at: www.statista.com/outlook/213/100/ebooks/worldwide (archived at https://perma.cc/H5AX-SRFC)

UKCCS (2020) UK Copyright Law [Online], available at: copyrightservice.co.uk/copyright/p01_uk_copyright_law (archived at https://perma.cc/WB5V-TETQ)

03

Targets

Setting objectives

This chapters covers:

- The importance and value that objectives bring to marketing plans.
- How to create effective marketing objectives using the SCALE framework.

The value of objectives

This brings us to the first T in the STRATEGY framework: **Targets**.

Using analysis, you can create or redefine existing marketing objectives, ensuring that they are aligned to achieving the business's objectives.

Objectives give a sense of **purpose** and **direction**. They help departments direct their activities towards the same goals in a consistent way. Objectives **motivate** staff to achieve them, particularly if they are tied into performance measures. Objectives give a **benchmark for control** so organizations can assess whether they are meeting the set objectives. Digital objectives are aligned with corporate objectives.

Objectives should be **acceptable** and **understandable** to internal managers and external stakeholders.

Influences on objectives

There are a number of factors that influence the choice and setting of objectives (Figure 3.1).

FIGURE 3.1 The influences on objectives

You may have seen objectives which include the following:

- increase sales;
- build brand awareness;
- grow market share;
- launch new products or services;
- target new customers;
- enter new markets internationally or locally;
- improve stakeholder relations;
- enhance customer relationships;

- improve internal communications;
- increase profit.

Let's discover how to create strategic objectives using the SCALE framework.

Building objectives that SCALE

The best approach to creating effective objectives is to use my SCALE framework. SCALE is an acronym that describes each aspect of an objective. SCALE objectives include all of the key elements which help you to align your marketing objectives to your organization's goals. They help to create solid objectives that include not only what you're trying to achieve but also when you need to achieve them by. By defining objectives that SCALE you will also create a marketing plan that has a good chance of succeeding.

The SCALE framework is set out in Figure 3.2. Let's break it down.

FIGURE 3.2 The SCALE framework

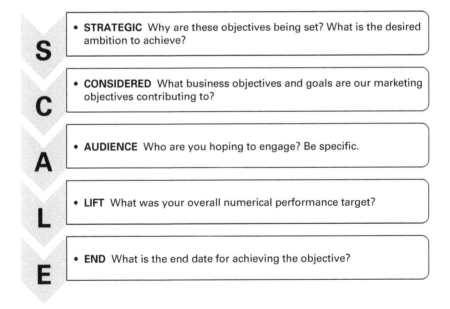

S
- **STRATEGIC** Why are these objectives being set? What is the desired ambition to achieve?

C
- **CONSIDERED** What business objectives and goals are our marketing objectives contributing to?

A
- **AUDIENCE** Who are you hoping to engage? Be specific.

L
- **LIFT** What was your overall numerical performance target?

E
- **END** What is the end date for achieving the objective?

S – STRATEGIC

Remind yourself where and why these objectives fit in with your overall strategy. We need to always keep strategic reasoning at the forefront of our minds when tracking results.

To keep things strategic, clearly define the objective of the marketing campaign. Is it to eradicate incorrect information about your product, like the Burger King example we discussed earlier, or is it to attract a different audience? Make these objectives easy for everyone in the organization to understand and support.

Avoid generalities as they only create confusion and can lead to poor results. Creating an objective to 'get more sales' is not helpful to anyone. Objectives should go much deeper than this. How many sales do you want to achieve? When do you want to achieve them? Are the sales for all products, or for specific items? Is there a particular target audience that you want to buy more of your products?

C – CONSIDERED

Realistic targets are those that your business can achieve with the resources you have. In many organizations, objectives are created before the organization's current context is analysed. When you set objectives first it's difficult to ensure that they are realistic within your context.

Understanding the current economic conditions through PESTLE and COMPETE analyses and the internal environment of the organization through SWOT, SWOTELL and VRIO analysis is crucial to setting realistic objectives.

For example, it would be unrealistic to set a goal of increasing sales if a recession is looming, or when new competitors have just entered the market.

Belief in the objectives set is important for their success. Everyone in the organization must agree the goals are achievable and that there are the tools and skills required to achieve the objectives.

A – AUDIENCE

When tracking the results of the campaign both while it's live and after it's complete, it is important to remain focused on the target audience you defined at the start.

For example, maybe there's been an increase in website traffic during your marketing campaign – but it's not from the audience you intended to target. You need to note this in your analysis, as it will help you to understand if and where your tactics may be misaligned (and enable you to pivot the campaign quickly if need be!)

L – LIFT

The KPI number chosen needs to be broken down into key milestones throughout the reporting duration of the campaign. If, for example, your campaign is running for three months, what numbers need to be generated (whether that's the number of leads, web visits, new customers, conversions) at each weekly, bi-weekly or monthly interval? Include milestones and goals to achieve. To be effective these should be very specific. A clearly defined measure of success is vital in understanding if the goal has been achieved.

E – END

Establishing a solid end date will help you to schedule your reporting, as well as helping to determine the timescale for reaching each milestone.

Schedule a clear end to achieve the objective. If there is no clear deadline, it's unlikely that goals will be reached, which means that people will become disillusioned and efforts towards achieving the goal will wane. The time-scale should be set with a specific end date, and everyone involved should be aware of the deadline set.

Clear endpoints also support measurement of your success during the key milestones running up to the end date.

SCALE-defined objectives

SCALE-defined objectives will help you to align your objectives with both the metrics that can help to measure progress, and with a timely reporting sched-ule. Speaking of which – the regularity of your reporting will depend a lot on the particular tactics you're using. For paid channels, reporting budget numbers on a weekly or even daily basis may be needed to ensure that spend doesn't escalate too quickly. Or, if you discover that the channels are not performing as well as expected, you may want to increase the frequency of reports in order to see whether any changes you've made to improve things are working.

Let's take this book as an example. An objective for this book is to become a bestseller in the marketing category within 12 months of publishing in the UK. There can be several KPIs aligned to this, such as the number of reviews, the number of 5-star reviews, the number of times the book is listed within the must-read lists, the number of universities including this book as a core resource and reaching the bestseller list. I can then break this down further to assign key milestones relating to what needs to happen within a particu-lar time frame to achieve this objective.

Areas to avoid when creating objectives

Avoid being vague. Be as specific as possible in your objective. If there's a target to increase the visits to your website, it should be 'increase website visits from new visitors by 5 per cent' (or something similarly specific).

Always include at least one KPI. If a KPI is not included, it's impossible to clearly measure the success or failure of the objective. Continuing my example from above, the KPI to measure is the existing new visitors to the website and the 5 per cent increase. If 1,000 people currently visit your website within 12 months, then 5 per cent increase in 12 months equals 1,050.

It's always good to focus on improving on a previous performance, but validate that the objective you are setting is attainable. Assess the resources, equipment, time and budget required to achieve the objective – are they all readily available? The same assessment can be done if an objective has been put upon you and the marketing team.

Is it realistic? If it isn't, you can build your case to management using the models, frameworks and tools in this chapter.

Time frame is absolutely key to achieving an objective. Ensure that it is as specific as possible and, as per the point above, that it is achievable with the constraints of the organization. This should always be in the back of your mind when creating any strategy and marketing campaign.

I created a SCALE objective for myself as a writer, to use as a goal to finish writing the book (see Table 3.1).

TABLE 3.1 Example of creating the SCALE framework to define objectives for this book

S	STRATEGIC	Write a book with 78,000 words about how to create a successful marketing strategy. Write a chapter a month, write 2,000 words each weekend for the next 39 weeks.
C	CONSIDERED	Measured by the 2,000 words in the timescale provided above. Write 2,000 words each weekend.
A	AUDIENCE	Finish my first rough draft within 39 weeks. Have the book ready to be proofread by May 2020 to provide enough time to make edits. My first audience is the one that will read the draft, ie a proofreader and marketing colleagues.
L	LIFT	During the week I'm busy running my business. The weekend is a time when I'll be less distracted and therefore able to spend more time and focus on writing to be able to achieve the 2,000 words per week for the next 39 weeks and achieve the end date.
E	END	Launch the book by May 2021.

TASK

Over to you! Using your SCALE framework template in Table 3.2, create SCALE objectives that define what the organization aims to achieve, are realistic and can be measured.

TABLE 3.2 Your SCALE framework template

S	STRATEGIC	
C	CONSIDERED	
A	AUDIENCE	
L	LIFT	
E	END	

Summary

Setting objectives is a huge step towards identifying the kind of strategy you'll need. By this point, you're well on your way to creating a winning strategy:

- We've discovered the importance of conducting situational analysis to inform objectives.
- We've identified the importance and value that objectives bring to marketing plans in providing direction and focus.
- We've established marketing objectives that SCALE using the framework.

Keep the objectives in mind throughout the remainder of this book. We will now progress to Chapter 4, where our focus shifts to understanding the needs and wants of your ideal customer.

04

Reach

Researching your customers

This chapter covers:

- Using data to identify and reach your customer.
- Discovering your customer's likes and dislikes.
- Positioning your organization's product or service.

We are now at stage R in the STRATEGY framework, which is where we find out more about who your existing customers are or who your new target audience is.

Constant developments in technology and devices have both led to changing marketing environments. This, in turn, has led to swift changes in customer behaviour, loyalty and focus. Who would have thought even three years ago that you'd be able to read an email through a smart speaker?

Companies are forced to keep up and stay ahead of the ever-changing likes, dislikes and behaviours of the consumer, or risk losing attention. Take location-tracking, for example. When it was first introduced, many thought it creepy or 'Big Brother-like', that an app could pinpoint your location and map your route. But when this technology began to provide value to consumers (like when Uber capitalized upon location-tracking to send convenient taxis right to people's feet) it quickly became the new normal. Now, many of us don't know what we'd do without location-tracking technology – if Google Maps can't put a pin in the right street, we get not only frustrated but lost!

So, we've moved from a position of mistrust to a place in which this previously 'creepy' technology is not only seen as normal, but as essential. From being worried about the capabilities of location-tracking, we've come to rely on it. This also demonstrates the importance of value. If there is value in sharing my location to get a taxi to arrive, then I'm more likely to see value in doing so, to and willingly share that information. As Tim Bond from the marketing governing body Data & Marketing Association (DMA) UK puts it in the interview at the end of this chapter, 'it's consumers that will lead the change'.

Interesting consumer psychology is at play here, and Maslow's Hierarchy of Needs captures this (McLeod, 2020). The Hierarchy of Needs (Figure 4.1) is a five-tiered triangle which demonstrates the position and relative urgency of human needs. The requirements at each level must be satisfied before the person moves up a tier.

You'll see that the second tier contains the essentials of feeling safe and secure. Uber could be placed here, with the availability to track a taxi. The customer is choosing this option ahead of a traditional taxi to satisfy their need to feel safe (and because it's convenient). By doing this, the customer is using new technology to meet this ancient psychological need.

FIGURE 4.1 Hierarchy of needs

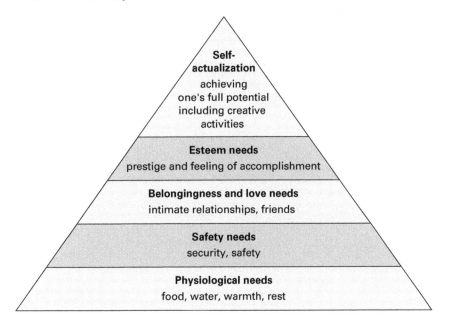

Question the psychological needs that your offering satisfies, as this is an area that can be mapped to the benefits of your product (which is explored in detail in Chapter 4). All of this will play an essential role in marketing your communications to engage your target audience.

Similar developments, while initially mistrusted, have rooted technology more deeply into our lives than we would ever have believed possible a decade ago. This is evident when comparing the most globally valuable companies in 2009 to those in 2019. Figure 4.2 shows the four largest US and Chinese companies in 2009, with oil companies heading the list.

By 2019 seven out of the 10 globally most valuable companies in 2019 are technology companies (Figure 4.3). The only company remaining in the list from 2009 is Johnson & Johnson, who are producers of medical devices, pharmaceutical and consumer packaged goods (Desjardins, 2019). This is as a direct result of our shift as consumers to both accept and welcome the need for technology in our lives.

FIGURE 4.2 Eight most globally valuable US and Chinese companies in 2009

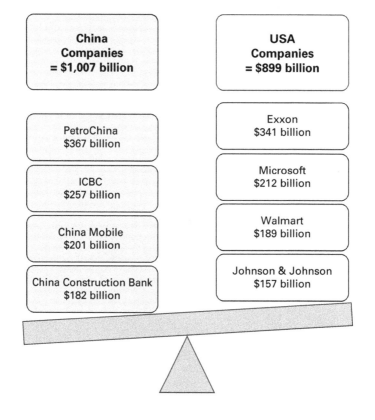

FIGURE 4.3 Ten most globally valuable companies in 2019

Microsoft $1,050 bn	
Apple $920 bn	
Facebook $546 bn	
Alibaba $435 bn	
Visa $379 bn	
Amazon $943 bn	
Alphabet $778 bn	
Berkshire Hathaway $507 bn	
Tencent $431 bn	
Johnson & Johnson $376 bn	

Visual Capitalist, 2019

Without even realizing it, people have developed expectations that their favourite brands will send them highly relevant and personalized content whenever and wherever it is needed. Now more than ever brands need to engage with customers on a personal level.

This isn't always an easy ask for brands and strategists – but we, too, can use technology to our advantage to enhance the customer's experience. And we should, because our customers are expecting it as standard.

The importance of understanding your customer

Ultimately, what your customers want from you is something of value to them. They'll be willing to pay for something they think will really benefit them. This is known as the value exchange (Day, 2000; Fill, 2015).

This starts with tailoring your marketing towards the kinds of people you think might want what you're selling. But the concept of value exchange can be carried further. It works for marketing, as well.

In the value exchange of marketing, the customer exchanges their valuable attention for the information about your offering. So, once you've identified a specific audience for your marketing, take things further. Look deep into who that audience is. Learn about them. Understand them. And think, while you're doing so, of the kind of marketing message which would engage them.

Make sure that the information is portrayed in a manner worth their attention. If you get it right, you'll gain the holy grail of marketing – value-added relationships. One-off customers will come back, brand loyalty will be fostered, and you may even get a collaborative relationship with your customers (perhaps with positive reviews, or friendly user-generated content!)

If you can increase the strength of this collaboration, you'll get a high Lifetime Value from your customers (more on measuring this in Chapter 8) as they continue their relationship with your brand, and even bring family and friends into your circle. But achieving this means providing constant value for and engagement with the customer. Michele Gettins, Global Category Manager at baby supplies company Tommee Tippee explains the importance of knowing your customers:

> For me one of the roles of marketing (and the marketing strategy) is to really understand consumers, their wants, needs and desires and to deliver innovation that delivers against those, and genuinely makes parents lives easier.

As Michele explains, the fundamental role of marketing is to truly understand customers. The marketing department (as mentioned in Chapter 1) should be the voice of the customer within an organization. It achieves this by understanding the customer's needs, wants and desires. The organization can then use this 'voice' to steer the direction of innovation or to change areas of the business in order to satisfy these needs, wants and desires.

This all relates back to the CIM's definition of the role of marketing as explored in Chapter 1 – *identifying*, *anticipating* and *satisfying* customer needs'.

Understanding your customer through data

Just as in real life, the best brand/customer relationships are based on mutual understanding.

If you're doing your job right, your potential customers already have plenty of resources where they can learn about you. So, now it's time to put in the work at your end. To build that all-important brand–consumer relationship, you need to learn about your customer.

Insights and understanding about your customers are vital for informing your strategic direction. You can gain these insights by digging into data.

Data will tell you everything you need to know about your customer's interests, behaviour, needs and wants. It comes in various types and can be gathered from multiple sources – from social media to website analytics to good old-fashioned face-to-face feedback.

But before we start getting too deep into data and what it can do for you, a quick word about the infamous GDPR and other data protection legislations, such as the CCPA in the United States and PIPEDA in Canada.

Data, controversy and privacy

You'll have heard a lot of bad things about data over the past few years – probably in conjunction with terms like 'Cambridge Analytica', 'scandal' and 'crisis'. The concern about privacy and data misuse is definitely justified. Unscrupulous methods of data harvesting, the unconsented sale of data to third parties, and a lack of transparency over data gathering have left people feeling vulnerable and exploited (*The Guardian*, 2020).

Part of the problem was that people were often unaware of the data trail they were leaving. Where permission was sought, it was usually done via the use of long and complicated small print. This had real-world impacts – for example, 91 per cent of Americans would consent to legal terms and conditions without reading them and therefore, didn't know how their data was being used (Deloitte, 2017). This is not how a brand–customer relationship should grow, and a lot of trust has been lost as a result.

However, that doesn't change the fact that data is now and always has been the primary method we marketers have of gaining an understanding of our audience, reaching our audience and learning how our campaigns are doing. If people had been more ethical, open and honest about how they gather and use data, I wouldn't now have to type 'data' like it's a dirty word. But they did, so here we are, struggling to give customers the content they want in a cyber world which is shutting us out.

As explained by Tim Bond from the DMA UK in the interview at the end of this chapter:

> The biggest shift over that time has been the number of organizations recognizing the benefits of the new laws. As businesses have implemented the necessary changes and come to terms with new processes, they've increasingly seen the positive impact to their businesses and marketing campaigns of putting the customer at the heart of everything they do – which is essentially what GDPR does.

People have always used 'data' in one form or another to get to know their target audience. When you're talking to your friends, you use 'data' (ie your knowledge of their likes, experiences and opinions) to keep your conversation exciting and relevant to them. As marketers, we do the same. The problem we began to encounter with the introduction of social media is that vast volumes of intensely personal data on social media users became available – and that data became an intensively traded commodity.

Data harvested unscrupulously by apps could be sold on to third parties (like political campaigns, in the Cambridge Analytica case), and then manipulated to target people with dishonest content designed to pique their darkest fears or most fervent desires. When the Facebook data scandal broke in 2018, people felt not only betrayed but violated. Many were unaware that their data had even been collected in the first place, and most were horrified at the way in which their data had been used. Henk-Frits Verkerk, Director at Sports Alliance, explains the challenge:

> … businesses face a challenge when it comes to gathering data. Why would you hand over your personal details to someone who wants to sell you energy, mobile phones, whatever? GDPR increases this challenge because companies need to be open about why they want the data. Businesses need to come up with a viable reason for clients to want to share their data. This is a real strategic issue.

What we're left with is a climate in which the actions of an immoral few have made everyone very wary of data gathering and usage. As Verkerk (2020) says, people are not keen to hand over any data to companies they believe will exploit them for profit.

But there's no need to throw away all the good things that data can offer us. We just have to ensure that our data policies are easy to read, transparent and honest, and place customers and their data protection centre stage.

Solving the data trust issue

The problem is not with the fact that data was used – the problem is that it was gathered without explicit and transparent permission, and that it was used in a dishonest, manipulative manner. If we can collect and utilize data ethically, using it to add actual value to enhance the customers experience, there is no problem. The best way to do this is to give the customer control and in full agreement with us. As Tim Bond explains, 'put the customer first' (Bond, 2020).

Here are a few tips to ensure that your data practice is ethical:

- Be transparent at every stage. When you're gathering data, *clearly* inform the customer that this is what you're doing.
- Give the customer the choice to opt in. In addition to informing the customer that you're gathering data, give them the choice as to what they

are opting in to. For example, if your website uses cookies to track customer behaviour, inform your online visitors that you're using cookies, and give them the option to browse your site with cookies disabled. However, be aware that the use of cookies, and tracking in general, is an ever-changing area and one that will reshape the way in which we, as marketers, have insight into our customer's online journey (Lardinois, 2020).

- Tell the customer how you plan to use their data and use it only for those purposes.

- Tell the customer where you plan to store their data, and for how long. Ensure you have the processes in place to make this happen.

- Keep all data secure and make your data privacy policies clear to the customer. The security of data should also be one that is continuously being monitored and controlled, ensuring that there are no lapses where hacks and breaches could occur.

- Do not sell data on to third parties unless it is explicitly clear at the time of providing consent that the data will be used in that way. For example, if you're an organization that hosts events for third parties and as part of that offering leads (in the form of data including subscribers to the event/webinar) are then shared with the sponsoring company. Make it clear at the point of sign-up that the attendees will be contacted by the sponsors. This not only enables the attendee to make an informed decision as to whether to share their data with your organization and the sponsor but will also reap a more engaged response from the sponsor's follow-up communication after the event.

If these practices are actioned, then there's no reason why you should not keep gleaning valuable insights from honestly gathered data.

How can you conduct audience research?

This may all seem very daunting. How can you research your audience if their data is so sensitive?

Well, it's not actually that difficult. In fact, when your customers are on board with what you're doing, it can actually be easier!

Here are some tips:

- *Be upfront and honest.* You'd be surprised at how willing people are to tell you about themselves – especially when you make it clear that you'll be using the data to improve their experience. So, ask! Questionnaires, preference centres and so on are all great ways to gather data in an upfront and honest way.

- *Give the customer control.* I've spoken above about choice and transparency in data. The same applies when gathering data for research. Make sure that the customer always has 100 per cent control over the data you gather and how you use it. Make this clear at all times and tell the customer how they can control their own data. Not only is this reassuring for customers, it's also a great way to build trust.
- *Add value.* There's nothing shameful in encouraging your customers! Offer incentives for them to participate in data gathering. Maybe discount codes, or entry into a prize draw.

With these ethical data principles and tips in mind, it's time to get into some market research.

What is market research?

Conducting market research is a useful way to gather information about your target audience and prospects. It will help you to develop customer personas (more on that in a bit), as well as giving you some insights into how successfully your product or service fits your targets' needs.

Market research can also help you identify who your prospects and customers go to first for information, for more options or to make a purchase. It's an excellent way of identifying trends and challenges in your industry, and can tell you a lot about influences on purchase decisions (which may impact future conversions).

The different types of market research

Primary and secondary research are the two main types:

- *Primary research* – is first-hand information directly from your target customer. This can be gathered by conducting interviews and surveys where an organization can ask specific questions.
- *Secondary research* – this is public record information such as trend reports, sales data available within your organization and industry content. This research is useful when analysing competitors.

HOW TO CONDUCT PRIMARY RESEARCH

Use your customer personas (as developed later in this chapter) to inform the type of people that are selected for focus groups. Plan the topics that you'd like more information about and create the questions to ensure that the sessions held with your target customers are as useful as possible. There are specialist companies in this area that can help you coordinate a focus group and surveys. There are also your existing customers. Ask them what they think, gather their feedback and insight to learn more about your target customers and what it is about your offering they value.

HOW TO CONDUCT SECONDARY RESEARCH

Review your competitors using G2 Crowd where you can review user ratings for your competitors based on the industry (www.g2.com/).

Market reports are available from companies such as Forrester and Gartner (go.forrester.com/, www.gartner.com/en). There are free and gated reports available that include annual industry analysis.

Social media can also be used to research what your target audience is saying about your organization and competitors. Brandwatch is an example of one of those tools (www.brandwatch.com/).

There's also the option to search for your competitors and review their activity on each social media platform.

Review your research into your competitors through your SEO and PPC activity (more on this in Chapters 6 and 7) and you may be surprised to learn that your competitors are not those you expected. Some useful tools to explore this further are Google Search Console (search.google.com/search-console/about), SEMrush (www.semrush.com) and Sprout Social (sproutsocial.com/). Discover the content that your target audience is interested in with SparkToro (sparktoro.com/).

Segmenting, targeting and positioning (STP) your organization with the target market

There's data which can tell you about your customers, data which can tell you about your performance, and data which tells you everything in between. Understanding what the data is telling you will ensure that your marketing is optimized.

The only way to do this is by having a clear strategy. Otherwise, you risk gathering data without a clear direction and will end up drowning in numbers.

TABLE 4.1 The four main types of segmentation

SEGMENTATION	INCLUDES	WHY IS THIS IMPORTANT?
Geographic	Regions, countries, counties, cities, neighbourhoods	The place where the target audience lives can affect their buying decisions. It can also affect the placement of bricks'n'mortar-based retail outlets.
Demographic	Age, gender, income, occupation, family size, family lifestyle, socio-economic status	Segmenting a market by, for example, income can inform a brand about things like the purchasing powers of the target audience. It is also one of the key factors involved in deciding whether to market the product as a need, want or a luxury. There are three different groups that are regularly used when segmenting by income: High income, Mid income, Low income.
Psychographic	Personality, lifestyle, attitude, beliefs	This works on the premise that a consumer's buying behaviour can be influenced by their character and beliefs. This level of segmentation can provide deeper and richer insights about the consumer than other, less personally-focused forms. These can influence the buying decisions and habits of a person to a great extent. For example, a person living a lavish lifestyle may consider certain purchases to be a need, whereas a person living a different lifestyle in the same city may consider those same purchases to be luxuries.
Behavioural	Those who know about the product, those who don't know about the product, former users, potential users, current users, first-time users, loyal customers, brand-neutral, loyal to a competitor, prospects. A combination of all can be used to create a segment, or just one.	This covers attitudes toward the product, use of the product and benefits the consumer expects to receive. This segmentation is based on an audience's behaviour, usage, preference, choices and decision-making. Segments are divided based on customers' knowledge of the product and their ways of using the product or service. Their knowledge and usage of the product can affect the buying decision of an individual.

Consulting with brands, I regularly get asked to review why their marketing activity is no longer working. Often, the problem is that the brand has been too business-focused and has neglected to truly understand their customers.

So, it's vital to ensure that you're getting to know your target audience in as much detail as you possibly can.

Segmentation

Segmentation is a useful way of splitting up a broad target audience into smaller groups with similarities. Think of it as similar to segments in an orange. Each segment is separate from the other, but they are all part of the orange as a whole. It's the same when segmenting a target audience. They are all similar in that they are suitable prospects for your product/service.

There are four ways to start segmenting the target market, outlined in Table 4.1.

The essential factor to keep in mind when segmenting is that each segment created must provide value to your organization. For example, if your customers were segmented by country but you only offer your product or service in the United States, then that segmentation basis isn't beneficial. It would be more appropriate to segment by the individual US State in which your target consumers are based.

Different segments should also have distinguishing features which make them unique. Segmentation can be used to boost conversions and to cut costs as it is a very effective use of marketing budget. By catering to the specific needs and wants of each segment, your marketing approach will be more effective. This enables you to optimize your messaging and offering to each segment.

Similar to the SCALE methodology for objectives that we covered in Chapter 3, the checklist below can be used to identify whether the segments you have created are effective:

CHECKLIST: SEGMENTATION

Here's a checklist to use to identify effective segmentation:

☐ Measurable – the segment needs to be of a size where results can be measured.

☐ Accessible – the data for each segment should be easy to reach and access.

☐ Substantial – the size of the segment is valuable to use.

☐ Differentiable – each segment is distinct from the other.

☐ Actionable – actions can be created using the segments.

TASK

Using Table 4.2, jot down the methods of segmentation that your organization or the one you have chosen previously is currently using. Which additional ones could you now use?

TABLE 4.2 Segmentation methods used in your organization

SEGMENTATION	DETAIL HOW THE METHODS BELOW ARE USED IN YOUR ORGANIZATION
Geographic	
Demographic	
Psychographic	
Behavioural	

Targeting your customer segment

Once your customer segments have been defined, the next step is targeting. The purpose here is to not target 'everyone' with the same message but to define the target group by identifying and understanding your particular niche. As Mark Ritson (2020) stated at the beginning of the book, your focus is on answering the question 'Who am I targeting?'

It's by understanding more about your target customers that you can then target them with relevant content, messaging and advertising that will

FIGURE 4.4 The four main types of targeting

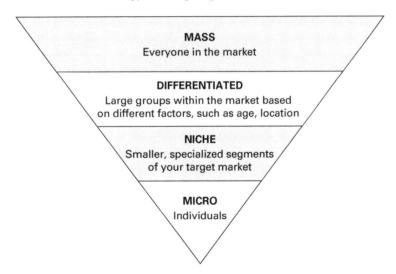

appeal to them. Conversions will increase the more insight that you have about your audience (which are key metrics we'll cover in more detail in Chapter 8). There are various approaches that can be used for this, as outlined in Figure 4.4.

Targeting can be used to evaluate the potential and commercial attractiveness of each of the segments you've defined above. The more clearly defined each target group is within its segment, the better you can understand how and where to reach your target audience.

To begin, broad categories can be used (eg homeowners), but ultimately, you'll need a lot more detail – such as the type of home that is owned (eg an apartment, bungalow, terrace house) to achieve success.

By using this approach, you won't stop people outside of these segments buying from you – you just won't be prioritizing them in your marketing strategy. However, to make sure you're not excluding markets with a lot of potential from your marketing strategy, you should conduct thorough audience research before defining your target audience.

CHECKLIST: TARGET MARKET

When defining your target market, consider the following:

☐ Market size – the market must be big enough for segmentation to provide value. If it is small, there may be little need in segmentation.

☐ Differentiation – as with the market size, there must be distinctive differences between each segment.

☐ Valuable – segmentation should provide value to the organization and not be costly without being profitable. The segments must also be able to receive marketing messages.

Positioning your organization competitively to attract your target market

Positioning is the approach taken by an organization to market its product or service. When establishing positioning the image or identity of a brand or product is created for consumers to view it in a certain way. A product or brand's 'position' is the place it occupies in the consumers' minds relative to competitors. It is influenced by the way in which the product is defined by consumers according to important attributes.

This is the stage in which a single image of the product is created based on its intended audience. Good positioning enhances the perception of a product/service with the target customer and moves from awareness to purchase. Specific positioning where the target audience is the core focus will increase the success of an organization.

As an example, when you think about music you probably think of Spotify. That's because it has been clearly positioned as 'a digital music service that gives you access to millions of songs' (Spotify, 2020). It's incredibly clear with no ambiguity. What's more, Spotify has stuck to this clear and precise position.

Building a competitive advantage through positioning

To build a competitive advantage through positioning, you first need to identify what makes your organization different from competitors. Spotify only provides an online streaming service. It hasn't diluted that offering with any other services, and it does that one thing exceptionally well. In doing so, it has built a competitive advantage, firstly by becoming incredibly recognizable as a music streaming service, and secondly by doing this better than competitors.

We went through this back in Chapter 2 when we discussed competitive advantages. But it's worth repeating here, as your competitive advantage is key for positioning yourself in the market.

Potential differentiators include:

- *Product differentiation* – a unique product not offered by competitors.

- *Channel differentiation* – perhaps you are using a unique and interesting channel, or using traditional channels in new ways.

- *People differentiation* – it may be that the employees at your organization make it stand out

- *Image differentiation* – this can be in the form of branding, tone of voice, image reputation, ie superior brand/value.

CHECKLIST: COMPETITIVE ADVANTAGE

The checklist for choosing the right competitive advantage is to ensure it is:

☐ Important to the customer.

☐ Distinctive – not a copy of the competition.

☐ Superior – provides a better experience.

☐ Communicable – you're able to effectively communicate it in marketing.

☐ Affordable – it's realistic given the organization's.

☐ Profitable – giving this differentiation isn't going to make the business bankrupt.

A lot of this can be established by going back to your customer personas and working out how they will perceive and/or react to the way you're presenting these factors.

Creating customer personas

It will be difficult to position your organization, product or service to meet customers' needs without knowing anything about those customers. A widely used method of getting to know your customers involves creating profiles or 'personas'.

A customer profile defines your ideal (or targeted) customer by establishing their likes, dislikes, habits, behaviour, where they work, income and so on. They can be known as customer personas or buyer personas (depending on where they are being used in the business) and will add value throughout all departments – not just marketing.

Customer personas should be based on market research and insights gathered from existing customers. Each persona is a fictional representation of an actual potential customer. Many marketers find it helpful to assign personas to their segments or target audiences, but they can also be used in product development, to ensure that the needs of your customers are considered during decision-making.

Customer personas are instrumental in the formulation of marketing strategies. They help you to illuminate who the buyers are, the situations they are faced with, their pain points and – most importantly – the goals they are attempting to accomplish. Personas help to provide context and 'reality' to your target customer for the rest of the organization. This can help to plan content, allocate resources and business planning. Your strategy is then aimed at attracting those customer personas to your business.

To develop a customer persona, you need to consider the following four identifiers: demographic, psychographic, environmental and behavioural (see Table 4.3).

There are many different types of personas, and they'll vary widely across different industries. They also vary within industries. Depending on your business, you may have one or many personas. Pinning your customer personas down accurately depends on getting the right data. Your objective is to identify personas for your different key groups of customers.

Researching your ideal customer

When creating a persona, the focus should be on making it as accurate and specific as possible. To do so, research ideally needs to be conducted on your actual customer base.

TABLE 4.3 The four main identifiers when determining a customer persona

DEMOGRAPHIC	PSYCHOGRAPHIC
Highlights the population segments of a company's ideal customer.	Helps marketers to understand the way their ideal customer thinks.
BEHAVIOURAL	ENVIRONMENTAL
Helps marketers to understand how a company's target customer behaves.	Helps marketers to understand the environment that their ideal customer lives in.

TIPS

Conducting audience research

1. Find out about your existing customers

Define potential new customers by understanding the characteristics of your existing customer base. Gather the information you can access about your existing customers in order to track trends and averages.

Data points to consider include:

- Age – this data may not be readily available, but if it is, it can be useful to identify the decade of life your customers are in.

- Geography – where do your existing customers live? This helps to identify the relevant operating hours for customer services and sales departments, as well as when to schedule social media adverts, send email marketing campaigns and so on.

- Purchasing behaviour – how much disposable income do your customers have to spend? Is there specific information they will be seeking when making a purchase?

- Interests – what do your customers like to do, besides using your products or services? What TV shows do they watch? What other businesses do they interact with? What social media channels do they use as this will help inform your communications plan later on.

2. Identify the life cycle stage your customers have reached

If you're selling in a business-to-business (B2B) environment, your categories will look different from those above. Collecting information about the size of the businesses that buy from you, along with information about job roles, titles, business structure (eg flat or hierarchical) and the people who make the buying decisions will also be useful insights.

Interviewing customers, potential customers or non-customers that resemble your target market – either in person, over the phone or online – can be a good way to discover what they like about your product or service. Ask questions about their job role and title if you're a B2B organization. In business-to-consumer (B2C), ask your customers what they like most about the product, and what they use it for (Newberry, 2020):

Listen. Take every opportunity to do so. There are so many customer touchpoints today, and everyone can generate insightful information about your customers. But the best source of insight is those customers.

SOURCE Bond, 2020

The messaging minefield

Some organizations, even now, persist with that old 'build it and they will come' attitude. These brands simply have not spoken to enough customers to validate their marketing tactics. Quite honestly, before you get even an inkling of what your target audience wants, you need to speak to a huge number of customers.

Social media is an amazing way of getting to know your customers. No, I don't mean in a creepy Cambridge Analytica data-mining sort of way! I mean in an honest, direct engagement way.

A well-managed social media account (or two) can be a great weapon in your strategic arsenal. In this first stage of building your strategy, it provides a great point of engagement with customers and prospects, which you can use to build your understanding of who your audience members are and what they want.

Use social media to ask questions about what your audience like, what they want, what they think of your brand. Take lessons from their comments. Analyse the demographics of engagement. And use your insights to inform your strategic understanding of your customers.

Of course, social media is not the only channel through which you can open conversations with customers. Email, polls, feedback, reviews – all of these are forms of customer communication. Keep engaging in 'social listening' – ie keeping your ears open to all the ways in which customers are communicating with your brand (and what they're saying!)

Lead scoring

If you're a B2B organization and don't know anything about your customers, you can try a method called 'lead scoring'.

Lead scoring involves allocating a score based upon activities which the lead/prospect has fulfilled. For example, if a prospect completed a form online, that may equate to a score of 2. If that customer also then subscribed to your email marketing, they receive a score of 3, making it a total of 5. This method enables you to understand more about how your customers 'behave'.

This is useful, because it tells you who is the most engaged, who is the most likely to convert, and the tactics which successfully increase your prospects' lead scores. For example, if you target a specific campaign to 3s and the majority of them rise to 5s, you know that this campaign is popular with your audience. It's also a good way to establish where customers are on their journey (more on that later).

Tailoring marketing

Once you've established your personas, it's time to start customizing your marketing towards them. Let's use personas defined by job role as an example.

In a B2B setting, two job roles could be the CEO and business development manager. Your strategy should be adapted to the buyer persona to target them effectively.

A CEO is going to be interested in different elements of a service or product than a business development manager. Your method of contacting each persona may also be different, as may the language used to communicate with each person.

Negative personas can also be created, which are focused on the characteristics of the people which aren't an excellent fit for your business. By understanding who's not interested in you as well as who is, you'll be able to segment out the unsuitable customers from the rest. This can help to reduce the costs of targeting the unsuitable customer and reduce the cost per lead in a B2B organization.

EXAMPLES: CUSTOMER PERSONAS

Below are examples of two customer personas.

The first example details the likes of the target audience for Action for Children (Table 4.4) as Sara Meikle (2020) details in the interview at the end of Chapter 7.

The second example of a B2B customer persona may focus on the key decision-maker. Attitude, reputation and job focus all play an important part in understanding how the company can relate to the decision-maker. This is different from the donor persona below, as the B2B persona's job role is a core element of focus.

TABLE 4.4 The specific likes as an example for an Action for Children donor

LIKES	Good causes – keen to support where possible. Family and friend events where everyone can be involved. Auction events that raise money for charity. Celebrities and their involvement in charitable causes. Prizes and giveaways. Challenges that they can get involved with.

The dangers of not knowing your customer

As one airline discovered, failing to understand customers and target audiences can be very, very costly.

In 1981, American Airlines introduced the AAirpass, offering unlimited first-class flights at a fixed price (EZMarketing, 2019). Their objective was to generate millions of dollars in sales.

However, the customers who bought these AAirpasses used them an awful lot more than American Airlines had anticipated. By 2007, AAirpass holders were taking thousands of free flights every year. This cost the company millions and therefore didn't achieve the objective of raising millions! (EZMarketing, 2019).

In a nutshell, the problem was that the purchase price of the pass didn't take into account customers using them for frequent trips. In an attempt to reduce their losses, the airline revoked passes. Which, not unreasonably, resulted in outrage and lawsuits (Rothstein, 2019). Breaking promises to your customers is never a good look.

American Airlines wanted to build loyalty and simultaneously rake in huge profits. But, ultimately, through the frequent-flying loophole and the lawsuits which followed, it achieved precisely the opposite of this.

How could they have made such a catastrophic error? Well, the company was so focused on raising funds quickly that they didn't research who the likely AAirpass purchasers would be. In doing so, they alienated long-time customers, lost huge profits and made a fatal error. Had they done something as simple as limiting rewards to a set number of flights per year, the offering would have been sustainable for the company. And something as simple as a bit of market research and persona-building could have ensured that this was built into the strategy.

The marketing lesson here is to set reasonable boundaries to any incentives being offered, to always deliver on the promises made, and to research who your customers are and (in the American Airlines case) what their usage of the incentive is likely to be (ie how often are they going to be using their AAirpasses?)

My target customer for this book is set out in Table 4.5 (as the reader of this book, is this you?).

TABLE 4.5 An example of the target customer for this book

BACKGROUND	Marketers, business owners, entrepreneurs, students
DEMOGRAPHICS	UK, Europe, United States, worldwide
PERSONALITY IDENTIFIERS	Skills in marketing, keen to learn and expand knowledge. Curious and interested in new methods and approaches
LIKES	Marketing, learning, expanding knowledge, reading
DISLIKES	Wading through stuffy texts; an absence of practical examples; little application provided

TASK

Complete the template in Table 4.6 to identify your target customer.

TABLE 4.6 Your template to identify your target customer

BACKGROUND	
DEMOGRAPHICS	
PERSONALITY IDENTIFIERS	
LIKES	
DISLIKES	

The 4Ps

To validate and provide depth to your positioning, consider using the 4Ps. We'll go into these in more detail when we study the Marketing Mix in Chapter 4, but they're worth mentioning here, too.

The 4Ps (Costantinides, 2006) are as follows.

Price

The psychology of pricing in marketing is something that can make or break a product's sales success. You'll undoubtedly have seen the use of 99p/¢ instead of £1/€1 /$1. The psychology behind this particular pricing method is that the item appears a lot cheaper even though it is only by 1p/¢. When making a purchasing decision, people perceive the difference between £1.99 and £2 to be bigger than it actually is (despite what they logically know). Human psychology is a strange thing!

On the other hand, it may not be a good idea to position your product too far towards the 'budget' end of the market. Many consumers associate a higher price with higher quality and vice versa. A product could be positioned as an alternative to more expensive competitors, but if the intention isn't to be seen as 'cheap', then the pricing level chosen would need to be centrally placed.

Place

The placement of where your product/service is available has an important role to play. At a basic level, if the majority of your target audience lives in city centres, having your product available in rural, hard-to-reach areas would not be productive positioning for this audience. The same principle applies online. Place or position your product or service as close to the target market as possible.

Promotion

This includes any method of advertising. The positioning element is important here because the same advertisement may not work for the intended audience when certain factors are different. For example, a television advert may not have the same impact on your target audience at 6am as it would at 7pm.

Product

The product includes all the attributes and benefits of the product with specific characteristics identified. This can also focus on the use and application of the product and the quality of the item.

Market positioning

You've already conducted an analysis of market factors back in Chapter 2. But it can help you to nail your market positioning if you really understand where you are in relation to your competition. It's also helpful in identifying which competitors are perceived as your closest rivals, and from whom you need to differentiate yourself most clearly.

One way to determine your organization's product or brand positioning is by using a perceptual map, also known as a positioning map. A perceptual map illustrates consumer perception of the products in your market.

This enables you to identify how competitors are positioned in comparison to yourself and allows you to identify any opportunities in the marketplace.

Figure 4.5 provides an example, with the positioning of car brands. This is my own perception of each car brand in terms of quality and price. You'll see that high quality and high price is where Rolls-Royce has been positioned. Lower price and lower quality have been assigned to Renault.

FIGURE 4.5   Example positioning/perceptual map

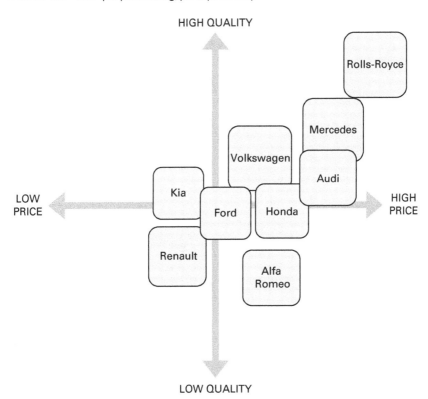

TASK

Plot the same organization as before for the previous tasks on a positioning map, using the template in Figure 4.6, including at least three competitors.

FIGURE 4.6   Your positioning/perceptual map template

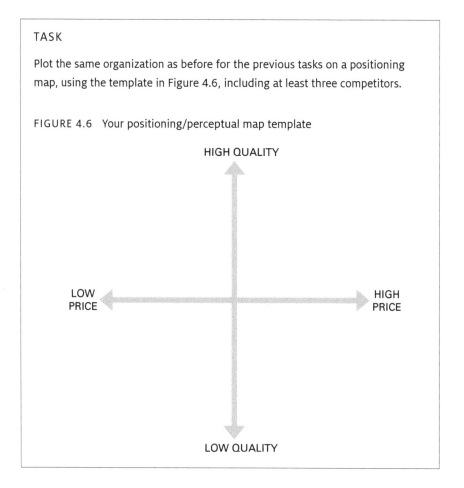

Creating a positioning statement

Once you've identified your market and product positioning, a statement can be created to communicate this across the organization. This positioning statement will detail how you want the brand to be perceived by consumers succinctly.

Here, for example, is the positioning statement of Rolls-Royce: 'Rolls-Royce pioneers cutting-edge technologies that deliver clean, safe and competitive solutions to meet our planet's vital power needs' (Rolls-Royce, 2020).

Here are some guidelines for creating a good positioning statement:

• make it simple, memorable and tailored to the target market;

• determine the uniqueness of your organization in comparison to competitors;

- clearly identify your current market position;
- make sure it is credible and that your company can deliver on its promise;
- make it unique to your organization, to ensure the brand can "own" it;
- ensure that it is ambitious enough to optimize for growth without overstretching;
- make it achievable.

To create an online value proposition, identify customer needs, then clarify a value proposition to meet those needs at a profit. Deliver your value proposition through the right product and service, the right channels and with consistent communication.

As an example, here's my value proposition for this book:

> A one-stop framework that is easy to digest and implement for all marketers when devising a marketing strategy.

TASK

Write down in one sentence what makes your organization different from competitors.

Neil Hopkins, Independent Communications Consultant from Neonadal has this to say about positioning statements:

> I believe that there are two myths stopping businesses from developing great communications strategies.
>
> Myth One: That the strategy needs to list everything that you need – or will ever need – to communicate meaningfully with your customers.
>
> Myth Two: That a strategy needs to include every single step on your journey and be completely prescriptive about every action that you'll ever take.
>
> Neither myth is true – but both are widely believed. And who, really, has the time to create lists of everything which are out of date as soon as you hit save? With that in mind, it's unsurprising that business leaders pressed for time and need to 'make something happen' often abandon important strategic development for instant tactical gratification.

A CAUTIONARY CASE STUDY
Tesco Clubcard email

If you fail to understand your customers properly, you can't communicate with them properly. Don't make the mistake Tesco made when announcing changes to their Clubcard policy in 2018 by email.

The copy used in this email was cold and factual. The only personalization – deployed in a very formal manner – was to include the customer's last name. Tesco Clubcard holders are likely to have been customers of the company across several years, yet this email does little to acknowledge that or to encourage the customer to keep coming back after the changes.

After receiving hundreds of customer complaints, Tesco delayed the changes to the Clubcard reward scheme in response to customer feedback.

It's important to know your customer in order to target your marketing efforts effectively. Otherwise, you'll be shooting in the dark and expending a lot of effort for very little return.

SOURCE BBC, 2019

As Tim Bond, Head of Insight at the DMA, stated, 'put your customer first'. And I couldn't agree more. This is an approach that is a common theme throughout this book because a marketing strategy should be focused on your customer to be truly successful.

Interview: Tim Bond

Tim Bond is Head of Insight at the Data & Marketing Association.

JT: *Tell us about yourself, your marketing background, what you do, who you work for and your passion.*

TB: I'm originally a social scientist by training, having studied for my MA in Sociology at Aberdeen University way back when. Before joining the DMA, I spent around 10 years in agencies working across communications and market research campaigns for a range of clients and sectors. As the Head of Insight at the DMA, a key part of my role is developing actionable insight for the data and marketing industry, which also supports the Association's core belief in putting the customer first and leading the business sector in creativity and innovation.

On a personal note, I'm a father, husband and geek. I've always been fascinated by how things work, which is probably why I've ended up in my current field. I'm also not great at doing nothing or sitting still, so hobbies like cycling and photography keep me busy when I'm not at work – as well as my daughter!

JT: *Data is a big topic in marketing. What are your three key pieces of advice for marketers who are using data to inform their strategies and campaigns?*

TB: Honestly, I think it's as simple as one: Put your customers first. It's the central principle of our DMA Code of Practice, but it's wonderful in its simplicity when it comes to data. If you think of your customer whenever you're making decisions about data, you shouldn't ever go far wrong.

JT: *You're heavily involved in research about the customer. What has been the most surprising finding you've come across?*

TB: Gosh, where do I start? There's so much! The one resounding thing I am continually surprised and reassured by is the resilience of channels now viewed by many marketers as 'traditional' or old hat. For instance, I hear many marketers espousing the power and influence of new channels, social media or the latest technologies to engage customers.

But we continue to find in our consumer research that email and mail are still the two most popular ways that people want to hear from brands. Whether it's pre- or post-purchase, across the customer journey email represents the central channel customers expect and confirm, which should serve as a strong reminder to brands not to overlook these established channels in favour of the latest shiny new toys at their disposal.

JT: *Do you typically see a difference between marketers' perception of what engages consumers in comparison to consumers' preference?*

TB: I regularly see differences in marketers' and consumers' perceptions, although this is often what I'm looking for when we conduct research too. It can also be explained in a few ways sometimes.

For instance, looking at email content that marketers believe is most effective, we see an agreement with consumers that discounts and offers work. This is much higher for consumers, but given the survey, the question is 'How much do you like the following emails from brands?' Can we really be surprised that people tick this option? Of course not.

But the interesting discrepancies come in areas like email receipts, offering access to other benefits or the effect of loyalty in getting customers to sign up to marketing in the first place. These are all areas where marketers appear to be undervalued, while consumers tell us they like and want this content.

JT: *Getting to know a customer group, segment or prospect is crucial in the stages of developing a marketing strategy. Do you have any tips on gathering insightful research?*

TB: Listen. Take every opportunity to do so. There are so many customer touchpoints today, and everyone can generate insightful information about your customers. But the best source of insight is those customers.

If you're using the data you already have at your disposal, make sure you're taking a step back first. Take it away from the campaign, the objectives and the performance. Listen and look at what it tells you about the customers first, then you can start to bring in these other areas to identify specific opportunities.

Don't be afraid to take this listening literally too. Feedback and surveys from customers are easily run over a range of channels these days, but one of the simplest ways to ask them questions is to do just that. Some of the best brands have not just customer or marketing teams, but their C-suite too who still walk into stores or pick up the phone to just speak to a customer – not to mention to their frontline staff too, who can offer just as much insight.

JT: *What are your go-to measurement metrics when analysing the success of a marketing campaign?*

TB: Ultimately, most organizations still tend to focus on sales or revenue as the arbiter of their marketing success. In fact, looking specifically at evaluating the effectiveness of email programmes, around half of the businesses say 'sales' is their key metric, closely followed by 'click-throughs', 'conversions', 'brand awareness' and 'engagement (active and inactive subscribers)' – all at around 40 per cent.

I'm encouraged to see awareness and engagement have grown over recent years when it comes to email at least, but I still believe there's a long way to go. Of course, money is always going to be part of the conversation, but fundamentally organizations need to define what their campaigns are being designed to do in the first place and then measure them to understand how effective they've been at that.

It's not good enough to just look at the ultimate goal of sales and say everything should be measured by that one metric, ignoring the entire purchase journey in the process. Moreover, in an increasingly complex and connected world, with so many ways to engage customers, even attributing that value to campaigns or even channels can be incredibly complicated – if not impossible.

JT: *What are the DMA's pillars of responsible marketing?*

TB: Beneath our central principle of putting the customer first, there are four pieces of advice that help explain what this looks like in the real world and are worth mentioning:

1 Respect privacy: act in line with the expectations of your customers.

2 Be honest and fair: make sure your organization is always honest, fair and transparent.

3 Be diligent with data: treat your customer's data with the care and respect it deserves.

4 Take responsibility: always act responsibly and be accountable for your actions.

JT: *How can marketers implement DMA's Six Pillars of Responsible Marketing into their marketing strategy?*

TB: The DMA Code and its principles set out the standards for the industry and represent the code to which all our members must adhere, in addition to all legal requirements, of course. But the Code is much more than just a rulebook; it's an agreement and commitment to always be fair and respectful to customers – understanding that this will also cultivate a profitable and successful commercial ecosystem too.

Under the hero principle 'Put your customer first', the Code promotes the evolution of marketing as an exchange of value between the business, looking to prosper, and its customer, looking to benefit. The DMA is committed to helping organizations put their customers at the heart of everything [they] do, in order that the business can prosperously grow to be enjoyed, prized and ultimately sustained by its market.

To help brands do that, we also have a host of best-practice advice, guidance and DMA award-winning case studies. These offer tangible examples and strategies every brand can look to in order to implement the principles we set out in the DMA Code.

JT: *Do you have an example of a marketing campaign that has used data effectively that you can share?*

TB: The DMA Awards offer a window into some of the fantastic work our industry has to offer, with specific categories dedicated to data too.

One of my favourites from last year's Gold winners is The&Partnership with the work they did for TalkTalk. Essentially, the brand realized they had households [using] products that didn't match their needs, but that there was no way to identify them either. This meant unhappy customers and high churn.

TalkTalk wanted to get the relevant customers to understand the benefits of switching to fibre, which would better meet their needs. To help, they created a new data feed called the 'Service Index' to identify customer broadband issues. Like a 'broadband MOT', it uses data from across the business to profile customers' broadband performance and identify service issues. This data feed was harnessed to contact customers with capacity issues due to multiple device use, creating a poor experience.

Customers were then contacted and shown why they should upgrade to fibre, but the proof is really in the pudding. Ultimately, the campaigns exceeded all its targets, successfully encouraging over 52,000 customers to make a move to fibre, resulting in an extra £3.7 million in revenue and an ROI for the campaign of 30:1.

The TalkTalk campaign really exemplifies, for me, both the power and ubiquity of data today. For consumers, it's a must-have. For brands, it's their most powerful source of insight on customers and to inform every marketing decision they make. Although I would add here that data-informed decisions, rather than blindly following what the data says, is what's important too. Sometimes it's the decision to buck the trend or take a more creative approach that can breed success.

JT: *Dare I mention GDPR? But what has been the biggest shift you've seen from the extensive research you've conducted?*

TB: We've been tracking concerns and sentiment around GDPR since the final text was agreed back in 2016. The biggest shift over that time has been the number of organizations recognizing the benefits of the new laws. As businesses have implemented the necessary changes and come to terms with new processes, they've increasingly seen the positive impact to their businesses and marketing campaigns of putting the customer at the heart of everything they do – which is essentially what GDPR does.

There are still clearly concerns around how compliant every organization is, particularly among the small to medium-sized business community where expertise and resources can be harder to come by. But broadly speaking, most businesses have taken the steps required to become compliant with the new laws.

My bigger concern is with the feeling that now May 2018 is in the rear-view mirror, an alarming number of organizations don't seem to see the importance of ongoing training in these key areas of data protection.

JT: *What future do you think artificial intelligence (AI) has in evolving the customer's experience with brands?*

TB: Machine learning (ML) and artificial/augmented intelligence (A/AI) have the potential to revolutionize customer engagement strategies, and the experiences brands can offer. From automation of processes through to building virtual sales assistants that utilize the latest technology – like augmented/virtual reality or smart devices/speakers.

However, it shouldn't be seen as a silver bullet either. There's a lot of work required to build these systems, and there will always be a need to monitor customer engagement touchpoints to ensure they are acting correctly too. The best ML and A/AI on the planet can only ever be as good as the data that goes into it and no data is entirely without bias. So, it's imperative that we continue to take a customer-centric approach to implement these tools, building in processes that hold to the principles of accountability and responsibility that we all work to as well.

JT: *What do you think the future of marketing holds?*

TB: Change, but not where you think. I'm a big believer that nothing stays the same and I love new things, but also a bit of a cynic at heart too. So, while I see the opportunities with so many technologies to change how we market today, I also see the barriers.

I also believe that we, as marketers, don't get to decide much of this either – which is why I say we won't know where the change is coming from. It's consumers that will cause the change. Just look at the trends that have exploded into our consciousness and then fallen by the wayside over the last 10 years. Ultimately, the customer is still king, and we'd do well to remember that – as well as listen to them a little more!

Summary

Let's recap what you've done in this chapter:

- Discovered your target audience's likes and dislikes through market research and social listening.

- You've created customer personas, and segmented your audience for better targeting.

- You've positioned your organization's product or service to match the value that your target customer is seeking.

The next step is to define your marketing strategy further by identifying the tactics that will be chosen to engage and communicate with your target consumer.

References

BBC (2019) Tesco delays Clubcard rewards cut after backlash, BBC [Online], available at: www.bbc.com/news/business-42715143 (archived at https://perma.cc/75CS-THXK)

Bond, T (2020) Head of Insight, The DMA [Interview] 11 March 2020

Costantinides, E (2006) The marketing mix revisited: Towards the 21st century marketing, *Journal of Marketing Management*, **22** (3–4), pp 407–38

Deloitte (2017) *2017 Global Mobile Consumer Survey: US edition, The dawn of the next era in mobile*, Deloitte [Online], available at: www2.deloitte.com/content/dam/Deloitte/us/Documents/technology-media-telecommunications/us-tmt-2017-global-mobile-consumer-survey-executive-summary.pdf (archived at https://perma.cc/R8YA-QXCH)

Desjardins, J (2019) A visual history of the largest companies by market cap (1999–Today), Visual Capitalist [Online], available at: www.visualcapitalist.com/a-visual-history-of-the-largest-companies-by-market-cap-1999-today/ (archived at https://perma.cc/8YZ6-RA9B)

EZMarketing (2019) Top Failed Marketing Campaigns, EZMarketing [Online], available at: blog.ezmarketing.com/top-failed-marketing-campaigns (archived at https://perma.cc/CN7T-3TWY)

Fill, C (2015) *Marketing Communications: Engagements, strategies and practice*, pp 235–37, Pearson Education, New York

Gettins, M (2018) Global Category Manager at Tommee Tippee [Interview] 20 February 2018

Hopkins, N (2020) Independent Communications Consultant at Neonodal [Interview] 28 July 2020

Lardinois, F (2020) Google want to phase out support for third-party cookies in Chrome within two years, TechCrunch [Online], available at: techcrunch.com/2020/01/14/google-wants-to-phase-out-support-for-third-party-cookies-in-chrome-within-two-years/ (archived at https://perma.cc/2SCM-UZSW)

McLeod, S (2020) Maslow's Hierarchy of Needs, Simply Psychology [Online], available at: www.simplypsychology.org/maslow.html (archived at https://perma.cc/RB42-3RLN)

Newberry, C (2020) How to find and target your social media audience [Online], Hootsuite, available at: blog.hootsuite.com/target-market/ (archived at https://perma.cc/D8L4-7UMV)

Ritson, M (2020) Marketing Thought Leader [Interview] 13 October 2020

Rolls-Royce (2020) Our vision and strategy, Rolls-Royce [Online], available at: www.rolls-royce.com/about/our-strategy.aspx (archived at https://perma.cc/5SKJ-BUM9)

Rothstein, C (2019) My father had a lifelong ticket to fly anywhere. Then they took it away [Online], *the Guardian*, available at: www.theguardian.com/lifeandstyle/2019/sep/19/american-airlines-aairpass-golden-ticket (archived at https://perma.cc/K8F5-5VH5)

Spotify (2020) Listening is everything, Spotify [Online], available at: www.spotify.com/pt/about-us/contact/ (archived at https://perma.cc/XLY2-MGPJ)

The Guardian (2020) The Cambridge Analytica Files, *The Guardian* [Online], available at: www.theguardian.com/news/series/cambridge-analytica-files (archived at https://perma.cc/8PFV-KLWV)

Verkerk, H (2020) Director at Sports Alliance [Interview] 23 September 2020

05

Awareness

Planning your marketing campaign

In this chapter we're going to:

- Explore the marketing mix.
- Learn how to use each of the 7Ps to plan the implementation of your marketing strategy.
- Identify the strategy needed to engage your target customer.

To recap:

- A strategy is a roadmap which takes you to your goals. I call this the 'who, what, when, where and why'.
- Tactics work hand-in-hand with strategy. Tactics determine the 'how' of a campaign. The 'how' should never be established before the who, what, when, where and why.
- Strategy = the who, what, where, why and when (planning an adventure).
- Tactics = the how (selecting the mode of transport).

In Chapters 2 to 4, we have analysed the business's Scenario, determined the Target ambition by defining our marketing objectives, and identified the Reach of our strategy. We're up to the A of the STRATEGY framework.

A stands for Awareness. It's all about using the information we have gathered on the marketing environment, competitors and our target audience to achieve the objectives we've set.

We will do this through the creation of a marketing plan.

The benefits of marketing planning

What's the difference between marketing planning and strategy?

Well, for starters, a marketing plan is part of a strategy, but it's not the whole thing. A marketing plan – rather than being a road map – is an assessment of the terrain you'll be covering. This is what we started in Chapter 2 when we analysed the external and internal contexts of the organization.

Marketing planning involves looking at the wider context in which your strategy will be operating. A good marketing plan informs the strategist about the state of the market, the competition, what resources are available and how the consumers are feeling.

Marketing planning has many benefits:

- It provides a structured means of analysing the marketplace, considering its dynamics and causing managers to both question and challenge.
- It provides a sense of direction, involving staff who can then take ownership of the plan.
- It identifies what resources are needed and where to focus.
- It improves communication of proposed actions.
- It provides a sound basis for control, because actual results can be measured against it.

A good marketing plan is a blueprint for marketing your products and services. Essentially, a marketing plan is a step-by-step guide which details how to deliver your marketing strategy. You have already started to 'plan' your strategic approach by analysing the macro and micro environments of your organization in Chapter 2. A marketing plan also identifies the resources needed, and the areas which require the most focus (we'll explore this in Chapter 7).

As we uncovered in Chapter 1, everyone in the organization must be moving in the same direction and fulfilling the organization's vision. Your marketing plan will improve cross-team communication, and make sure that everyone knows what's required of them to achieve the brand's goals.

The detail of the activities required to implement the plan such as budget, timescales and resources are included in Chapter 7. The measurement for each activity is covered in Chapters 8 and 9. Because, once the plan is defined, it doesn't stop there. It's an ongoing process.

Let's start by planning and determining how we are going to implement your strategy to achieve the objectives you defined in Chapter 3.

The marketing mix and why it's still valid

An excellent model to use to ensure that your marketing strategy is equally weighted and not overly focused on one area is the marketing mix – otherwise known as the 4Ps or the 7Ps (Table 5.1).

If you remember from Chapter 4, the 4Ps are Product, Price, Place and Promotion. These were introduced by E Jerome McCarthy in 1960 (Costantinides, 2006).

As the services industry grew (explored in the history of marketing in Chapter 1), the marketing mix was extended to include three more Ps – People, Process and Physical Evidence.

The marketing mix is invaluable. It's a method that has existed for more than 60 years and it's my go-to approach when creating a marketing plan to implement a marketing strategy. Why? Because the 7Ps ensures that all of the Ps are considered. As a result, your marketing efforts are equally weighted across all of the 7Ps, without all of the focus on product and price.

Many organizations spend a considerable amount of time, money and resources on developing a brilliant product, only to then not put the same level of effort into determining the place in which it will be sold, the promotional methods that will be used to engage prospective customers and a price that is relative to its perceived value.

If the product doesn't fulfil your target market's needs, then it will provide little value. This will then impact the success of the pricing approach used. If it's not being sold where the target market is, the same problem applies.

Let's say you'd like to promote your offering on social media platform TikTok. This would be a great choice if you have identified in Chapter 4 that your target customers are also there, but if they aren't then the messaging won't be seen, the consumer will not be engaged, and the budget will be wasted.

TABLE 5.1 The marketing mix

1	P	PRODUCT	Design, technology, usefulness, convenience, value, quality, packaging, branding, accessories, warranties
2	P	PLACE	Retail, wholesale, mail order, internet, direct sales, peer-to-peer, multi-channel
3	P	PRICE	Strategies: skimming, penetration, psychological, cost-plus, loss-leader
4	P	PROMOTION	Special offers, advertising, endorsements, user trials, direct mailing, leaflets/posters, free gifts, competitions, joint ventures
5	P	PEOPLE	Employees, management, culture, customer service
6	P	PROCESS	Especially relevant to service industries. How are services consumed?
7	P	PHYSICAL EVIDENCE	Smart, run-down, interface, comfort, facilities

Your marketing strategy should be focused on engaging your customers, so always concentrate all 7Ps on your target audience when creating your marketing plan and align to the research, data insight and customer personas from Chapter 4.

Let's break the marketing mix down into more detail and uncover how you can use each P in developing your marketing plan.

Product

The focus here is on creating a product that will satisfy the needs and wants of your target market.

During the product development phase, marketers need to conduct extensive research into the benefits of the product being created. There is a great tool that I highly recommend using for this. It's called Augmented Product, a model created by Kotler and Armstrong (2010).

I have often used this model to help product and business owners identify the benefits that customers gain from their offering. Often, I find that they hadn't previously considered many of the benefits that the model identifies.

Augmented product breaks down a product into three levels. Each 'level' provides marketers with an opportunity to identify the core benefits customers would gain. For a car, the first 'level' of benefit would be the ability to travel from A to B. The second layer would take into account other features of the actual product which could benefit the customer – the quality, the style, the colour of the car and so on. Then there is the 'augmented level'. This includes the service and additional items provided after purchase, such as aftercare, warranties, deliveries and ongoing customer care.

The findings in each layer should inform marketing messaging. In the car example, it becomes much more than a mode of transport. The marketer can now communicate all the benefits that a customer gets from buying the car – not just the surface-level benefits.

Let's look at each level in more detail.

Level 1: Core product

This is not the physical product itself. The 'core' describes the basic benefit/purpose of the product, ie the elements that make it valuable to the target consumer. For example, the core purpose of a razor is removing hair. Its core benefit is a clean-shaven face.

Level 2: Actual product

This level is the physical product. Level 2 is focused on what the consumer would think about the product when first seeing or testing it. This can be in terms of the quality, the colour, the style, the branding and so on. For instance, with a shaving razor, the weight of the handle, the material it is made from and the brand can all impact the perceived quality.

Level 3: Augmented product

This level involves the non-physical part of the product. Level 3 is all about added-value elements which the customer may or may not pay a premium for. If we continue with the example of the razor, the 'augmented' benefit could be a life-time warranty, or impeccable customer support. If your offering provides things like free delivery, in-home installation, free software updates, etc when the product is purchased, you'll be doing well for Level 3.

The augmented part of a product is a meaningful way to tailor the actual product to the needs of a customer. Features of a product can be transformed into benefits for individuals and used in promotional communication in marketing campaigns. It also gives you additional dimensions on which to set yourselves apart from your competitors and stand out from the crowd.

How can I use the augmented product model?

This model is particularly useful to ensure that product design focuses not only on practical elements but also on the benefits to the customer. Many technology companies focus heavily on the features that their tool provides but fail to align these to the customer's actual wants and needs.

A feature is only as useful as the benefit it gives the customer. If it is challenging to communicate this effectively, it will be difficult for a customer to see the benefit.

There can also be an additional level to this model called the *Potential Product*. This encapsulates what the future product may include. Returning to the car example, the potential product could include things like AI-driven vehicles. Philip Kotler named this the fifth level in his book, *Marketing Management* (Kotler and Armstrong, 2010).

TASK

What's your augmented product?

Review your product and consider the different aspects that you'd include within the core, actual and augmented part for your offering.

Remember to use the analysis of your target customer which you conducted in Chapter 4, as well as your Scenario analysis from Chapter 2. Reflect on your choices through the eyes of your target customer, questioning what they would deem a benefit.

The findings from reviewing your product can then be used to inform the detail in your marketing communications which we'll cover in Chapter 6.

The life of a product

A product also has a life cycle which is important to take into account when defining your marketing plan because for existing vs new products, the approach and communication will be different at each stage. The product life cycle also impacts other Ps (such as Price and Place). The product life cycle model is illustrated in Figure 5.1.

WHAT IS A PRODUCT LIFE CYCLE?

The product's life cycle is broken down into four key stages, as outlined below. Each stage will require a different marketing approach. The price may change as the introductory offer ends and demand grows, the place in which the item is being sold may expand as the product begins to mature in the market, and the promotional channels used can vary at each stage too.

1. Introduction   A product has been introduced to a market and will require investment to drive awareness that it is now available. Before this stage, there would have been research and development (R&D). If R&D is extensive, it may be a good idea to add this as a new stage.

During this stage, you could use things like introductory offers to encourage the target audience to try out your product and to switch from established competitors.

FIGURE 5.1   The product life cycle

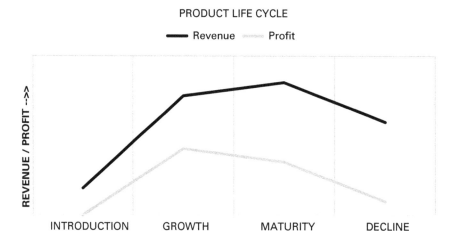

PRODUCT LIFE CYCLE

━━━ Revenue   Profit

2. Growth   If the product launch in the introduction stage is successful, the popularity of the product will grow. During this stage, production will increase to fulfil expanding demand. Places where the product can be purchased may also grow, so you'll need to establish more distribution options to help fulfil the increasing demand. It's at this stage that product reviews and testimonials will be useful, as they support your growth and will help to amplify it further. Costs may be quite high to achieve increases in distribution so that would need to be considered.

3. Maturity   As a product matures, it enters the most profitable stage. The costs of producing should begin to decline thanks to economies of scale. Awareness of the product has also developed, and so has the market, which means the need to drive 'awareness' about the new product has switched to retaining loyal customers and encouraging repeat purchases.

4. Decline   Competitors begin to launch competing products or make enhancements to existing ones, which could result in the product losing market share. This is where differentiation marketing is vital. At this stage, it's crucial to promote the unique selling points (USPs) of your product in comparison to competitors, as the product is no longer 'new'. Remember, competitors entering the market with new products are starting at Stage 1, where your product's life began.

You'll see from Figure 5.1 that profit declines as the product moves through its life cycle. This isn't always the case. Not all products go through every stage of the life cycle. Some don't reach the final stage and others may continue to grow. However, it is useful for marketers to have an understanding of where your product is today. As you'll see, the life cycle impacts all of the 7Ps in some way.

The length of the life cycle can vary from product to product. Some products may move quickly to the growth stage, others may see a quick decline.

HOW CAN I USE THE PRODUCT LIFE CYCLE MODEL?

There are marketing approaches which can be used to extend the life of a product before it goes into decline. Adding new features to the current product, for example, or reducing the price to attract more customers. New markets, different customer segments and so on could be explored to increase sales opportunities.

Lucozade is a great example of a company that has extended its product's lifespan several times.

In the 1950s and 1960s, Lucozade was advertised as a benefit of being ill! As the general population became healthier, the 1970s witnessed a decline in sales. In the 1980s, Lucozade was repositioned as an energy drink for busy, energetic and successful people (*Campaign*, 2005).

Just a few short years later, Lucozade pivoted to target athletes and people involved in fitness. Scientific terminology that linked back to its heritage began to creep in, with 'glucose' mentioned in the late 80s and words like 'isotonic' making their appearance in the 90s. Lucozade wanted to be seen as a drink to keep athletes energized. This product range was expanded further in the 1990s with the launch of the Lucozade Sport range (*Campaign*, 2005).

Today, Lucozade continues to market itself as an energy drink – in fact, it's the most popular energy drink in Great Britain (Statista, 2020).

TASK

Now over to you! Whether you have an existing product or are planning to launch a new product, plot where your product is today on the life cycle diagram (Figure 5.1).

Make notes on why you consider your product to be at that particular stage in the life cycle.

Price

Your pricing should reflect the product's positioning (as covered in the perceptual map in Chapter 4) and business objectives. It should also cover the cost per item and aim to achieve a profit margin unless the goal is to undercut competitors by being a loss-leader to gain market share. However, if the objective is to grow, a price too low can hinder a business's growth and risk not delivering enough profit to sustain the operation.

The pricing method you use can be influenced by where your product is in its life cycle (as detailed above). For example, if your product is new to a market, you'll probably want to give it a lower 'introductory' price to drive interest and awareness, and to draw consumers away from established competitors.

The following are the main pricing methods used:

- *Cost-plus* – this takes the production cost and adds an additional profit, which is factored into the price. The thing to consider here is whether your production costs are variable or fixed, as this could impact the profit gained.

- *Value-based* – this pricing strategy uses the customer's own perception of the product's value to determine the price. The quality of the product and the company's reputation will influence the perceived value.

- *Competitive* – to use competitive pricing, you need to conduct research into the pricing approach your competitors are using for similar products. The decision is then to either price lower, the same or higher than your competitors. Prices should also be monitored, and the company needs to have the ability to respond to any changes.

- *Going rate* – this pricing approach is mostly used in markets where companies have little to no control of the market price. The price of the product would be based on the going rate of similar items. This can fluctuate regularly.

- *Skimming* – if the product is of high quality, the price will be high to target affluent customers and to 'skim-off' maximum profits. When the market becomes saturated, the price is typically lowered as the product becomes more 'mass market' and available to everyone.

- *Discount* – for old stock (or to sell excess stock), the advertised price is discounted.

- *Loss-leader* – everything has production costs. A loss-leader is a product whose retail price is lower than its production costs. The rationale behind using this pricing strategy is to attract customers to your website or into your store and convert them to add more items to their basket; this is known as 'upselling'. For example: a customer visits your website or store with one purchase in mind, and is either converted to purchase a higher-priced equivalent (ie the premium version) or to add more items that they didn't originally intend to buy.

- *Psychological* – the most commonly used psychological pricing method is to use a price that isn't rounded off to the nearest whole number. For example, pricing an item at 99p instead of £1: the 99p looks more attractive and appears a lot cheaper than a £1 item.

Several new pricing approaches are increasingly being used, such as:

- *Subscription* – pricing that is based on a set monthly subscription package each month. Disruptive companies such as Netflix have made this pricing approach popular. As a result, there are more and more subscription-based offerings available for pretty much everything, from shaving products to organic food packages, all delivered directly to the customer's door each month.

- *Pay-per-view* (PPV) – a widely used approach with the increase in online streaming is for customers to pay for each view online or through a smart TV. This provides the flexibility to only pay when you view something such as a film, rather than paying a monthly subscription. This approach does come with the risk of setting an incorrect price. If the price is too low, it may not generate a profit. If too high, customers won't bother with it. Understanding your customer is crucial for establishing the ceiling of PPV pricing, as this is almost entirely dictated by the customer's perception of the offering's worth. This is one of many cases in which a good strategy really can make all the difference.

Place

The 'place' factor concerns where or how your product is bought.

There are various ways in which a product can be sold, including through intermediaries such as distributors, wholesalers, retailers or direct to the consumer via your website. Placement is vital to ensure that your product reaches the right target audience at the right time.

Your placement could be where your business is located in a business-to-business (B2B) environment, or where the retail store is located in a business-to-consumer (B2C) market. In terms of distribution, it is also essential to consider where the products are stored and how quickly they can be transported to their final destination, be that direct to the consumer or to a retail store/warehouse.

Distribution channels

How your product is distributed is also an aspect of Place in the 7Ps. Ask yourself: how does your product get from the factory where it is produced to the hands of your customers?

You may be thinking 'why is the distribution of the product important for marketing?'. Well, it's important to be aware of the distribution methods either already being used for an existing product, or to choose an appropriate option, as the way they receive your product will have an impact on your customer's experience of it. The distribution channel chosen will also be dependent on your target market, the industry in which you are operating and the life cycle of the product.

There are four main types of distribution channels available.

DIRECT: PRODUCER TO CONSUMER

This is where the manufacturer directly provides the product to the consumer. The business owns all the elements of the distribution channel, or may sell through a specific retail location. An example of this would be a company selling directly to consumers via its website.

The advantage with direct distribution is that the company has complete control over both the product and the customer's experience. However, it does mean that there is additional responsibility placed on the organization to not only promote and sell the product but also to ensure that it is delivered to customers. The business must also provide the after-purchase customer care.

New start-ups with a brand new product in the introductory stage typically firstly sell directly to the consumer. This helps the organization to gain direct feedback from the consumer and retain control of the distribution of their product.

INDIRECT: PRODUCER > WHOLESALER > RETAILER > CONSUMER

In this model, the producer/company uses an intermediary, for example, a wholesaler who then distributes the product to retailers.

This method of distribution could increase costs as each intermediary will receive a percentage of the profits or charge a fee as a result of providing that service. Typically, this option is best for large producers who are selling through lots of small retailers. In the product life cycle, a product which is in the growth stage would be better positioned to start including indirect distribution to ensure that they fulfil the growing demand. Different types of intermediaries are detailed in the next section.

DUAL

This distribution channel is a combination of direct and indirect. The product could be sold directly to the end consumer and also sold through intermediaries. This option can reach more consumers but can also cause a risk of conflict or crossover between the direct and intermediate distributors. The consumer experience may also vary, and product marketing risks becoming inconsistent.

Products within the growth and maturity stages of the product life cycle will typically use dual distribution so that their product can be sold both directly via their website and through an intermediary in order to increase the scope of customers that purchase their item.

REVERSE CHANNELS

A consumer who sells their product back to the company they had purchased from is using reverse channel distribution. For example, when a customer recycles their old phone with the company that sold them the item, they are making money from the activity and are effectively reverse selling the item to the original distributor.

Auction websites such as eBay are good examples of reverse channels in which the original consumer of the item also becomes the seller of the product.

INTERMEDIARIES

There are various types of intermediaries. The four main types are:

- *Agents* – an agent is independent of the organization. They are representatives of the producer to the consumer. An agent doesn't have ownership of the product and is usually paid in the form of commissions or fees for their services.

- *Wholesalers* – typically purchase from the producer in bulk and in doing so receive a discount. The wholesaler then sells the items in smaller amounts, adding a margin to make a profit. Wholesalers could sell to another intermediary such as a retailer, or directly to the end-user.

- *Distributors* – a distributor will only stock and sell products from one company or brand. This is unlike a wholesaler, who may stock several products from different companies. There is likely to be a close relationship between the distributor and the producer to retain their loyalty.

- *Retailers* – retailers stock the goods that wholesalers and distributors have sold to them. Retailers will then sell to the end-users at a profit.

Promotion

This P is focused on advertising and communicating your product or service to let your target customer know what you're offering.

To engage your target audience, your promotional activity needs to:

- explain what the product or service is;
- explain how to use it;
- tell the audience why they should buy it – how does it benefit them?

Linking back to the analysis of your target customer you conducted in Chapter 4, it's important that your promotional content engages that customer. You need to grab their attention in a way that convinces them to convert.

The promotional method chosen to convey your message to the target customers will (in the majority of cases) use more than one marketing channel. The vast array of marketing channels, media and tools that can be used to promote your offering, and how to use them, are detailed in Chapter 6, but to start with here is a short summary.

Above-the-line (ATL)

This uses mass media methods. The advantage of using this type of promotion is that it attracts a large audience. The disadvantage is that anyone and everyone would be exposed to marketing, not just the target customer. ATL marketing channels include:

- radio;
- TV;
- print / leaflets;
- newspaper;
- magazines;
- outdoor locations such as billboards.

Below-the-line (BTL)

The company can control BTL promotion methods – for example, in-store offers and direct selling. Smaller audiences are reached through targeted advertising. The advantage of using BTL promotion is that the company has more control and can target specific groups of customers. This enables marketers to be more efficient in the budget being spent.

Below-the-line methods include:

- trade marketing;
- sampling;

- roadshow;
- door to door;
- event management;
- direct mail;
- email marketing;
- online retargeting;
- social media;
- PPC;
- PR;
- search engine optimization (SEO).

PPC, SEO and social media marketing can also be used to target everyone, but most typically and most effectively, they are used to target specific audience groups, specific search terms and locations. I'll go deeper into the specific tactics you can use to implement your strategy and how to use them in Chapter 6.

People

The P of People was added within the extended marketing mix of the 7Ps during the rise of the services industry. It has since become one of the most important elements of the marketing mix.

Even with the best product in the world, people are required at some stage in the buyer's journey. The customer may encounter people who are selling directly, shipping the product or answering queries post-purchase. A bad experience with a person from the organization at any stage could end the life of a product or company.

People includes everyone who is involved, either directly or indirectly, in the product or service. Not all of these people will be in contact with customers, but these people all have a role to play in the production, marketing, distribution and delivery of the products or services to the customer.

For services, people are crucial. The customer experience can be altered dramatically by the person who is providing the service. Attitude, skills and appearance all have important roles to play with people in an organization.

The importance of people also doesn't disappear with products. Retail outlets, for example, require people to help answer prospective customers' queries. If the people in the store aren't approachable, friendly or helpful this could deter a customer from completing their purchase.

Let's take a visit to the hairdresser as an example. If the hairdresser doesn't cut your hair to the style you requested and if they don't provide a welcoming service, you'll probably not return to that salon.

The importance of people doesn't just apply to the employees who are engaging directly with customers. Everyone in the organization has an impact. For example, if the IT developers at a software company don't truly understand how customers use their product, they may create features that the user either doesn't use or doesn't find at all useful. This was unlike my experience with the Hollister staff as detailed in Chapter 1, where they embody the brand even down to showcasing the clothing which is worn as a 'uniform' in-store.

People can also be a differentiation factor for an organization. The head chef of a restaurant will be known by their reputation. A well-known and well-respected chef will bring in customers purely on the strength of their reputation. On the other hand, if the waiter serving your table is rude, then, however delicious the meal is, you're unlikely to ever dine at that restaurant again.

This all relates back to implementing the vision that we covered in Chapter 1 throughout the organization. If half of the people at the organization are pulling in one direction and the other in another direction, this will limit the success that the company is able to achieve.

Even with the right product, an organization can still fail if the people in the company don't share the same attitude, skills or vision.

Personal selling

Personal selling is where the business has representatives who sell directly to consumers. They aim to inform the customer and persuade them to purchase. Typically, personal selling is conducted by sales representatives who communicate the benefits of the product or service to the customer and, while receiving instant feedback, can adapt their approach specifically to their unique prospect.

It's vital that the sales representative portrays the same marketing message as set out in the marketing plan and demonstrates the same vision, values and attitudes of the organization. Training is important to ensure that the people within the organization have the appropriate knowledge and feel confident in their roles.

Here are some questions to ask yourself about the people from your organization:

- What training do the employees need to provide the standard of customer service required?

- What will be the process for the people to follow when handling customer queries and complaints?

- What skills does each team require and what type of people are required for each role?

- What training will be provided for new people who join the organization?

- What will be the regular training provided?

- How will the people in your organization sell and promote your product or service?

Process

Process is focused on the systems and processes that deliver a product to a customer. It could include the process of making transactions on your website, website design, the process of providing customer service support to your customers, etc.

The process of engaging a prospective customer doesn't just start when an order is placed. The processing element includes all of the operational aspects of being able to service a customer. Having your website up and running 24/7 without any downtime is a 'process'. The ability to respond to customer queries, the process of promoting your offering, the systems and resources required to deliver all of those processes – all of these and more come under this P. Process covers the customer experience across their journey. There are also the processes involved in creating your promotional activity, which we will explore in more detail in Chapters 6 and 7.

EXAMPLES: THE MARKETING PROCESS

Here are two examples to help you build a picture of a marketing process from the customer's point of view.

1. An all-inclusive holiday

From the time of booking with personalized online 'manage your holiday' portals to the moment that you arrive at the airport, you receive a personalized experience. You are greeted at the airport, your baggage is taken onto the coach and then you are personally delivered to your hotel. You are greeted and checked into your room. You have two weeks of services from restaurants and evening entertainment to casinos and shopping. This is a highly focused marketing process and is an example of the importance of process in enabling delivery of the customer proposition.

Another way of looking at this example is that there is end-to-end service support, which has enabled transactions between the company and its customers. The process is quick and efficient. It is also sustainable for the company – they are able to provide the time, money and resources needed to undertake these processes.

2. Supermarket shopping

One process that is changing is the process of purchasing food at a supermarket. Amazon has created supermarkets called Amazon Go (Vincent, 2019) that don't contain any checkouts, changing the process drastically for buyers. A buyer only needs their smartphone (and for it to be connected to their bank account). The buyer adds the items they'd like to purchase to their basket or trolley and then, when they are finished, they walk out of the store; their items are automatically scanned and their smartphone automatically pays for the items purchased.

This removes the process of a buyer waiting in a queue to pay for their items in-store. This is a process that makes the experience more efficient, saves time for the consumer, and also doesn't infringe on the consumer's time or space as they are very likely to have a smartphone to complete the transaction.

Physical evidence

The marketing mix is a blend of both physical and psychological factors.

For services, don't forget to consider the physical elements. For a hotel, for example, this would include the building, the hotel rooms, the décor, etc. The atmosphere and general feeling when experiencing the service can also contribute towards physical evidence.

For products, physical evidence includes the actual product, the retail store (or the website that it is sold on), how easy it is to use, testimonials, reviews, etc.

There are several ways to break down physical evidence; let's review these in more detail below.

Environment

This is the space in which you are situated when you consume the service. The physical environment may include several other factors on this list, such as the atmosphere, the space within the environment, functionality and so on.

Ambience

Can include temperature, colour, smell, sound, etc. The combination of these can consciously or subconsciously improve or hinder the experience of the service. This is why spas are focused on creating a relaxing and calm atmosphere with soothing music and fragrances.

It's the marketer's role to establish and create an ambience that matches the service being delivered. If, for example, you delivered the experience of classic fine dining in a restaurant, but the music was very loud and there was bright lighting, the ambience would not match the service being delivered. The ambience should be relaxed, friendly, inviting, with background music and soft lighting to reinforce the fine-dining experience.

Layout

The spatial layout and design of your store are important when shaping the customer experience. If the layout is unclear, cluttered or confusing, or if the store is dirty, then customers may ultimately not want to experience it again. The same applies to a company website:

- it should be easy to navigate;
- information about the company and its product/service offering should be easy to find and understand;
- products or services should be clearly displayed;
- a contact or support option for customers who have purchased or prospects looking to ask queries should be provided;
- it should have complementary design, colours, text and imagery reflecting the company's brand.

Signage

Corporate branding contributes to physical evidence. For example, the signage of your favourite clothing store is instantly recognizable and reassures you that this is indeed where you can find that style you love.

Buildings like company headquarters all add to the public perception of a company. If the company is trying to establish itself as a leader in its industry, yet is operating out of a shed, this may not represent the right kind of image. The same concept applies to digital evidence, like social media profiles, email marketing, direct mail, business cards, employee uniform, brochures and so on.

The physical evidence should always reflect how an organization wants to be seen by its customers.

The 7Ps: summary

Your marketing plan will use the marketing mix to plan the activities which are aligned to your objectives in order to achieve your strategy.

Your target customers should be in the centre throughout your planning and each of the 7Ps should be aligned to their needs and wants. Resources required to implement each of the 7Ps will be identified in Chapter 6, where we'll create an action plan.

Table 5.2 presents my application of the 7Ps for this book.

TABLE 5.2 An example of applying the 7Ps to this book

1 P		PRODUCT	Two versions of the book: printed and digital. Online resources for readers, study pack for lectures and students.
2 P		PLACE	Dual distribution being utilized through bookstores and retailers, direct distribution – online via Amazon.
3 P		PRICE	Introductory offer as part of initial launch, list price £29.99.
4 P		PROMOTION	Marketing events, content marketing – via the blog, interviews, podcasts, webinars.

(continued)

TABLE 5.2 (Continued)

5 P		PEOPLE	Me, the author, publishers – editor, book designer, printing partner, readers and marketers' reviews, bookstores and retailers, expert opinions and marketing bodies, colleagues and peers – teachers and marketers.
6 P		PROCESS	Order direct via my company's website, Amazon, publisher's website, bookstores and retailers, online resources, templates, additional reading.
7 P		PHYSICAL EVIDENCE	Book reviews, testimonials, quotes from experienced marketers and business owners and tips within the book.

TASK

Using the template in Table 5.3, identify two factors per P for your organization.

TABLE 5.3 Your 7Ps template

1 P		PRODUCT	1... 2...
2 P		PLACE	1... 2...
3 P		PRICE	1... 2...

(continued)

TABLE 5.3 (Continued)

4 P		PROMOTION	1.. .... 2.. ....
5 P		PEOPLE	1.. .... 2.. ....
6 P		PROCESS	1.. .... 2.. ....
7 P		PHYSICAL EVIDENCE	1.. .... 2.. ....

The 4Cs

Let's add another layer to our marketing mix by tightening focus on the consumer. We can do this by using the 4Cs.

Robert Lauterborn created this alternative method to the 4Ps in 1990 (Smalley, 2017). The focus is on targeting niches in a similar way to segmentation, rather than mass markets. The 4Cs focus on understanding what the consumer truly wants from a product or service.

The 4Cs add the consumer layer to the 4Ps as illustrated in Figure 5.2.

Let's look at the 4Cs in more detail.

FIGURE 5.2 The 4Ps aligned to the 4Cs

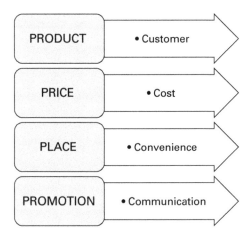

Customer

The focus here is on selling products that the consumer will want to buy. The aim is to understand the value that the product or service delivers to the customer through the eyes of both the organization and the consumer.

Cost

The price is typically the first thought when considering the cost of a product/service. But the price is only a small part of the total cost when producing a product or providing a service. The cost reflects the total cost of ownership, not just the price the consumer pays. The price of the product/service is one of many elements that make up the total cost to satisfying the customer's needs. There are several influences on cost, such as the time spent acquiring the product or service, the cost of conscience when it comes to consuming the product (Belyh, 2018), and the cost of changing to another item or implementation of a new product.

If we refer back to the COMPETE framework in Chapter 2, there could be a cost to the consumer for not using a competitor's offering. A huge amount of focus is on the price of a product in marketing, but it is the positioning of the value provided by the item or service which should retain the focus. Shifting the focus on the cost of satisfying the customer ensures that more than just the purchase price is considered. This will drive the focus on the customer's experience. In turn, this creates value beyond the benefited value that the product delivered, adding to the consumer/brand value exchange I mentioned earlier.

Communication

This C shifts promotion from only being one-directional and focuses our attention as marketers on creating a relationship. The focus is on the entire buying experience, led by the buyer. A dialogue with prospects needs to be established by focusing on their needs and challenges, not the organization's. All communication should be designed to build meaningful relationships to create a more collaborative conversation. This includes any form of marketing, adding another layer to the promotion P of the 4/7Ps.

Convenience

The location at which a consumer can purchase your product or experience the service is important for many businesses, but there is another layer here, and it involves understanding how the target market prefers to purchase.

A great example of this is what happened when Netflix entered the DVD rental industry, competing with the well-known and established Blockbuster. Blockbuster only provided one location for DVD rental and that was their physical stores, typically located within retail parks. At the time of Netflix's entry to the market, the internet and online shopping adoption was beginning to grow. Initially, Netflix provided its customers the service of an online subscription to order a specific number of physical DVDs each month that were sent by post. Now, Netflix is available as a solely online streaming service in more than 150 countries worldwide. Blockbuster did not evolve and subsequently went bankrupt. They didn't adapt to the changing needs of their consumers, and they did not provide their target market with the preferred way to buy, which was and is now online (Levin, 2019).

Ease of purchase is important when creating buying experiences that will delight your ideal consumer. How easy is it for your consumers to purchase your offering? The quality of the buying experience should also be explored, as this is becoming increasingly important for the modern buyer.

TASK

Complete Table 5.4 created by Smart Insights that contains the 4Cs for your organization.

TABLE 5.4   Template to review your organization using the 4Cs

	Current situation in your organization	Competitor A (repeat for others)	How your business could enhance its offer?
Consumer wants and needs			
Communication			
Convenience to buy			
Cost to satisfy			

Reproduced with the kind permission of Dave Chaffey from Smart Insights (2020). The table is based on the Bob Lauterborn 3C model from his 1990 article in *Advertising Age* (1990)

What makes service marketing different?

Marketing of services is different to the marketing of physical products. While the fundamental strategic principles (segmentation, research, creative thinking, tactical innovation) remain present, there are fundamental differences in the marketing mix. These differences can provide challenges for service-sector marketers. Usually, these challenges centre around five basic factors, of which every service marketer needs to be aware:

- *Intangible* – services are not 'things' in the same way that, say, face creams are. You can't judge their quality by sight, smell, touch, etc. Or, at least, not as effectively as you can with physical products. People are therefore a bit more wary about 'impulse buying' services, and tend to research them more heavily.

- *Inseparable* – a service is tied to the person or organization providing it. This means that the customer often comes into contact with the service provider. Therefore, every exchange needs to be done right the first time. A bad first impression could doom the sale.

- *Perishable* – services can't be stored in the fridge and consumed later. They're 'produced' and 'consumed' at the same time. Once you've used a service, you may get a similar experience by hiring that service again, but you can never have the exact same experience. This has an impact on pricing to manage demand:

  o when travelling during peak times the fares will be higher than at off peak;

  o cancellation fees for beauty and physio appointments because of a no-show means that time has gone and cannot be recovered, costing the organization time and money.

- *Lack of ownership* – what does the customer get to take away from the service they've used? As no goods change hands, customer experience and customer satisfaction are paramount when marketing services. If the service is not effective for the customer, they have absolutely nothing to show for the money they've spent. If you hire someone to clean your house, and the house is still dirty when they leave, you've wasted your money and you don't even have a physical trinket to show for it!

- *Heterogeneous* – services are difficult to standardize, as every service deliverer's methods will vary. A user's experience of a service is likely to be different every time, influenced by factors such as people, time and location.

Summary

In this chapter:

- You've explored the marketing mix.
- You've learned how to use each of the 7Ps.
- You've identified the importance of keeping your target market in the centre of your plans.

Next, we'll explore the variety of channels, media, methods and tactics available to promote your offering.

References

Advertising Age (1990) New marketing litany; Four Ps passe; C-words take over [Online], Crain Communications, Inc, available at: rlauterborn.com/pubs/ pdfs/4_Cs.pdf (archived at https://perma.cc/3LG6-6T6D)

Belyh, A (2018) Understanding the 4Cs of the marketing mix [Online], Cleverism, available at: www.cleverism.com/understanding-4cs-marketing-mix/ (archived at https://perma.cc/H32L-8W6X)

Campaign (2005) Superbrands case studies: Lucozade [Online], *Campaign*, available at: www.campaignlive.co.uk/article/superbrands-case-studies-lucozade/232378 (archived at https://perma.cc/T5AB-YFTE)

Costantinides, E (2006) The marketing mix revisited: towards the 21st century marketing, *Journal of Marketing Management*, **22**, (3–4), pp 407–38

Kotler, P and Armstrong, G (2010) *Marketing Management*, 15th edn, Pearson, London

Levin, S (2019) Netflix co-founder: 'Blockbuster at us... Now there's one left' [Online], *the Guardian*, available at: www.theguardian.com/media/2019/sep/14/ Netflix-marc-randolph-founder-blockbuster (archived at https://perma.cc/ M8CS-MSGJ)

Smalley, T (2017) What are the 4Cs of marketing? [Online], Stratomic, available at: www.stratomic.uk/blog/what-are-the-4cs-of-marketing/ (archived at https:// perma.cc/JVQ5-BL3A)

Smart Insights (2020) The 4Cs marketing model [Online], Smart Insights, available at: www.smartinsights.com/marketing-planning/marketing-models/4cs-marketing-model/ (archived at https://perma.cc/G6S5-G6XD)

Statista (2020) Brands of energy drinks (excluding colas or mixers for alcoholic drinks) ranked by number of users in Great Britain from 2018 to 2019 [Online], Statista, available at: www.statista.com/statistics/308493/leading-brands-of-energy-drinks-excluding-colas-or-mixers-for-alcoholic-drinks-in-the-uk/ (archived at https://perma.cc/F4SS-U5KZ)

Vincent, J (2019) Amazon reportedly plans bigger cashierless supermarkets for 2020 [Online], The Verge, available at: www.theverge.com/2019/11/20/ 20974037/amazon-go-cashierless-2020-expansion-supermarkets-pop-up-stores (archived at https://perma.cc/TD5P-CE7C)

06

Tactics

Selecting the right channels

This chapter covers the conventional marketing channels to use in your marketing strategy, which include:

- Digital marketing (online):
  - SEO;
  - PPC;
  - affiliate marketing;
  - social media;
  - email marketing;
  - website and e-commerce;
  - content marketing;
  - PR marketing.
- Traditional marketing (offline):
  - trade shows/exhibitions;
  - direct mail;
  - out-of-home (OOH);
  - TV;
  - radio.

All of the above will help you determine which tactics are appropriate to use in your own marketing strategy. 'Finally, with that strategy in place, we select the appropriate tactics to deliver the strategy and win the day' (Ritson, 2020) and in this chapter we are going to focus on this selection process.

Marketing channels and tactics

A marketing channel is the main route taken to promote your offering such as SEO, social media and PPC. The way that channel is implemented is the tactical element. Marketing tactics are the promotional elements and, in some cases, the 'fun' part of marketing. People often mistake tactics for marketing strategy, but tactics are the vehicles used to reach your destination.

Digital marketing channels (online)

Digital marketing tactics

According to Hootsuite (2020) there are three main areas to focus on when using digital marketing tactics:

1 *Building confidence*: Linking back to the 'People' P from the 7P's as covered in Chapter 4, 67 per cent of global consumers state that a good reputation will encourage them to try a product, but they also need to trust the company to continue their custom (Edelman Trust, 2019). They lend a human face to a brand – which brings us neatly to the second focus…

2 *Providing connection*: Consumers want to receive less corporate-focused content and more human communication. Focus on creating a sense of a meaningful relationship.

3 *Enabling convenience*: Via digital, organizations are theoretically capable of reacting to user needs within minutes. Modern consumers expect this ability to be utilized. Realistically, however, this kind of instant service can be difficult for small businesses to provide, so it's essential to set expectations.

These are all valid areas of focus, but I would like to emphasize no 2 – 'providing connection'. Now that it's being enhanced by artificial intelligence (AI), the human element is more critical than ever. Yes, we can use technology to automate and even create the content of our marketing messages, but if it sounds robotic people will simply not engage with it. Who wants to express themselves to something without empathy?

Victoria Peppiatt advises, 'Only use AI when you have defined the problem you need to solve.'

If the problem isn't clearly defined then how can it be determined that AI is the right tool for the job? That's an important distinction to make. The dos and don'ts of using technology and tools are covered in detail in Chapter 7.

Empathy and context are crucial when attempting to engage an audience. Continuing to broadcast a marketing campaign that isn't relevant to the context is not just a waste of time and resources; it could also alienate your audience.

With these focus areas in mind, let's take a look at the most frequently used digital channels and how you could implement them in your strategy.

SEO

SEO stands for 'search engine optimization'. The focus of SEO is to ensure that the content on your website is optimized to appear in the results when relevant search terms are entered into a search engine.

Moz, an SEO platform, has adapted Maslow's Hierarchy of Needs, as explored in Chapter 4, to reflect the principles of good SEO (Figure 6.1).

When enhancing your SEO, you should start with the most basic and functional of questions.

CAN SEARCH ENGINES CRAWL YOUR WEBSITE?

Crawling is how the search engines read your website; they 'crawl' through all of the pages of your site to determine the topics it covers. If there are any issues in crawling the content on your website, it may not appear in the search results (or appear for the wrong reasons).

Your website can be as beautiful and content-rich as possible, but if it cannot be found, it won't provide any value to a business.

FIGURE 6.1 Mozlow's Hierarchy of SEO Needs

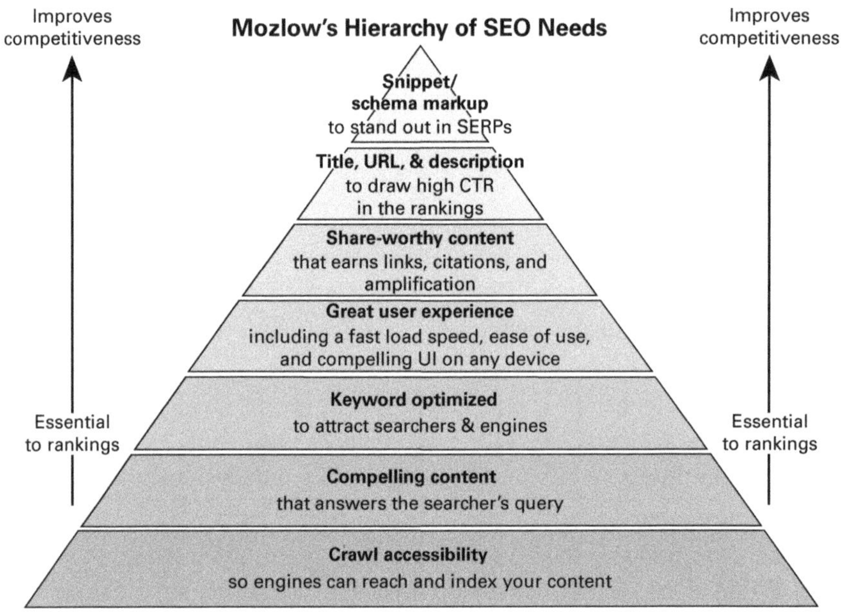
Improves competitiveness
Mozlow's Hierarchy of SEO Needs
Improves competitiveness
Snippet/ schema markup to stand out in SERPs
Title, URL, & description to draw high CTR in the rankings
Share-worthy content that earns links, citations, and amplification
Great user experience including a fast load speed, ease of use, and compelling UI on any device
Keyword optimized to attract searchers & engines
Essential to rankings
Essential to rankings
Compelling content that answers the searcher's query
Crawl accessibility so engines can reach and index your content

Reproduced with the kind permission of © MOZ (Moz, 2020a)

As described by Moz (2020b) search engines have three primary functions:

1 crawl;
2 index;
3 rank.

If your website can't be crawled, you have some technical issues to fix.

Once search engine bots can crawl your website, we move on to the next hurdle: indexing.

Your crawled content will be indexed. The index positions the crawled results according to how relevant the bots consider them for the query. For example, if I were to google my company 'Let'sTalk Strategy', the bots would crawl through several websites with these terms, and rank mine highly, as both the title and the content 'answer' the user's 'query' in the most direct and relevant way.

Search engines always seek out the most relevant content first and will order each subsequent piece of content accordingly. This is called ranking. There are many factors taken into account by search engine algorithms when ranking results and these factors change and are updated regularly.

Search engines can crawl your page, and they are displaying it on the search index. Now, you need to improve your ranking.

This takes us to the next stage of the hierarchy: compelling content. The most critical area of focus when optimizing your website for SEO is to ensure that your content will be relevant, useful and of value to your visitors. Solving a searcher's query, providing them with the information they are looking for, being specific in your product information and so on are just some of the ways you can create compelling and relevant content.

Keywords research is the starting point here. Keywords research allows you to identify common search queries being entered into search engines. There are many tools available to help with this research, such as SEMRush, Google AdWords (more detail in the PPC section below) and Moz Keyword Explorer, to name a few.

Once you've completed your keyword research, you can then tailor your landing pages to answer queries according to what your research has indicated. Try not to over-engineer the keywords aspect of the content. The holy grail of SEO content marketing is useful pieces of material which include the keywords organically. Search engines are well aware of the practice of 'keyword stuffing', and know how to filter quality content from keyword-laden dross.

HISTORY OF SEO

It's debated within the industry as to when SEO began. In 1991, the first website in the world was launched by Tim Berners-Lee (Stern, 2015). Six years later, the first web search engine started, giving birth to the need for content optimization.

Baker (2017) breaks down SEO to include the following:

- search engine placement;
- search engine positioning;
- search engine ranking;
- search engine registration;
- search engine submission;
- website promotion.

In 1994, as more and more websites were developed, Yahoo created a directory where developers could manually add their websites. Ask Jeeves and Google launched in 1997, with the aim of helping to improve and simplify the indexing and delivery of data (Stern, 2015). In 1999 the first-ever search marketing conference took place. It was called Search Engine Strategies (SES), and it featured Danny Sullivan, who is a widely respected SEO guru. Danny launched Search Engine Watch and Search Engine Land (Stern, 2015). Then came a turn of events that changed the SEO landscape forever.

In 2000, Yahoo partnered with Google, who then powered their organic search results. At that time, which may now be difficult to imagine, Google was a relatively unknown search engine. This agreement helped to raise the profile of Google, as every search result made in Yahoo included the message 'Powered by Google'. On-page content, domain names, site structure known as 'breadcrumbing' and the ability to be listed on directories were all-important ranking criteria at that time. Google's web crawler and PageRank algorithm were revolutionary in the search space (Baker, 2017). On-page and off-page factors were reviewed. This included the quantity and quality of external links pointing to a website.

During this time, there was a lack of sophistication in SEO. Search engine results could be manipulated with keyword stuffing, excessive tagging and spammy backlinks. Now recognized as black-hat SEO techniques, these approaches get penalized by the search engines as their algorithms have become increasingly sophisticated over time.

The measurement of links also started with Google Toolbar when it became available on Internet Explorer in 2000. This meant that SEO practitioners could see their PageRank score between 0 and 10, ultimately assigning a value to links. This started the increase in spammy link-building practices, where links were sought purely based on a number and not for quality or relevance. AdWords also started in 2000, enabling paid ads to appear above, below and to the right of Google's organic results.

From 2004, search engines started to improve results based on several factors such as geographical intent (ie displaying local websites based on where you had searched). YouTube, Google Analytics and Webmaster tools all launched in 2006. Google Analytics received such an influx of users that when it initially launched it couldn't handle the volume and the website went down. It remains a much relied-upon analytical tool today.

XML sitemaps gained universal support in 2006. It helped search engines to crawl more intelligently. From 2007 onwards, the focus was on improving the user experience and in 2008 Google CEO Eric Schmidt said the issue of SEO was becoming a 'cesspool' and identified brands to help with a solution (Keane, 2008).

Microsoft Live Search became Bing in 2009 and joined forces with Yahoo to challenge Google's large share of the search market. Social media platforms began to make headway in the late 2000s, and Google made its attempt with Google+.

Two of the most significant algorithm updates for Google that have left a lasting effect on SEO were in 2011 with Panda and 2012 with Penguin. These focus on quality content and take pains to eliminate the spam tactics that were still being exploited at that time to manipulate search results. Knowledge Graph was a further attempt in 2012 to interpret keyword strings to understand semantics and intent. 2015 was the year of mobile-first for SEO, and it continues to be an important area today.

THE FUTURE OF SEO

The future for SEO continues, with AI, machine learning and voice all starting to add another dimension to the channel. Google also dominates the search space with 86 per cent market share (Statista, 2020a). To dig deeper into the future of SEO, in 2020 I interviewed Digital Strategist and Marketing Technologist Jono Alderson, who manages Special Projects at SEO WordPress plugin Yoast for his thoughts on the future and the approach required for success:

> Historically, setting an SEO strategy meant identifying tactical opportunities for content production and outreach, and prioritizing technical fixes. What little 'big picture' existed was often limited to chasing vanity goals ('We want to rank first for [competitive keyword]'), or driving short-term ROI from links and PR coverage.
>
> Whilst there's still a place today for improving your pages and courting influencers, a modern SEO strategy requires that you think more broadly. Rather than just researching commonly searched keywords or chasing yet another link, you must become the brand which solves the problems of your audience.
>
> Google's objective is to solve the problems of *their* users. They do that by highlighting the best answers, products and services for a given user, for a given search. But articles, links and other traditional SEO value signals were only ever a poor proxy to help Google to understand the *quality of fit*. As they continue to get better at understanding, the effectiveness of those types of tactics diminishes. If all you have are tactics, you'll never be able to demonstrate that you deserve those top rankings.

That means that you have to deeply research and understand the types of content which your audiences want to consume and identify where you can add value. You must create and promote content which aims to help, support and contribute to conversations – rather than just to sell.

To do this, we must stop thinking of SEO as a direct response channel. We live in an age when consumers control their own research and decision-making processes, and search is the mechanism through which they form opinions and build brand preferences. Whilst organic search certainly *can* be at the end of the funnel, the real impact of SEO happens much earlier on.

Consider the behaviour of a consumer who's researching a purchase decision. They may search multiple times, visit multiple websites, and gradually develop (and refine) a consideration set based on what they see. Each touchpoint affords an opportunity to influence what happens next, leading to the final purchase decision. A good SEO strategy manages these experiences. It considers how to position the brand as the best solution for the user's problems – not just how to attract clicks at the end of the funnel.

So, a futureproof SEO strategy must focus on improving (and *demonstrating*) your product–market fit. Instead of producing articles to match keywords, you should aim to solve real problems and meet real needs. Rather than soliciting links from influencers, you should have a product or a service which naturally gets talked about, reviewed or cited (and amplify that). Rather than chasing short-term ROI, you must see your SEO strategy as the key to reaching consumers earlier in their purchase cycles, before they're swayed by competitor messaging. And, to remain competitive, you must do all of this on a technically perfect, lightning-fast, accessible platform.

None of these tactics will show a short-term ROI, but they'll increase your chances of accessing a shrinking marketplace, and of winning hearts and minds.

No matter what type of website you're optimizing, or which market you're in, your SEO strategy must make you a better business. If it doesn't, and if all you're focusing on is how to squeeze some more visits from the search results, you're going to get left behind.

PPC (pay-per-click)

Another key channel is PPC (pay-per-click). When you are using a search engine (such as Google or Bing), ads appear at the top of the results and on the right-hand side. What you're witnessing there is PPC in action.

PPC involves brands paying for their ad to appear in search results based on several criteria, including:

- specific keywords;
- the location where the search is taking place;
- time of day;
- day of week;
- device.

Advertisers and companies 'bid' (through specific, coveted keywords) for the position in which they would like their ad to appear. For highly competitive search terms, first place could cost thousands of an advertising budget. Every time the ad is clicked, that visitor is sent to the website of the advertiser. The advertiser then pays a fee to the search engine.

There are a lot of moving parts to fit together when creating a PPC campaign. The keywords need to be specific to your target audience, so keyword research plays a big role. Any keywords you've identified then need to be organized in campaigns and ad groups. From experience, dedicated PPC landing pages that are optimized for the specific search query generate the best results, as they will be the most useful in providing the visitor with all of the information they are seeking. This is crucial to success with PPC, as the search engines reward companies that focus on the visitor's needs and will penalize those that try to manipulate the search results with irrelevant landing pages that generate high bounce rates.

HISTORY OF PPC

In the mid-1990s, flat-fee directory listings websites became the first monetized search engine results page (SERP). These operated in a similar way to how *Yellow Pages* sold their advertising. In the beginning: the advertiser willing to pay the most per click would secure the highest position for their ad on a SERP.

As explored in the history of SEO, by 2000 search engines were the world's primary source for finding web content. As their popularity continued to grow, so did web content. This meant that it was getting increasingly competitive for an organization's website to be at the top of the results. It was during this time that Google launched AdWords, the auction-based, pay-per-click model which became the standard that we see today.

Google introduced the quality score in the mid-2000s as a way to determine which ads should appear on the results page and in which order, based on various optimization factors. This also ensured that the ads which generated the most revenue (ie got the most clicks) would get pushed to the top. Yahoo and Microsoft followed suit with this method.

PPC is big business: Google generated $134 billion in 2019 from ad revenue (Statista, 2020b).

FUTURE OF PPC

There have been many changes to PPC advertising over the last couple of years. The basics of engaging a visitor enough to click on your ad and land on your website remain the same. However, how the algorithms will rank your performance will remain heavily focused on optimizing their searchers' experience and in turn, that needs to be the focus of your PPC advertising campaign.

Affiliate marketing

Affiliate marketing is based on performance in which an external partner receives a reward, typically a commission (Target Internet, 2020) for delivering a specific result to a merchant or advertiser. The affiliate searches for a product related to their website/offering, then promotes that product and receives a commission from each sale. The tracking of sales from one website to another takes place through specific links that are created for each affiliate.

For affiliates, it's vital to promote and engage visitors to click through to purchase. If successful, the affiliate receives a commission from the sale. For example, it may be that the ingredients of a cooking recipe are included as affiliate links on the blogger's website to promote the items they used. If the reader of the recipe then clicks the links of the ingredients and buys them, the blogger is paid a commission (Enfroy, 2020).

Affiliate marketing spreads the distribution of communicating about a product or service to individuals from the seller to the affiliate or advertiser. This helps to support the marketing team's effort, as the affiliate becomes another source of promotion. At times, the level of control and influence an organization has over an affiliate can be limited. The affiliate operates independently, which is different from corporate advertising where the company has full control of message and placement.

HISTORY OF AFFILIATE MARKETING

Many believed that Amazon created affiliate marketing, but actually it was created in 1989 by William J Tobin – known as the world's first internet marketer. It was Tobin who created the concept of affiliate marketing. He launched his programme on the Prodigy Network for his company, PC Flowers & Gifts (Abad, 2015).

This involved paying a commission on every sale generated. By 1993, it generated $6 million annually for Prodigy (Abad, 2015).

In 1996 Amazon launched its Associates Programme, making it the first global affiliate programme. Their model paid commissions based on a percentage of the price of the product sold. This remains as a widely used affiliate model.

During this same time, Johnson and Samuel Gerace established BeFree, and Stephen and Heidi Messer launched Linkshare (now known as Rakuten Affiliate Network). Commission Junction followed these in 1988. And went on to become the world's biggest affiliate marketing provider (Abad, 2015). These networks for the first time enabled smaller retailers to get involved in affiliate marketing.

Rules and regulations began to tighten around affiliate marketing in 2000. The US Federal Trade Commission published guidelines for affiliate marketing which required clear disclosures about commissions earned. This legislation was updated in 2008, requiring bloggers to disclose their relationships when promoting other companies' products. In 2017 celebrities including Rihanna and Kim Kardashian faced controversy from US regulators for not making it clear that some of their Instagram posts were sponsored (Lawrence, 2017). Posts must be clear they contain ads including hashtags such as #SponsoredAd, #Ad.

In 2001, the world experienced the dot-com burst. This caused significant changes in affiliate marketing. Online businesses that had been built during the commercial rise of the internet crashed. Suddenly, people were out of jobs and looking around for new sources of income. A flurry of books and articles were written promoting tips about affiliate marketing. In 2003, the Affiliate Summit was created by Missy Ward and Shawn Collins to educate those in affiliate marketing with the latest updates and trends.

By 2007 more than £3 billion was generated in the UK from affiliate marketing (Marketing Charts, 2008). By 2017, 6 per cent of the UK's whole online economy was generated by affiliate marketing and was generating £9 billion in sales (IAB, 2018).

WHERE IS AFFILIATE MARKETING TODAY?

Affiliate marketing remains popular today and does continue to provide potential, particularly with the rise of online shopping. It is a great way to raise awareness of new products/services and build relationships with relevant affiliates (Abad, 2015).

Social media

Buffer (2019) describes social media marketing as a way to '... connect with your audience to build your brand, increase sales and drive website traffic'. Content is published in a variety of formats on the social media platforms to engage audiences, and discussions take place to listen to and to partake in. Advertisements can also be promoted on the platforms and results of both organic and paid-for content can be analysed.

3.8 billion people use social media worldwide (Buffer, 2019). The average daily time spent by individuals on social media globally is 144 minutes (Statista, 2020c). Social media users spend this time engaging with friends, family, peers and brands.

Around 90 per cent of internet users aged 16 to 64 watch online videos, 70 per cent listen to music streaming services, 47 per cent listen to online radio, 41 per cent listen to podcasts and 51 per cent watch vlogs (Kemp, 2020). There are a variety of social media platforms engaging with different ages and demographics – some of which will include your target market.

HISTORY OF SOCIAL MEDIA

Many would consider Facebook as the pioneers behind social media, but it began in 1971 when computer engineer Ray Tomlinson sent the first email. The email was sent from one computer to another as a test (Centre for Computing History, 2020a).

In 1988 Internet Relay Chat (IRC) was developed as an open protocol that allowed users to exchange text messages in real time over the internet. This was one of the first chat systems that allowed more than two people to join in a discussion (Allen, 2017).

In 1997, Six Degrees was founded. This is widely considered to be the very first social networking site. Friendster then followed in 2002, and by 2003 Google wanted to buy it for $30 million. A Malaysian-built platform that doesn't exist now was regarded as the pioneer of social media (Ahmad, 2018).

LinkedIn launched in 2003 and now has more than 500 million users. In 2004 Facebook launched, and is now regarded as the king of social media, boasting more than 2.4 million users (Ahmed, 2018).

In 2005 YouTube launched, allowing users to share, upload and watch content online. It was followed in 2006 by Twitter where users could easily interact with celebrities, and at the time there was a limit of 140 characters for each message. WhatsApp launched in 2009 without any ads. In 2019 it had 1.5 billion users and was continuously growing. The selfie revolution then began, with Instagram launching in 2010, Snapchat in 2011, Selfie in 2013 and Filters in 2015.

TikTok, the video-sharing platforms where users can edit their video and share with everyone, first launched in 2017, and at the time of writing it is enormously popular. But with huge popularity comes controversy, with India banning it in June 2020 (Pahwa, 2020) and the United States attempting to do the same in September 2020 (Paul, 2020). And recently there has been the launch of Clubhouse, a new, voice-only social media platform.

WHAT'S THE FUTURE FOR SOCIAL MEDIA?

Publishing was the starting point of social media. Content is shared to generate website traffic, followers and fans of an organization's offering. But to truly engage a social media audience, it should be a place to have conversations, not to simply broadcast content.

Similar to SEO and many other tactics, AI and machine learning will have significant impacts in the future, especially in helping to curb the spread of fake news (McFadden, 2018). New platforms will come and go, but the fundamentals of sharing new content in various formats of imagery, video and text will continue.

WHAT IS SOCIAL MEDIA USED FOR TODAY?

Social media can be used in several ways. Brands can monitor what is said using social listening, and respond to conversations that are relevant to them or their product. Social media can also be used by businesses to understand what is performing well with analytics and to uncover the interests of a particular audience (Buffer, 2019). And new talent can showcase their skills using social media (on TikTok, for example), growing their following and raising their profile (Kastrenakes, 2020).

Getting down to practicalities, let's take a brief look at top-line demographic usage of each platform and the total monthly number of users (Table 6.1). This is useful information to understand in depth so that you can plot your target market to the appropriate platform(s).

Further reading and research into the users of each social platform are available at Wearesocial.com who publish quarterly and annual in-depth usage reports.

Influencers also have a part to play when engaging an audience. 'Influencers' are influential people who have a very large following and presence. Often these influencers are celebrities, but we are increasingly seeing the rise of

TABLE 6.1 Monthly active users and interesting facts about social media platforms

SOCIAL MEDIA PLATFORM	MONTHLY ACTIVE USERS AND INTERESTING FACTS
Facebook	2.5 billion monthly users, 56% of Facebook's advertising audience is male, majority of monthly users are between 25 and 34 years old (Wearesocial, 2020).
YouTube	2 billion users, one billion hours watched on YouTube each day, 45% of users are female, 55% male. Top search queries reveal that the userbase still focuses heavily on using YouTube to watch music videos. With 7.22 billion video views, Luis Fonsi's and Daddy Yankee's *Despacito* is the most viewed YouTube video of all time (Wearesocial, 2020).
WeChat	Messaging app heavily used in China, 1.15 billion users (Wearesocial, 2020).
Instagram	928.5 million users, 50.9% ad audience is female (Wearesocial, 2020).
TikTok	New entrant that has rapidly grown its global user base with more than 800 million monthly active users, 60%+ of users are based in China (Kemp, 2020).
LinkedIn	663.3 million people that can be reached via ads, largely a work- and career-based networking platform, but every LinkedIn member also has a life outside their work! Don't write off LinkedIn if you're B2C rather than B2B (Wearesocial, 2020).
Reddit	430 million active worldwide monthly users, 199 million new posts were published to the platform in 2019 (Wearesocial, 2020).
Snapchat	381.5 million people that can be reached with ads, 61% of users are female (Wearesocial, 2020).
Twitter	339.5 million users, heavily male-dominated, within the age bracket 25 to 49 years. Interesting fact: Barack Obama has the most followers in the world (at the time of writing that was 123.7 million) (Wearesocial, 2020).
Pinterest	322 million monthly users on Pinterest (169 million can be reached by advertising), the majority of its user base are aged between 25 and 34 years, 72% are female (Wearesocial, 2020).

'micro-influencers'. Micro-influencers may not have the 1 million+ range of celebrities, but they do have a lot of followers in their niche area. For example, a parent who has a large influence on other parents through their online blog or community could provide value to a brand with a product that is targeting the same demographic.

Email marketing

Email marketing is an electronic method of communicating to an audience known as 'subscribers'. Subscribers can be made up of both customers and non-customers, but both groups will have an interest in the company, the brand and/or its product or service.

The term 'email marketing' describes commercial emails that are sent from a company to a prospect or customer. All email marketing should be sent to people who have provided their consent.

HISTORY OF EMAIL MARKETING

In 1971 Ray Tomlinson sent the first email as a test to himself from one computer to the other (Centre for Computing History, 2020a). The following year the first email management system was developed by Larry Roberts, which let users list, select, forward and respond to email messages (Chugh, 2020).

In 1978 the first 'email blast' (the same email sent to multiple recipients) was sent by Gary Thuerk, a marketing manager at Digital Equipment Corporation. This first 'mass mailing' consisted of 400 emails sent to Arpanet advertising machines, generating $13 million in sales (Chugh, 2020).

In 1982 'email' got its name, when users stopped referring to their digital communication as an 'electronic mail message' (Phrasee, 2016).

In 1989 Lotus Notes was launched and AOL recorded their famous 'You've Got Mail' track (Chugh, 2020).

By 1991 companies and college students weren't the only ones using the internet; everyone was. Email marketers, therefore, had the opportunity to reach the vast majority of potential customers (Phrasee, 2016).

By late 1990, Microsoft developed and released Internet Mail which is today known as Outlook, and Hotmail launched to the public in 1996 (Left, 2002). HTML was also introduced to add characters to emails, using custom fonts, colours, graphics and formatting.

In Europe, the EU Data Protection Directive was enacted in 1995, and in 1998 the UK introduced the Data Protection Act, which was designed to protect personal data stored on computers or in an organized paper filing system (UK Government, 1998).

By 1998 the term 'spam' had been introduced and added to the Oxford English Dictionary (Cnet, 1998).

2003 saw the United States introduce the CAN-SPAM Act, which created a standard for sending commercial emails. Businesses had to reduce unsolicited emails and include sender details and an unsubscribe link in every message (FTC, 2009).

Responsive emails were introduced in 2009 (Uplers, 2020), which enabled marketers to effectively transfer their message from one device to another, allowing the recipients to use their desktop, smartphone or tablet to access and read emails.

In 2018 in the European Union, the original Data Protection Act was updated to the General Data Protection Regulation (GDPR). This is one of the most significant changes in legislation for marketing in a decade, intending to provide enhanced rights and controls to individuals of their data. Although the legislation is not solely focused on email marketing, consent did play a large part, and as a consequence, many email marketers found themselves responsible within their organizations for ensuring that they were adhering to the new law. Gathering opted-in consent has already been best practice for email marketing; the GDPR made this law.

WHERE IS EMAIL MARKETING TODAY?

Email marketing has stood the test of time. Four decades on and it remains one of the most effective and revenue-generating marketing channels. Email marketing provides marketers with the opportunity to build a relationship with its subscribers and customers. It also uniquely features at several touchpoints along a customer's journey as both a push and pull channel.

Email marketing is the channel that consistently drives the highest ROI, at £35.41 for every £1 spent (DMA, 2020). Email marketing can be used to attract new customers from a company's website or in-store by signing up to receive regular email communications. Email marketing is also effective at retaining the engagement of customers throughout their journey with a company, from placing their first order to being a loyal customer. Since many other channels use an email address as a unique identifier, email remains an important part of the promotional mix.

Email marketing also provides the ability to learn more about your customer, and gather information about their interests, as Sara Meikle explains below and in more detail in the interview in Chapter 7:

> … as we gained so much insight about these supporters from the information
> they supplied when registering, we are able to make intelligent decisions
> and offer 'products' that are relevant to them. For example: asking a family
> participant when they signed up how old their children are so that we can
> promote a specific age-related child-led or family product.

Website and e-commerce

E-commerce is the ability to buy and sell products on the internet. To enable businesses to provide this online service to its customers, an e-commerce store is used. This enables organizations to handle both online marketing and sales activities as well as logistics and fulfilment functions that are required to make an e-commerce store operational (Hicks, 2020).

HISTORY OF WEBSITES AND E-COMMERCE

In 1969 CompuServe was founded with technology harnessing a dial-up connection (Moore, 2020). In 1979, electronic shopping was created by English inventor Michael Aldrich when he connected a modified TV to a customer via a telephone line. This became the foundation for e-commerce. It was during this time that there were several developments in e-commerce such as the Boston Computer Exchange launching in 1982, becoming the world's first e-commerce company (Moore, 2020).

In 1991, the internet opened for commercial use and made e-commerce possible. The first online book marketplace was launched in 1992 by a company called Book Stacks Unlimited. Netscape Navigator launched its web browser in 1994. Since that date, thousands of businesses have developed a website. In 1995 Amazon launched as an e-commerce platform for books. PayPal launched its e-commerce payment system in 1998. In 1999 Alibaba launched.

2000 saw the dot-com collapse which did lead to the disappearance of many e-commerce companies. However the traditional 'bricks and mortar' retailers saw advantages in e-commerce and started to add e-commerce elements to their websites, enabling customers to buy products online. This gave customers the ability to compare prices with the click of a mouse (Chrisos, 2019).

In 2000, Google introduced Google AdWords as covered in the PPC section above. By 2000, Confinity, owners of PayPal, had been acquired by Elon Musk's online banking company, X.com, which changed its name to PayPal and continued to grow (Moore, 2020).

Amazon introduced Amazon Prime membership in 2005, Etsy launched in 2005, Square launched in 2009, BigCommerce launched in 2009, and Google Wallet in 2011 as a digital payment method. Facebook rolled out sponsored stories in 2011, Stripe payment processing launched in 2011. Apple Pay introduced its mobile payment method in 2014. Jet.com also launched at this point, providing customers with the lowest price in exchange for longer shipping times and ordering in bulk (Moore, 2020).

Shoppable Instagram was introduced in 2017. Cyber Monday and Black Friday e-commerce sales days continue to deliver record online sales figures with these discount events now extending into month-long periods (Ecommerce-Land, 2004). E-commerce revenue is estimated to grow close to $476.5 billion in the United States alone by 2024 (Statista, 2020d).

WHAT IS IT USED FOR?

The primary use of e-commerce now is in company websites. Most brands engaged in e-commerce will have websites which can accept online orders and payments. The typical e-commerce website will also automatically calculate stock inventory and, for more sophisticated systems, the potential dispatch of deliveries.

As with SEO, PPC and social media marketing, the effectiveness of a company's website is critical in converting visitors into customers and in generating sales. For websites that are unable to fulfil orders in their entirety online, the website is there to convert prospects into marketing qualified leads that the sales team can then follow up – and (hopefully!) convert into a sale. For both instances, it's vital that the website is easy to use, easy to navigate, has a secure and reliable payment provider, is compatible with a variety of devices such as mobile and laptops, and includes testimonials to instil trust and convert visitors into customers.

The following two channels, content marketing and PR, can be used in both online and offline contexts, but are included here as they are increasingly being used as digital media.

CONTENT MARKETING

Content can take many forms such as videos, blogs, infographics, podcasts, whitepapers, leaflets, emails, books, press releases and much more. Content marketing has evolved from traditionally printed content to digital marketing and electronic formats. Used across all marketing channels and tactics, it's an important area to optimize.

HISTORY OF CONTENT MARKETING

It's often assumed that content marketing is something new and recent. Content marketing has been around for a long time. In 1835 there was the Great Moon Hoax, during which *The New York Sun* became the largest newsletter (in circulation at the time) to run a series of articles about the 'scientific discovery' of life on the moon. This was later revealed to be a hoax, but it continued to grow their readership and proved the timeless power of unique content (History.com, 2009).

The first magazine containing printed adverts appeared in 1895 when the first issue of John Deer's *The Furrow* was printed. In a few decades, this agricultural magazine reached millions of customers and remains in print today. This movement then continued into the 1900s. 1904 saw the first recipe book (something which we have access to every day!). It was created by Jell-O who created gelatine- and pudding-inspired dessert recipes door-to-door. Brands such as Michelin followed, publishing travel guides to increase people's interest in cars (Gabriel, 2018). Procter & Gamble ventured into audio content marketing with their branded radio and TV programmes (more about radio and TV later). In 1987 LEGO launched its *Brick Kicks* magazine, now known as the *LEGO Club Magazine* (Steck, 2017).

From 1994, content marketing evolved into the digital age with the first website and a large proportion of content being made up of blogs, e-books, articles, reports, whitepapers and more (Digital Marketing Institute, 2020). In the year 2000 marketing guru Seth Godin introduced his *Unleashing the Ideavirus* e-book for free, which was a revolutionary idea at the time. It has since been downloaded over 1 million times and created the inspiration for a new content format (Steck, 2017).

During 2004, Merriam-Webster's Dictionary declared 'blog' the word of the year (BBC News, 2004). Content then continued to expand into video, podcasts and webinars. It was also at this time that social media was born, as explored in the history of social media section in this chapter. 2006 saw Blendtec pioneer a fun new way of promoting their blenders using video content uploaded to YouTube. They have blended a Rubik's Cube, silly putty and even an iPhone and have over 700,000 subscribers (Rachel, 2018).

Content marketing saved Marcus Sheridan's pool business when he used the power of content by blogging answers about common customer questions. River Pools and Spas is now the most-visited pool website in the world (Stelzner, 2017). Content Marketing Institute (CMI) launched a range of conferences, publications and benchmarking reports all focused on content in 2011 (Content Marketing Institute, 2020).

At that time, Kraft started to focus all of its marketing around content. This resulted in a four-fold increase in marketing ROI over what it was achieving with advertising (Brenner, 2016). This occurred at the same time (as we explored in the history of SEO) that low-quality content was becoming a major challenge for search engines. As search engines cracked down on spammy content, brands had to concentrate their efforts on high-quality, customer-centric content with a strong distribution strategy.

2016 saw the growth of personalized experiences linked to a focus on ABM (account-based marketing) (Rusonis, 2020). Marketers and sales representatives started to work more closely together to create targeted streams of content to help close sales.

WHERE IS CONTENT USED TODAY?

Content is everywhere. It is used across all channels and comes in a variety of formats. Content is there when you look up at a billboard, when you read an email, visit a website, watch a video. Content marketing has evolved to include more sophisticated techniques such as storytelling, which we look at in more detail in Chapter 7. Content is now the very cornerstone of effective marketing.

When crafting an engaging piece of content, consider what you want to achieve with it. Align these goals with the interests of your target audience based on the persona research conducted in Chapter 4. Make sure that your content answers their needs, interests, queries and so on.

Developing great content takes time, skill, expertise and patience. Testing and learning are also crucial to pinpoint exactly what engages your audience. Bloggers can also be influential when partnered with a relevant company, product or service. There are more than 600 million blogs on the internet covering a wide range of topics (Lin, 2020). New and existing products can be reviewed by independent bloggers to share their experience with their audience.

Public relations (PR)

Public relations (PR) is a form of using communications to inform, raise awareness, influence and maintain a positive reputation of an organization (Siddiqui, 2014). This can be focused on the company, the products/services, employees, or showcasing customer success stories.

HISTORY OF PR

The very beginnings of PR can be traced back to Ancient Greece when classical philosophers like Plato and Aristotle wrote about using the art of rhetoric to persuade people. PR was also put to good use during the British abolitionist movement in the late 17th century, when books, leaflets and lectures were used to sway public opinion in favour of abolishing the global slave trade (Siddiqui, 2014).

As advances in education gave more people access to the written word, printing was used increasingly for PR purposes. For example, in 1893 Germany, industrial company Krupp started its own news bureau.

Before long, professional PR began to creep into corporate life. In 1903, for example, Standard Oil and the Rockefeller family suffered a blow to their reputation after their reactions to the coal mine strikes (Siddiqui, 2014). Ivy Lee, a journalist for several New York-based newspapers, encouraged Rockefeller to visit the mines and interact with the miners to improve their reputation (Siddiqui, 2014).

In 1990 the Publicity Bureau was established, becoming the first PR agency in the United States (Siddiqui, 2014). It was Ivy Lee who was behind the first-ever press release, after a major rail crash in Atlantic City in 1906. In 1910, the Marconi company in the UK sent out its first news (Watson, 2012).

Edward Bernays believed that political propaganda could be used by corporations to influence public behaviour (Siddiqui, 2014). With his background in psychology, he approached PR as a science. He is attributed with refining the press release process and developing PR theory in his book *Crystalizing Public Opinion*.

During the 1950s and 1960s, the emphasis on developing public relations was growing, especially in Europe, and the International Public Relations Association (IPRA) was developed (Watson, 2012).

1965 saw wide adoption of the 'Code of Athens'. From then on, there was an increasing number of organizations adding corporate communication departments (Watson, 2012).

During the 1960s and 1970s, the main focus of PR was on developing relationships with the media. This remains a significant part of the practice today. However, it is now expanding to include the social mediascape (Watson, 2012).

European University education began to include PR in the 1980s, and in the 1990s the International Communications Consultancy Organisation (ICCO) came into existence in response to the rising number of public relations entrepreneurs. Technology and the birth of the internet meant that the speed of communicating had increased dramatically compared to the fax machines and postal services that had previously been used. PR, as it stands today, was developed during the 20th century with the birth of mass communication. This saw a massive growth of PR professionals, and by the 21st century, PR had become a major communication practice (Watson, 2012).

HOW IS PR USED TODAY?

To remain relevant, PR needs to keep up with the changing landscape and adapt to the new ways of communication. The changes and developments in methods used to communicate have an impact on the form of PR. Today, channels such as social media are used as a way to communicate with target audiences; thought leadership articles are developed to showcase the skill set of a particular employee in an organization and as a technique to raise the company's awareness in the marketplace. In the past, this would have been by telephone, fax and post.

PR is similar to content marketing in that it is used across multiple channels.

Traditional marketing channels (offline)

Trade shows and exhibitions

Trade shows and exhibitions (also known as Expos) provide excellent opportunities for brands to showcase their product or service offering within a specific industry. Typically, they are more prominently used in B2B industries where attendees are within a particular industry and are ideally at the point of purchasing or searching for a new product/service. They are an opportunity for a company to showcase their expertise and knowledge about a particular topic, with stages available for speakers to present their ideas.

HISTORY OF TRADE SHOWS

Trade shows began during the ancient bazaars in the Middle East. Medieval Europe then also utilized trade fairs where farms and artisans travelled to display their offerings at local markets (Trade Show Advisor, 2020).

Exhibitions were regularly held in Europe and North America during the 1700s (Trade Show Advisor, 2020). Today, there is still a demand for exhibitions to showcase services and products. There is a broad range of events of all sizes from small local fairs to multimillion-pound shows in huge exhibition venues with a growing demand for virtual events on the web.

Direct mail

Direct mail refers to physically printed and posted promotional messages. Direct mailing may involve a 'door drop' campaign in which content is sent directly to the target customers' door.

Direct mailing can take several forms, including leaflets, brochures, letters and postcards. Many charities rely on this method of communication if an email address isn't available.

For particular demographics (such as those 70+ years old), this is often their preferred method of communication and, due to their lower use of the internet, it may be the only way to get your message in front of them.

The disadvantage in using this method of marketing is the cost, the impact upon the environment (printing and paper), and timescales. It takes a longer time to deliver the campaign and generate results online and can also be challenging to track results.

HISTORY OF DIRECT MAIL

The first known direct marketing comes from 1000 BC, where an advertisement was written on a piece of papyrus by an Egyptian. The offer was for gold in return for a runaway slave. That papyrus now stands in the British Museum in London (Central Mailing Services, 2020a).

1440 saw a massive leap with the invention of the printing press. In Europe William Caxton used this technology to create printed pamphlets to order from Westminster Abbey (Central Mailing Services, 2020a).

The faster output that printing presses enabled made direct mailing possible on a much larger scale. Garden and seed catalogues were distributed in the 18th century in the nascent American colonies before the Revolutionary War (Central Mailing Services, 2020a).

In the 1960s bank credit cards were introduced and direct mail was used to promote them to customers. At the time, this was viewed as the most personal way of reaching their customers. Colour was introduced in the 1970s, and bold graphic designs were added to grab attention (Central Mailing Services, 2020a).

WHERE IS DIRECT MAIL TODAY?

Technology continues to evolve and has enhanced direct mail further by creating heavily targeted campaigns that previously wouldn't have been possible. The design of direct mail campaigns has continued to move forward, with the inclusion of augmented reality (AR) and virtual reality (VR) to capture the recipient's attention (Central Mailing Services, 2020b).

Out-of-home (OOH)

Out-of-home advertising is any form of advertising that is promoted to customers outside of their home, such as ad wraps on transport, on benches and billboards, to name just a few. Billboards come in many forms, from a traditional poster to ever-changing digital formats. Roadsides, sides of buildings, shopping centres and bus shelters are where they can be found. The aim of billboards is to grab attention. Due to their size, they can be seen by many, especially in areas of high population.

HISTORY OF OOH

The first billboard was created in the 1830s by Jared Bell, advertising circus acts. They were often large posters displaying colourful pictures. The unique features were promoted for each of the upcoming shows (bmedia, 2019).

In the 1860s, it became possible under new legislation for businesses to purchase outdoor space for advertising, which increased the popularity of billboard advertising. Often the creatives were hand-drawn and hand-painted, making them very labour intensive (OAAA, 2020).

The Paris Expo in 1889 unveiled the first-ever 24-sheet billboard, which then became the standard for billboards everywhere (bmedia, 2019).

As the manufacture and popularity of cars grew, infrastructure was developed to accommodate better roads and motorways. This prompted new advertising opportunities where messages could be advertised to drivers. Many businesses used this method to advertise, with Coca-Cola and Palmolive designing humorous signs to entertain bored drivers (OAAA, 2020).

In 1965 new legislation passed that set limits on the number of billboards that could be placed along the motorway, as well as regulations on size, spacing and lighting. This didn't end billboard advertising but did create a new design format (bmedia, 2019).

THE FUTURE OF OUT-OF-HOME ADVERTISING

Many billboards today are digital. Developments in technology in areas such as AR have added a third dimension to the once hand-drawn advertisement, bringing the ad to life.

Radio advertising

HISTORY OF RADIO

The exact date of the first radio advert is debatable. The transmission of voice and sound across the airwaves was introduced in the early 1900s. While there was some experimentation at the time, it is thought that it was in 1920 in the United States that the first radio advertisement aired. Radio remained heavily regulated and ad-free in the UK at the time. The first paid-for radio commercial was aired in 1922 in the United States at the cost of $1 a minute, totalling $50 for 50 minutes of airtime. The commercial promoted the sale of apartments in New York's Jackson Heights (*Campaign*, 2016). Many department stores built their broadcast stations that same year to finance the streaming of programmes and generate returns.

As time went one, more and more people had a radio at home. Audiences grew, and so did the promotional potential. It was during the 1940s that commercials were invented. As the popularity of TV started to increase in the 1950s, radio was losing its position as being the most popular medium. As a result, companies became less interested in radio (Harsch, 2013). The solution to this was to change the approach from trying to target the masses to focus on distinctive and smaller groups instead. This approach made it easier for companies to reach their exact target audience, increasing the strength in radio as a marketing channel.

In the UK, the first radio commercial wasn't aired until 1973 and was a 60-second spot promoting Bird's Eye fish fingers (Birds Eye, 2020).

Radio advertising has come a long way from then, and now we have everything from podcasting to DAB broadcasting. There are several formats available:

- The live read: a fully written radio commercial that is voiced live on air. Influencers and celebrities often voice these reads.

- The jingle ad: this is also used for TV ads. Jingle ads use distinctive music to incorporate a marketing message. These appear less disruptive to listener experience, as the radio listener is expecting to hear music.

- The personified commercial: where a customer or someone who has experienced the promoted product/service talks about that experience on the radio.

- The sponsored ad: this is typically used to raise awareness. It could come in the form of sponsoring a show – eg 'Brought to you by Brand X' (Harvey, 2020).

The radio may seem to be a dated format when compared with others but it does have a place when promoting and raising awareness of products/ services. In the UK, 89 per cent of people still listen to the radio at least once a week (Ofcom, 2017). Digital streaming and podcasts add another, often more interactive, dimension to the traditional analogue radio format.

The cost of radio advertising is cheaper than other marketing channels, and audiences can be heavily targeted based on listenership.

TV advertising

Advertising on television is typically for a slot of 30 seconds, but can be anything between 10 and 60 seconds or longer (Thinkbox, 2019). They feature within the 'break' of a television programme or before/after the start of the next showing.

HISTORY OF TELEVISION ADVERTISING

The first television commercial airing during World War II (Mertes, 2020). In 1941, Bulova Watch Company aired the world's first TV commercial. It was a short ad at only 10 seconds long. Over 4,000 people saw the ad in New York at a cost between $4 and $9. The 1950s saw sponsored programmes with brand names like Colgate, Mattel and Coca-Cola (Mertes, 2020).

In 1952 Mr Potato Head became the first toy advertised on television. In the first year of launching, nearly two million were sold. Jingles were born in the 1960s and became a popular feature in adverts. In 1965 the RCA included a cartoon character singing about coloured TV in their ad (Mertes, 2020).

The first-ever UK TV ad was broadcast on ITV. This first commercial was for Gibbs SR toothpaste. Featuring a block of ice, a tube of toothpaste, and commentary about its 'tingling fresh' qualities. The ad was only available on special TV sets in 100,000 homes in London and the South-East (Content Works, 2020).

1958 saw the ban on subliminal advertising in the UK after panic was caused when US researchers reported that they'd managed to increase popcorn sales by 18.1 per cent from quickly flashing 'Eat popcorn' during a movie (Love, 2011). Since then it has been banned. In 1961, the Committee of Advertising Practice was formed and agreed on the importance of ads being trusted by consumers. As a result, the advertising industry joined forces to form the Committee of Advertising Practice (CAP), who then went on to produce the first edition of the British Code of Advertising Practice (ASA, 2020).

In 1965 the UK banned smoking cigarettes in TV ads (Feronspecial, 1965), and in 1971 the Public Health Cigarette Smoking Act in the United States banned cigarette ads on TV and radio. In 1991 adverts for tobacco and cigarette firms were banned altogether (The Drum, 2016a).

The first colour TV ad, for Birds Eye peas, was broadcast in the UK in 1969. Owned by Unilever at the time, Birds Eye was reported to have bought the slot for £23. In the same year, the first car advert launched. There was a secret gentleman's agreement between the main car manufacturers at the time (Ford, Vauxhall, Chrysler, British Leyland and Datsun) which was why there was little car advertising. However, in 1969 Japanese car manufacturer Datsun broke that agreement by launching their first car advert (Roderick, 2015).

The first commercial for China debuted promoting Shengui Tonic Wine in 1979 (Mertes, 2020). Most of the population had never seen an ad before, so naturally, at 90 seconds, it generated a lot of confusion (Roderick, 2015).

One of the most iconic TV ads of all time was broadcast in 1979 with Coca-Cola's commercial with Mean Joe Greene leading the Pittsburgh Steelers to a victory during Super Bowl XIV. The timing of the ad was right at the end of the Civil Rights Movements, changing people's perceptions (The Drum, 2016b).

In 1982 Nike launched their first TV ads, featuring the *Chariots of Fire* theme song and showing the evolution of running from cave people to marathon racers. Two years later Apple released their '1984' commercial. In only three months $155 million worth of Macintosh computers were sold (Roderick, 2015).

The late 1980s saw the first interactive ad, in which car manufacturer Mazda instructed viewers to video record their ad and play it back frame by frame. By participating, viewers were entered into a competition to win a Mazda car (Roderick, 2015).

1992 saw the first ad for football's recently launched Premier League on Sky Sports (Hurrey, 2020). The 'Holidays are coming' debuted in 1995 with Coca-Cola's Christmas truck ads. They've since become iconic – so much so that Coca-Cola even tours their 'Christmas lorry' around the UK to cash in on the ad's cult status (Coca-Cola, 2017).

1996 saw the first alcoholic drink to be promoted on TV, with Seagram advertising their Crown Royal. Up until that point, promoting alcohol on TV had been banned (Elliott, 1996).

The first ad to be filmed in space was created in 1997 to advertise an Israeli drink called Tnuva Milk, making its way into the *Guinness Book of World Records*. One of the best ads ever was aired in 1999 by Guinness with their ad called 'Surfer' (Roderick, 2015). It is worth checking out (youtu.be/U3JEORDUEqc).

In 2004, the first TV ad was banned by the ASA (Advertising Standards Authority). The banned advert was part of Tango's 'You know when you've been Tangoed' campaign. Four complaints were received by the watchdog from people who feared children could copy the commercial by slapping people in the face (Timms, 2004).

Dove made a statement about beauty conventions in 2006, with a television advert showing the transformation of a woman into a model using photoshop (Leonard, 2008). And one of the most iconic ads in the 2000s was Cadbury's 2007 drumming gorilla ad, where a gorilla plays the drums to Phil Collins' track *In The Air Tonight* (youtu.be/TnzFRV1LwIo). John Lewis became famous for its television ads back in 2011 with 'The Long Wait' featuring a young boy impatiently waiting for Christmas. LinkedIn released its first TV ad in 2006, and Snapchat launched its first in 2018 (Roderick, 2015).

Streaming services like Netflix and Hulu were launching from 2007 onwards (Wallace, 2019), and have changed the way we watch television and consume video content.

THE FUTURE OF TV ADVERTISING

While there are growing audiences using online streaming services, TV still has a place and one that is evolving within the 'smart' interactive world. As the smart TV experience continues to improve, this will disrupt the TV advertising space. Demand will increase for relevant TV ads based on what the viewer is currently or about to watch. Misplaced ads that are irrelevant to viewing behaviour will frustrate and annoy viewers to the point of switching off or muting during the broadcast. The expectations for interactive ads, I think, will grow, but will become more intuitive to the viewer; placing an interactive ad that has a link to view a product on your website in the middle of a film is not going to win any favours, but one that is placed at the end of a programme related to what someone has just watched will gauge interest.

What does the future hold for marketing tactics?

There are many developments taking place, particularly within the tech sector. One key development that I recommend tracking is the growing trend to own a smart home device — for example, a Google Home or an Alexa. A smart device starts to add a voice to a brand and its offering.

However it also means that these devices become gatekeepers. We're no longer only marketing to the consumer: we are marketing to a smart device which is then, in turn, determining what is relevant and what does not apply to the consumer. For SEO and email marketing, this is already starting to change interactions. For example, Alexa can read emails in the inbox and will highlight to the user if an email is going to take longer than one minute to read. She then asks the user to confirm if they'd like Alexa to continue reading. The chances of a user saying 'yes, please continue reading the email to me' start to diminish. This means that the content of each email needs to be short, snappy, concise and have a very clear call to action.

SEO is also witnessing changes. Now, users can use their voice to ask their smart device to solve their query. Again, like email marketing, this shifts the focus of optimizing from the search engine and transfers it to the smart device. Expect to see 'smart device optimization' entering marketing very soon! Test to discover what your brand sounds like when your marketing is read out, and if your offering is presented back to you for a related query.

In addition to channels, there are many tools, software and technologies available. Two of these are artificial intelligence (AI) and machine learning (ML). Both of these provide marketers with the possibility of automating tasks faster and at a larger scale than humans. But this doesn't mean that technology and tools replace marketers — the two work hand-in-hand. AI and ML, in particular, add another layer to marketing efforts as Victoria Peppiatt, the COO and co-founder of AI company Phrasee explains in the interview below.

Interview: Victoria Peppiatt

Victoria is Chief Operating Officer and co-founder of Phrasee, a marketing technology company that empowers brands with AI-powered copywriting, helping boost marketing performance and revenue.

JT: *Tell us about yourself, your marketing background, what you do, who you work for and your passion.*

VP: As COO, I lead the day-to-day running of Phrasee's operations across the US and UK markets where most of our team are based. I'm passionate about building strong relationships with our awesome customers but also managing and motivating our incredible team.

Since we launched Phrasee in 2015, 300 million people across four continents have received an email with a Phrasee-generated subject line and we count global brands like eBay, Domino's, Groupon and Virgin Holidays as customers.

I am a passionate supporter of women in technology and devote a lot of my time to mentoring young entrepreneurs, notably working with an inspiring organization called BelEve.

Prior to launching Phrasee, I founded and ran The Pink Group, a leading creative and branding agency, for 11 years.

JT: *There are a few misconceptions about what artificial intelligence means. How do you describe AI?*

VP: Artificial intelligence is an umbrella term for many different forms of technology. This includes everything from machine learning to image recognition, natural-language processing to robotics, and clustering to deep learning.

We created a glossary of terms to help marketers understand the landscape and we describe AI as follows:

Artificial Intelligence (AI) is the theory and development of computer systems able to perform tasks that normally require human intelligence – eg visual perception or language processing.

JT: *How do you use AI to improve marketing?*

VP: The language a brand uses in its marketing is the crux of all marketing efforts. And yet before Phrasee, there was no technology that could make it better, that was quick to use, and that didn't sound spammy or robotic. Phrasee's vision is to empower brands with AI-Powered Copywriting, boosting marketing performance and revenue.

Phrasee (www.phrasee.co/) has developed the most advanced AI-Powered Copywriting technology on the planet.

Our world-leading technology draws upon two areas from the field of AI: natural-language generation and deep learning:

- Phrasee's natural-language generation system writes human-sounding language variants, at the touch of a button – and in a brand's voice – at scale.

- Phrasee's deep learning engine predicts what language will and won't work with greater accuracy than any human. This removes human bias from the equation. The deep learning engine breaks the language down into thousands of linguistic parameters and uncovers microscopic patterns invisible to the human eye.

JT: *In your experience is AI easy to use?*

VP: AI should be used to solve a problem. It is about the application of AI and technology you choose to use to solve that problem. Phrasee, as a platform, is extremely easy to use, yet is solving a much more complicated problem.

JT: *How long does it take for brands to incorporate AI into their marketing activity?*

VP: The challenge is to define the initial problem, and then find an AI solution that can help. The inverse of this doesn't work and takes much longer. Phrasee, as an example, is a simple SaaS platform which is up and running in three to four weeks.

JT: *Have you experienced any challenges that brands have had to overcome to use AI in marketing?*

VP: The real issue when implementing revolutionary technologies within a business is often inertia and not wanting to disrupt the status quo. In the case of Phrasee, some marketers can be nervous about the technology because of the myth around AI taking people's jobs and there's often a lack of understanding about AI as a whole, which presents a challenge. A recent study by Vitreous World among global marketers confirmed that 67 per cent don't fully understand how to make the most of AI to deliver results and 68 per cent think AI has become a buzzword that marketers don't really understand.

Our vision at Phrasee is to *empower* brands with AI-Powered Copywriting, optimizing short-form marketing language. This includes email subject lines, headline copy and CTAs, push notifications, SMS and Facebook ad copy, and importantly leaves copywriters to focus their skills on long-form creative writing.

A real-life example of this working in practice would be eBay, one of our longest-standing customers. eBay was looking for a way to optimize language at scale, which is why Phrasee was brought on board initially.

In the early days, it took some convincing for eBay's creative team to really embrace and adopt Phrasee. We worked together successfully to overcome a few initial challenges:

1 Copywriting reservations – the creative team had initial concerns that robots were coming to take their jobs away.

2 Brand team concerns – there were worries that eBay would not be able to trust the natural-language generation [NLG] to sound human and in their brand voice.

3 Buy-in from all stakeholders – could AI really empower eBay to drive more revenue?

A strong customer relationship was the key to overcoming these concerns – but most importantly, it was the results. Eventually Phrasee became an extension of the creative team, working in harmony together.

JT: *How do you make sure that the machine has the right tone of voice of each unique brand?*

VP: We build NLG models from a brand to brand basis. These models can produce limitless copy that adheres to a brand's voice and business model.

The NLG models are created with various constraints in place – constraints like brand guidelines, business model considerations or even corporate governance practices. This is the balance; the check is a mandatory review/approval process so our customers can verify that the created language is on point.

JT: *How do you know AI is the right tool for a client to use?*

VP: It goes back to sourcing the problem, then looking for a solution. You can spend £/$ millions on every different AI solution out there, but if you don't know why you are using it, then it's pointless.

If a brand is looking to overcome stagnant engagement rates, a hyper-competitive marketplace, and mega-cluttered inboxes with brand-compliant language, then Phrasee is the answer!

JT: *What are your tips for using AI in marketing?*

VP:

- Only use AI when you have defined the problem you need to solve.
- Only use AI if it will save you time or make you money (or both!).
- Only use AI if you have a clear control group to measure success.

JT: *AI and marketing working together – is that the future?*

VP: The recent surge in online content has created an unprecedented demand for skilled copywriters. These talented folks are in short supply, however, and brands can't afford to hire all the copywriters they need to keep up with the demand. Tech companies have poured millions of dollars of research into applying AI to many facets of the marketing mix – segmentation, personalization and the like. But not copywriting. No one believed it [was] possible for AI to write... not just like a human... but better than a human. This is just one example of where AI has transformed marketing. There are many others.

Optimizing the repetitive, short-form copy that humans struggle to write means marketing teams get their long-form copy seen! The way we like to see it is that Phrasee is to copywriting what Photoshop is to design.

Marketing teams are always looking to quantify the effectiveness of their work and improve KPIs, but not at any cost. The key is to improve metrics without resorting to cheap clickbait tactics, and ensure the improvement lasts not just today, but tomorrow as well. That's the role AI can play.

JT: *Do you think AI has a role in a marketing strategy?*

VP: Marketing technology is a critical component of any marketing strategy today. The marketers of the future are already building it into their plans.

We've applied high technology to every part of the marketing mix... except copywriting. Because we've always assumed that language was the unique domain of humans, and humans alone. But what if we were to apply the same level of rigour to copywriting that we do to every other part of the value chain? That's what Phrasee does, and that's the game we're changing and why it should be a component part of any strategy.

JT: *What do you see from your experience working with brands as the common pitfalls marketers fall into when creating a marketing strategy?*

VP: One of our biggest competitors is the status quo, ie marketers not necessarily moving with the times or embracing the opportunities that new technology like AI brings. We did some research recently which showed that most global marketers don't fully understand how to make the most of AI to deliver results and think it's a buzzword. So one issue is not embracing the technology that could generate £/$ millions in incremental revenue as part of a wider plan.

At the other end of the spectrum, there are the marketers who know AI is game-changing but don't necessarily have a clearly defined use case.

To be clear, it's not marketers who are at fault here. It is confusing. AI is a buzzword; it is difficult to cut through the hyperbole and understand what's actual AI and what's BS. And it's hard to know the tech that will make a real difference and where tech exists for tech's sake. We've actually committed to training marketers about AI to help the whole industry understand what's possible.

JT: *Do you have any examples of clients that you can share where AI has been used successfully to achieve a marketing strategy?*

VP: Yes! Global enterprises such as Groupon, eBay and Domino's are using Phrasee to generate more revenue and underpin brand transformation.

Dixons Carphone used Phrasee's advanced tech to ignite its CRM strategy (phrasee.co/futureaihub/how-dixons-carphone-ignited-its-crm-strategy/), and eBay pioneered the use of Phrasee to lay the groundwork for marketers everywhere (phrasee.co/futureaihub/how-ebay-pioneered-the-use-of-ai-powered-copywriting/).

Summary

In this chapter:

- You have explored the history of each traditional and digital channel in order to understand more about their heritage and story so far.

- You have identified how the channels are being used today to assist you when determining which channels to use in your marketing strategy.

- We talked with Victoria Peppiatt (2020) about the usefulness AI and machine learning provide marketers – and discovered that they are most valuable when aligned to the marketing strategy.

References

Abad (2015) A brief history of affiliate marketing [Online], Moreniche, available at: moreniche.com/blog/a-brief-history-of-affiliate-marketing/ (archived at https://perma.cc/5C99-ME9V)

Ahmad, I (2018) The history of social media [Infographic] [Online], SocialMedia Today, available at: www.socialmediatoday.com/news/the-history-of-social-media-infographic-1/522285/ (archived at https://perma.cc/NZ62-3Q7U)

Alderson, J (2020) Special Ops at Yoast, [Interview] 23 October 2020

Allen, J (2017) The history of social media [Online], Future Marketing, available at: www.future-marketing.co.uk/the-history-of-social-media/ (archived at https://perma.cc/LA6B-J23E)

ASA (2020) Our history [Online], ASA and CAP, available at: www.asa.org.uk/about-asa-and-cap/our-history.html (archived at https://perma.cc/X3HU-8NSM)

Baker, L (2017) 20 years of SEO: A brief history of search engine optimisation, *Search Engine Journal* [Online], available at: www.searchenginejournal.com/seo-101/seo-history/ (archived at https://perma.cc/D6Y2-ZXSU)

BBC News (2004) 'Blog' picked as word of the year [Online], BBC, available at: news.bbc.co.uk/1/hi/technology/4059291.stm (archived at https://perma.cc/QR8N-HHZD)

Birds Eye (2020) Birds Eye History [Online], Birds Eye, available at: www.birdseye.co.uk/our-brands/birds-eye-history (archived at https://perma.cc/M75Z-T3CE)

bmedia (2019) History of billboard advertising [Online], bmedia Group, available at: www.bmediagroup.com/news/history-of-billboard-advertising/ (archived at https://perma.cc/638N-W3YH)

Brenner, M (2016) The secret to Content Marketing ROI [Online], Content Marketing Institute, available at: contentmarketinginstitute.com/2016/05/secret-content-marketing-roi/ (archived at https://perma.cc/54FQ-KZ5W)

Buffer (2019) What is social media marketing [Online], Buffer, available at: buffer.com/social-media-marketing (archived at https://perma.cc/Y8MA-TS7D)

Campaign (2016) History of advertising: No 160: The first radio commercials [Online], *Campaign Live*, available at: www.campaignlive.co.uk/article/history-advertising-no-160-first-radio-commercials/1381044 (archived at https://perma.cc/G8P6-959C)

Central Mailing Services (2020a) History of Direct Mail [Online], Central Mailing Services, available at: www.centralmailing.co.uk/blog/history-of-direct-mail/ (archived at https://perma.cc/RP4P-JSPQ)

Central Mailing Services (2020b) History of Direct Mail part two [Online], Central Mailing Services, available at: www.centralmailing.co.uk/blog/history-of-direct-marketing-part2/ (archived at https://perma.cc/7J9Q-AV4Z)

Centre for Computing History (2020) First network email sent by Ray Tomlinson [Online], The centre for computing history, available at: www.computinghistory.org.uk/det/6116/First-email-sent-by-Ray-Tomlinson/ (archived at https://perma.cc/W2MS-ULXF)

Chrisos, M (2019) Top benefits of Ecommerce for Retailers [Online], Tech Tunnel, available at: www.techfunnel.com/fintech/top-benefits-of-ecommerce-for-retailers/ (archived at https://perma.cc/49TX-84BR)

Chugh, R (2020) The evolution of email: A complete timeline [Online], fresh marketer blog, available at: www.freshworks.com/marketing-automation/email-marketing/complete-timeline-of-email-blog/ (archived at https://perma.cc/3PC3-GHAH)

Cnet (1998) Oxford dictionary adds Net terms [Online], Cnet, available at: www.cnet.com/news/oxford-dictionary-adds-net-terms/ (archived at https://perma.cc/Y8P6-GV54)

Coca-Cola (2017) Truck Tour [Online], Coca-Cola, available at: www.cocacola.co.uk/en/trucktour/ (archived at https://perma.cc/T3X6-W4EL)

Content Marketing Institute (2020) About the Content Marketing Institute [Online], Content Marketing Institute, available at: contentmarketinginstitute.com/about/ (archived at https://perma.cc/FV3B-RU9B)

Content Works (2020) The History of Television Advertising [Online], Content Works, available at: contentworks.agency/the-history-of-television-advertising/ (archived at https://perma.cc/972M-KKR2)

Digital Marketing Institute (2020) The evolution of digital marketing: 30 years in the past & future [Online], Digital Marketing Institute, available at: digitalmarketinginstitute.com/blog/the-evolution-of-digital-marketing-30-years-in-the-past-and-future (archived at https://perma.cc/5UQT-VEYQ)

DMA (2020) The Marketer Email Tracker 2020 [Online], DMA, available at: dma.org.uk/research/marketer-email-tracker-2020 (archived at https://perma.cc/W6WC-R65F)

Ecommerce-Land (2004) History of Ecommerce [Online], Ecommerce-Land, available at: www.ecommerce-land.com/history_ecommerce.html (archived at https://perma.cc/9B6K-2HQY)

Edelman Trust (2019) *Edelman Trust Barometer Global Report* [Online], Edelman, available at: www.edelman.com/sites/g/files/aatuss191/files/2019-02/2019_Edelman_Trust_Barometer_Global_Report.pdf (archived at https://perma.cc/6BTP-T3U8)

Elliott, S (1996) Liquor industry ends its ad ban in broadcasting [Online], *The New York Times*, available at: www.nytimes.com/1996/11/08/business/liquor-industry-ends-its-ad-ban-in-broadcasting.html (archived at https://perma.cc/4AZ2-9WJD)

Enfroy, A (2020) Affiliate Marketing in 2020: What it is and how you can get started [Online], Big Commerce available at: www.bigcommerce.co.uk/blog/affiliate-marketing/#how-does-affiliate-marketing-work (archived at https://perma.cc/C96H-YQ4S)

Feronspecial, J (1965) British will ban cigarette ads for reasons of health; Britain will ban TV cigarette ads [Online], *The New York Times*, available at: www.nytimes.com/1965/02/09/archives/british-will-ban-cigarette-ads-on-tv-for-reasons-of-health-britain.html (archived at https://perma.cc/SZ2P-FSQ2)

FTC (2009) Can-Spam Act: A compliance guide for business [Online], Federal Trade Commission, available at: www.ftc.gov/tips-advice/business-center/guidance/can-spam-act-compliance-guide-business (archived at https://perma.cc/H2EV-TJC4)

Gabriel, T (2018) Infographic: A brief history of content marketing [Online], The content strategist, available at: contently.com/2018/04/02/infographic-brief-history-of-content-marketing/ (archived at https://perma.cc/RSW3-337G)

Harsch, C (2013) Radio advertising. Why radio commercials are more effective than advertisers think [Online], Grin, available at: www.grin.com/document/437822 (archived at https://perma.cc/CJL2-ZNKX)

Harvey, S (2020) The history of radio advertising [Online], Radio Fidelity, available at: radiofidelity.com/history-of-radio-advertising/ (archived at https://perma.cc/3LTM-PN8K)

Hicks, K (2020) What is ecommerce? [Online], HostGator, available at: www.hostgator.com/blog/what-is-ecommerce/ (archived at https://perma.cc/2QWB-55RJ)

History.com (2009) 'The great moon hoax' is published in the 'New York Sun' [Online], History.com, available at: www.history.com/this-day-in-history/the-great-moon-hoax (archived at https://perma.cc/K2JQ-T57U)

Hootsuite (2020) The future of customer engagement [Online], Hootsuite, available at: hootsuite.com/pages/landing/future-of-customer-engagement (archived at https://perma.cc/ZKB7-FDLK)

Hurrey, A (2020) '90s heroes: The best Sky Sports Premier League adverts [Online], The Set Pieces, available at: thesetpieces.com/latest-posts/90s-heroes-best-sky-sports-premier-league-adverts/ (archived at https://perma.cc/6R4M-BC5C)

IAB (2018) IAB/ PwC affiliate marketing study 2017 [Online], IAB UK, available at: www.iabuk.com/adspend/iab-pwc-affiliate-marketing-study-2017 (archived at https://perma.cc/YZ3M-ZH26)

Kastrenakes, J (2020) Meet Ricky desktop, the most viral beatmaker on TikTok [Online], The Verge, available at: www.theverge.com/21504619/ricky-desktop-tiktok-beat-creator-interview-musician-viral-hits (archived at https://perma.cc/8H9W-55WG)

Keane, M (2008) Google CEO calls internet a cesspool, thinks brands are the solution [Online], Wired, available at: www.wired.com/2008/10/google-ceo-call/ (archived at https://perma.cc/2H6X-XVKJ)

Kemp, S (2020) Digital 2020: 3.8 billion people use social media [Online], Wearesocial.com, available at: wearesocial.com/blog/2020/01/digital-2020-3-8-billion-people-use-social-media (archived at https://perma.cc/ANJ5-D4CG)

Lawrence, H (2017) Celebrities told to make it clear when they're advertising on Instagram [Online], Metro, available at: metro.co.uk/2017/04/20/celebrities-told-to-make-it-clear-when-theyre-advertising-on-instagram-6587665/ (archived at https://perma.cc/2MZQ-RCC6)

Left, S (2002) Email timeline [Online], *the Guardian*, available at: www.
theguardian.com/technology/2002/mar/13/internetnews (archived at https://
perma.cc/N935-E5Y8)

Leonard, T (2008) Dove's real beauty ads 'were retouched' [Online], *The Telegraph*,
available at: www.telegraph.co.uk/news/worldnews/northamerica/usa/1939646/
Doves-real-beauty-ads-were-retouched.html (archived at https://perma.cc/
T9EM-397D)

Lin, Y (2020) 10 Blogging statistics you need to know in 2020 [Online], Oberlo,
available at: www.oberlo.com/blog/blogging-statistics (archived at https://
perma.cc/Z3SP-4KHA)

Love, D (2011) The shocking drink and incredibly coke history of subliminal
advertising [Online], Business Insiders, available at: www.businessinsider.com/
subliminal-ads-2011-5 (archived at https://perma.cc/3FDE-9FRB)

Marketing Charts (2008) Affiliate marketing drove £3b in UK sales in 2007
[Online], Marketing Charts, available at: www.marketingcharts.com/industries/
travel-and-hospitality-3237 (archived at https://perma.cc/9H2F-TKG8)

McFadden, C (2018) A chronological history of social media [Online], Interesting
Engineering, available at: interestingengineering.com/a-chronological-
history-of-social-media (archived at https://perma.cc/GF7H-L329)

Mertes, A (2020) History of TV ads [Online], Quality Logo Products, available at:
www.qualitylogoproducts.com/promo-university/history-of-tv-ads.htm
(archived at https://perma.cc/J3XX-VDL7)

Moore, K (2020) Ecommerce 101 + The history of online shopping: what the past
says about tomorrow's retail challenges [Online], BigCommerce, available at:
www.bigcommerce.com/blog/ecommerce/ (archived at https://perma.cc/2P9V-
ZEYN)

Moz (2020) Beginners Guide to SEO [Online], Moz, available at: moz.com/
beginners-guide-to-seo (archived at https://perma.cc/AT3K-W7NS)

Moz (2020) How Search Engines Operate [Online], Moz, available at: moz.com/
beginners-guide-to-seo/how-search-engines-operate (archived at https://perma.
cc/QD5X-7JN7)

OAAA (2020) History of OOH [Online], Out of Home advertising Association of
America, available at: oaaa.org/AboutOOH/OOHBasics/HistoryofOOH.aspx
(archived at https://perma.cc/M5GA-57F2)

Ofcom (2017) *Communications Market Report* [Online], Ofcom, available at:
www.ofcom.org.uk/__data/assets/pdf_file/0014/105440/uk-radio-audio.pdf
(archived at https://perma.cc/C7AV-D5AJ)

Pahwa, N (2020) What Indians lost when the government banned TikTok [Online],
The Wire, available at: thewire.in/tech/india-tiktok-ban-government (archived at
https://perma.cc/9DD9-7VUY)

Paul, K (2020) Trump's bid to ban TikTok and WeChat: where are we now? [Online], *the Guardian*, available at: www.theguardian.com/technology/2020/sep/29/trump-tiktok-wechat-china-us-explainer (archived at https://perma.cc/5Q8P-3W7S)

Peppiatt, V (2020) COO and co-founder at Phrasee [Interview] 20 October 2020

Phrasee (2016) A brief history of email: dedicated to Ray Tomlinson [Online], Phrasee, available at: phrasee.co/a-brief-history-of-email/ (archived at https://perma.cc/555H-GA3B)

Rachel, P (2018) The curious case of Blend techs viral 'Will it Blend' videos [Online], Contentwriters, available at: contentwriters.com/blog/curious-case-blendtecs-viral-will-blend-videos/ (archived at https://perma.cc/S3J5-D7J9)

Ritson, M (2020) Marketing Thought Leader [Interview] 13 October 2020

Roderick, L (2015) TV ads at 60: History [Online], *Marketing Week*, available at: www.marketingweek.com/tv-ads-at-60-a-history/ (archived at https://perma.cc/W58D-BQ3Z)

Rusonis, S (2020) If your Account-Based Marketing Strategy isn't personalised you're missing the point [Online], Optimizely blog, available at: blog.optimizely.com/2016/04/21/account-based-marketing-strategy/ (archived at https://perma.cc/ME3U-MKR7)

Siddiqui, Z (2014) The History of PR [Online], Curzon PR, available at: www.curzonpr.com/theprinsider/from-the-beginning-the-history-of-pr/ (archived at https://perma.cc/AK68-QK26)

Statista (2020a) Worldwide desktop market share of learning search engines from January 2010 to July 2020 [Online], Statista, available at: www.statista.com/statistics/216573/worldwide-market-share-of-search-engines/#:~:text=Google%20has%20dominated%20the%20search,revenues%20are%20generated%20through%20advertising (archived at https://perma.cc/3S8G-5CCR)

Statista (2020b) Advertising revenue of Google from 2001 to 2019 [Online], Statista, available at: www.statista.com/statistics/266249/advertising-revenue-of-google/ (archived at https://perma.cc/T7MT-GXN3)

Statista (2020c) Daily social media usage worldwide 2012–2019 [Online], Statista, available at: www.statista.com/statistics/433871/daily-social-media-usage-worldwide/ (archived at https://perma.cc/3JDG-SQQT)

Statista (2020d) Retail e-commerce sales in the United States from 2017 to 2024 [Online], Statista, available at: www.statista.com/statistics/272391/us-retail-e-commerce-sales-forecast/ (archived at https://perma.cc/LG57-GNN9)

Steck, E (2017) A brief history of data and content marketing, plus where they are headed [Online], Quietly, available at: blog.quiet.ly/industry/a-brief-history-of-data-and-content-marketing-plus-where-they-are-headed/ (archived at https://perma.cc/ACK5-EH9Q)

Stelzner, M (2017) Content marketing success: Why answering questions sells [Online], Socialmedia Examiner, available at: www.socialmediaexaminer.com/content-marketing-success-why-answering-questions-sells-marcus-sheridan/ (archived at https://perma.cc/SY6R-W795)

Stern, T (2015) The evolution of SEO trends over 25 years [Online], Search Engine Land, available at: searchengineland.com/evolution-seo-trends-25-years-223424 (archived at https://perma.cc/RER6-PTJZ)

Target Internet (2020) A marketer's guide to affiliate marketing [Online], Target Internet, available at: www.targetinternet.com/a-marketers-guide-to-affiliate-marketing/ (archived at https://perma.cc/BT59-VMTD)

The Drum (2016a) 1871: Congress bans cigarette advertising on TV and radio [Online], The Drum, available at: www.thedrum.com/news/2016/03/31/1971-congress-bans-cigarette-advertising-tv-and-radio (archived at https://perma.cc/ZH4W-JLML)

The Drum (2016b) 1979: 'Mean' Jo Greene stars in iconic Coca-Cola commercial [Online], The Drum, available at: www.thedrum.com/news/2016/03/31/1979-mean-joe-greene-stars-iconic-coca-cola-commercial (archived at https://perma.cc/8XER-M7AM)

Thinkbox (2019) TV ads explained [Online], Thinkbox, available at: www.thinkbox.tv/getting-on-tv/tv-advertising-basics/tv-ads-explained/ (archived at https://perma.cc/PNC2-9QFQ)

Timms, D (2004) Tango ad pulled off air over safety fears [Online], the Guardian, available at: www.theguardian.com/media/2004/nov/11/advertising.uknews (archived at https://perma.cc/39W3-G5NT)

Trade Show Advisor (2020) History of trade shows [Online], Trade Show Advisor, available at: www.trade-show-advisor.com/history-of-trade-shows.html (archived at https://perma.cc/4LEC-A3HG)

UK Government (1998) Data Protection Act 1998 [Online], available at: www.legislation.gov.uk/ukpga/1998/29/contents (archived at https://perma.cc/GU5D-974F)

Uplers (2020) Theory of Email Evolution [Online], Uplers email, available at: email.uplers.com/infographics/evolution-of-emails/ (archived at https://perma.cc/S69C-TQ7V)

Wallace, K (2019) The history and future of television advertising [Online], Oracle Data Cloud Blog, available at: blogs.oracle.com/oracledatacloud/the-history-and-future-of-television-advertising (archived at https://perma.cc/3QE2-R9C7)

Watson, T (2012) A (very brief) history of PR [Online], Communication Director, available at www.communication-director.com/issues/b2b-or-not-b2b/very-brief-history-pr/#.X5MLOVNKjOQ (archived at https://perma.cc/9VM9-W9BE)

07

Execution

Implementing your marketing strategy

This chapter covers:

- A brand's tone of voice.
- Brand guidelines and how to structure them.
- Roles and responsibilities of your marketing team.
- The areas to focus on when implementing your marketing tactics.

Congratulations for getting to this stage! By this point you've put in an enormous amount of work. You've analysed the internal and external marketing environment; you've identified and learned about your target audience; you've analysed the marketing mix and created a plan; you've chosen channels and tactics. Now, it's time to set all of this into motion, and execute your plan.

The importance of consistency

The key area to focus on when rolling out your strategy is consistency. Consistency is crucial to ensuring that your message is clearly understood. If for example, your tone is inconsistent, things will quickly become confusing for your audience. Confusion is a block to understanding, if a customer doesn't understand your brand or your message they are unlikely to buy. Take, for example, Marks & Spencer (M&S) clothing – who is it for, what is its USP? No one clearly knows, it is confusing and the end result is poor performance (Russon, 2020). You want your prospects and potential new customers to be completely clear about the products and services you provide. If things aren't 100 per cent clear or it's difficult to understand what you do, you won't engage your audience.

In my experience, there are usually common denominators involved when a brand's marketing starts to lose consistency. One is not clearly identifying as a business what you do, the benefits that the product/service on offer provides. In many cases each department in the organization and the individuals have a different interpretation of what the organization does and in turn the benefits being provided also differs. This translates into not pre-establishing a clear tone of voice and a coherent way of explaining what the organization does.

The second is visual inconsistency, which is where brand guidelines come in. The guidelines structure the use of colour schemes and graphic styles to visually represent the brand. The graphics that you use on your social media page, the colours that are displayed on your website, everything should be aligned to a pre-established guideline to ensure that there is consistency. More on how to ensure consistency and how to create tone of voice and brand guidelines further in this chapter.

Branding

A brand is how a person perceives and identifies an organization or person (if it's their personal brand). This perception can be influenced with what are known as branding elements, such as logos, a specific slogan/strapline, designs, symbols, and (most importantly) the feelings which the products or services evoke.

A brand is more than a product or service; it is the combination of all of these elements. Together, branding elements portray the core message of the company.

A brand is an incredibly valuable asset to an organization and this value can be measured through brand equity. Brand equity is what a company generates from a recognizable name, logo, design, symbol or experience. Brand equity can be enhanced by creating products or services that are memorable, easily recognizable, superior in quality and reliability.

As an example, Coca-Cola's brand is worth $84 billion in 2020 (Statista, 2020). The elements that Coca-Cola have used to build this brand equity and the longevity include remaining consistent across their marketing (using the 7Ps) and their incredibly clear and recognizable visual identity.

Consistency (explored in more detail in Chapter 10) and a clear definition through tone of voice (ToV) and brand guidelines are vital to grow the value of a brand.

Brand audits

To determine the health of your brand, a brand audit is a useful exercise. The brand audit can identify where brands may need more support, brands that aren't adding any value or those that require changes to be made in areas such as positioning or to suit changing customer preferences.

Key questions to ask during a brand audit include:

- Does your brand deliver benefits that consumers deem valuable?
- Does the brand positioning reflect the desired outcome?
- Is there clear internal positioning of the brand?
- How is the brand supported and maintained?

Finding your brand's tone of voice (ToV)

Let's first look at the difference between tone and voice.

One of the ways in which we make our content empowering is to be very aware of our voice and our tone.

'Voice' and 'tone' are closely related concepts but are not entirely the same. For example, when you speak to your friends in everyday life, you generally use the same 'voice'. Unless you're making a special effort to do an impersonation of someone else, your voice sounds roughly the same. You tend to speak with a particular accent, for example. The sound of your voice is recognizable and unique to you.

However, your 'tone' will differ considerably depending on the circumstances of your conversation. You would not use the same ToV when addressing a scared child as you would when joking with your sibling, would you? In both cases, your voice remains identifiable as your own voice – but the tone you're using is entirely different based on the situation in which you're speaking.

This applies to marketing and when we should all be trying our best to sound human, it's the element that is often incorrectly overlooked.

Here's an example of voice/tone guidelines.

MAILCHIMP: VOICE/TONE GUIDELINES

Creating this brand was a key element in connecting with customers but it walked a very thin line between the fun and the silly. Mailchimp made this fine balance seem easy and natural but there was a lot of work that went into getting it right.

As Ade Lewis, Marketing Director at Mailchimp explains in the interview at the end of Chapter 9, a lot of effort was put into the creation and documentation of Mailchimp's ToV (Lewis, 2020). Mailchimp's 'Content style guide' (styleguide.mailchimp.com/voice-and-tone/) details the voice and tone, along with how to write for a variety of different channels using Mailchimp's voice.

Mailchimp's voice as detailed in their Content Style Guide reflects the founders' (Ben Chestnut and Dan Kurzuis) entrepreneurial experience. The way the copy should be written to reflect Mailchimp's voice is documented within the guide such as 'we are plain spoken' and 'we are genuine'.

The tone of Mailchimp is also defined as 'usually informal' but with the importance of clarity emphasized over being entertaining.

There is also a clear distinction made of Mailchimp's mascot Freddie, who does not have a voice.

'Mailchimp created a point of difference in their brand with the now iconic Freddie logo and a sense of the fun and quirky that small business owners understood' (Lewis, 2020). And that was important, because Mailchimp's target customers are small business owners. This enabled the company to 'understand and connect with their customers' (Lewis, 2020). From connecting with its target customer, Mailchimp has become one of the world's biggest email marketing platforms (Cannon, 2020).

It can also be helpful to include what your voice and tone is not, along with any words to avoid – especially when sharing ToV guidelines with external partners.

Brand guidelines

Documents like this are hugely useful for keeping all marketers and contractors on the same page. Copywriters in particular love it when you include guidelines like this in the brief, as it saves them a lot of back and forth trying to nail your voice!

Creating comprehensive and consistent brand guidelines should involve all stakeholders. You need your instructions to cover everything from your voice to the way you represent your products/services, and the visual 'feel' of your brand. This will include the colour representation of your brand with pantone numbers.

As with everything involving input from multiple viewpoints, nailing down your brand ToV guidelines can be a long and complicated process, but it's worth persevering at.

Your guidelines shouldn't be hundreds of pages in a huge PDF document hidden away on a G.Drive where nowhere uses it. Less is more when it comes to guidelines. The core information to include is detailed below.

I often find that organizations do not focus closely enough on an instantly recognizable handful of colours, icons, dedicated fonts and so on. I've worked with companies which have documented their brand guidelines across 20 or more pages, and which included every colour of the rainbow and more!

There's also the issue of version control. It's healthy for the brand guidelines to evolve along with the company, but older versions that are now obsolete should be archived and replaced with the new version. I'd also recommend not updating the guidelines constantly. There needs to be a moment of 'completion' to embed the new or revised guidelines. The guidelines should remain in place for at least six months unless there are major flaws or major company changes with the direction of the company, the target audience or vision change. There's a misconception that a new marketing direction will always update and remap the brand and the guidelines 'because that's what they do' (to quote an anonymous client)! If the guidelines are robust and succinct then there is no need to reinvent the wheel. The major prompts for adjustment are when the company pivots to a new offering or new target audience or the current guidelines are not viable for digital assets.

For example, it may be that the core colours identified include one that does not display correctly online but looks beautiful in print. If the colours are mainly used online rather than offline, then this wouldn't necessarily represent the brand correctly and would be inconsistent with offline assets. The best brand guidelines take into account all use cases, whether it be at a physical event or on the company's website; the font, the colours, the logo size need to work in all those different situations.

Many times I have worked with clients and inherited brand guidelines that may have a great story to tell but were far too complicated, too long, included a full palette of over 100 colours, fonts that aren't online friendly – and didn't include rules for how the logo should be displayed. Each of these instances would prompt a slight adjustment to the brand guidelines. If there is too much room for individual interpretation you risk the creep of inconsistency.

When the remit of choice is this big, it's very open to individual interpretation and, while personal innovation and creativity is useful, it always needs to be allied to clear ToV guidelines. When the guidelines give too much choice, inconsistencies quickly arise. This can lead to the website presenting itself as a different colour to the product, which has a distinct visual representation again to the presentation decks. The core essence of the brand and its message becomes confused, unclear and unfocused. Brand guidelines are the rules to come back to whenever visually displaying the brand. They should ensure consistency across all brand assets.

By pairing your brand's visual identity down to a few core elements, it becomes much easier for the rest of the business to interpret and for external suppliers/agencies to implement. Figure 7.1 gives an example of my marketing agency Let'sTalk Strategy's brand guidelines.

It's a one-page brand guideline. There are clear dimensions for the full logo at the top and for the shortened version below. These are useful to maintain appropriate spacing whenever it is used. Then there are three core primary colours and five secondary colours. The primary colours are the ones that are most used and which provide the predominant visual 'feel' of the brand. When choosing your colours, it's essential to consider where and in what context they will be used – eg on the website, in a presentation, in an email etc. This is important, because choosing colours which do not show up well in certain media or on certain devices will make a massive difference to the accessibility of your brand material.

FIGURE 7.1 Example of brand guidelines used at marketing agency Let'sTalk Strategy

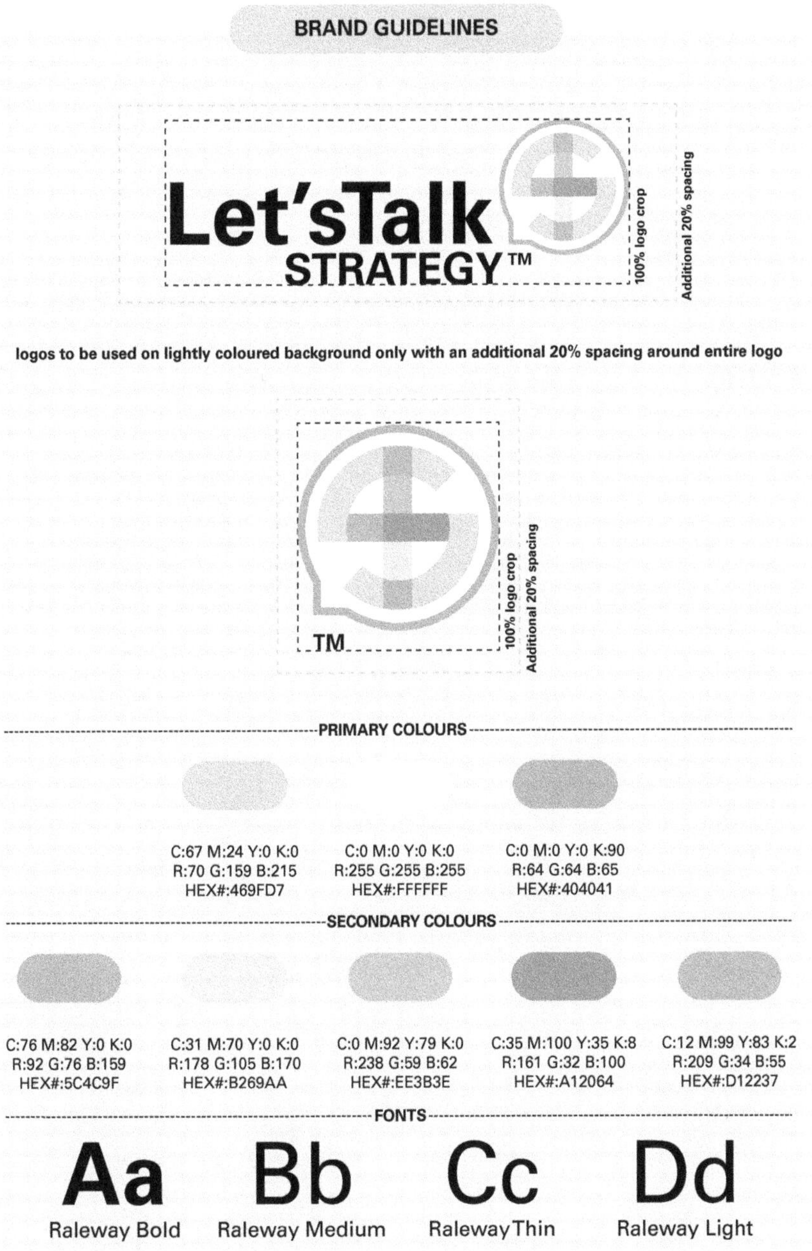
BRAND GUIDELINES
Let'sTalk
STRATEGY™
100% logo crop
Additional 20% spacing
logos to be used on lightly coloured background only with an additional 20% spacing around entire logo
TM
100% logo crop
Additional 20% spacing
PRIMARY COLOURS
C:67 M:24 Y:0 K:0
R:70 G:159 B:215
HEX#:469FD7
C:0 M:0 Y:0 K:0
R:255 G:255 B:255
HEX#:FFFFFF
C:0 M:0 Y:0 K:90
R:64 G:64 B:65
HEX#:404041
SECONDARY COLOURS
C:76 M:82 Y:0 K:0
R:92 G:76 B:159
HEX#:5C4C9F
C:31 M:70 Y:0 K:0
R:178 G:105 B:170
HEX#:B269AA
C:0 M:92 Y:79 K:0
R:238 G:59 B:62
HEX#:EE3B3E
C:35 M:100 Y:35 K:8
R:161 G:32 B:100
HEX#:A12064
C:12 M:99 Y:83 K:2
R:209 G:34 B:55
HEX#:D12237
FONTS
Aa
Raleway Bold
Bb
Raleway Medium
Cc
Raleway Thin
Dd
Raleway Light

Reproduced with the kind permission from Let'sTalk Strategy (2020)

Then there are the fonts underneath and the four varieties that can be used. The important thing with fonts is to ensure that the one you use can be replicated across all channels and, if it can't, that there is a viable alternative. For example, if your preferred font is not compatible with specific email clients, will it be replaced with something that works nearly as well?

The next layer that could be added to a guideline document is examples of how your brand guidelines will look in practice, for example, in different heading sizes, on a website and in an email signature.

Clearly set out the rules for when and how colours, fonts and icons are used, along with how to display the logo. All visual assets should refer back to your guidelines. I particularly recommend creating templates in order to make things even more consistent.

Implementing your guidelines

Having decided on your brand guideline for tone and voice, you now need to roll them out across your operation.

It's vital that everyone in your business knows that there are new guidelines to follow – and to make a pretty big deal out of this in order to drive the point home! The last thing you want to end up with is a hybrid of new and old. You need to make sure that everyone is entirely on board with and using the latest guidelines from Day 1.

If your new guidelines are a significant change from what's gone before, your best bet is to treat the launch of your new guidelines as you would treat launching a new marketing campaign. Host a party in the office, or virtually (depending on your organizational set-up), share newly branded goodies if your budget will allow. Get everyone involved, and get everyone enthused!

Update all of your templates so that everyone can start using the new assets straight away, rebrand assets that are in regular use and archive the old versions. In a large organization, it may be possible to assign brand ambassadors responsible for implementing the new guidelines within each team. These ambassadors will be responsible for ensuring that their department implements the new guidelines correctly. Schedule regular check-ins and reviews, in order to answer any queries and to review the documents being used.

And always remember – consistent voice and visual identity is key to a consistent message.

Engaging your audience with your brand voice

Getting your colleagues on board with your brand voice guidelines is critical – but let's not forget who you'll be using that voice.

Think about how you're going to use this new, consistent voice to communicate, in order to get people engaged with your marketing strategy. This is where voice and tactics start to integrate. Your brand voice is crucial to the success of your marketing tactics – but you also need to know how to implement those tactics in order to give your voice the most significant possible impact.

EXAMPLE: STRAPLINES

The strapline for my agency Let'sTalk Strategy is simply this: 'Straightforward marketing strategy'.

It's simple, it's concise, and it makes it totally clear what the agency is all about. It does what it says on the tin.

Straplines should embody your brand's voice while clearly summarizing what you do. Think of them like dating profile bios. Anyone who's done online dating will have worked hard to get a wealth of information about their personality across in a succinct one-liner. Your brand strapline is like the dating bio for your organization. And it's a great place to start when establishing consistency in voice and tone.

Here are some tips for nailing your strapline:

- Simplicity is key:
  - Your strapline needs to be immediately comprehensible and engaging. Make it as simple as you can while staying within your brand voice.
  - Make it snappy. A concise strapline is not only simpler, it's also easier to remember. Not to mention that it's easier to fit on your signage.
- Link it to your vision:
  - Remember all of the tips in Chapter 1 about Vision. Your Vision needs to connect everything you do, and it should be at the forefront when it comes to your strapline.

o This is especially important when it comes to nailing a consistent voice and tone in everything you do.

o Every time you're considering new marketing content, think: Is this tone, or this voice, or these graphics, or this colour scheme consistent with our brand Vision? For example, a company with a holistic, ecological vision could perhaps express this by using green branding, leafy imagery and so on. A voice and tone involving bold red capitals and aggressive sales pitches would be inconsistent with their vision.

How can we do that? Let's dive into campaign implementation and find out.

Bringing your campaign to life

Using the information that you have gathered from Chapters 2, 3, 4 and 5, your tactical timings should reflect when your audience is most likely to engage with your content. The topic that you choose, while aligned to your marketing objectives, should be one that is of interest to your target audience.

When defining and implementing your campaign, think about the issues identified in Table 7.1.

Defining roles and responsibilities is, in my experience, something that many companies struggle with. Let's dig into it a little further

TABLE 7.1 The key focus areas and questions to ask when defining and implementing your marketing campaign

Messaging	What are you trying to say? What is the process of getting this message across? Who are the stakeholders of your message?
Channels	How will you get this message across? Consider things like events, research, PPC, paid social, your website and email marketing (more detail in Chapter 6).
Action	When considering 'action', draw up a schedule to implement your tactics. Consider: What needs to be done, who will do it, when they will do it?
Resources	What do you need in order to put your plan into action? Do you have all the skills you need in-house, or will you need to outsource?
Roles and responsibilities	When implementing any marketing campaign (or even individual tactic) you need to clearly define roles and responsibilities. What will each role consist of? What will be the remit of each person?

Roles and responsibilities

Roles and responsibilities should be clearly defined across your marketing team, including any external agency that may be supporting your marketing activity, and across the business if you're a smaller organization. What's important is that each person involved in the implementation of your marketing strategy is aware of what is expected of them – including things like deadlines, KPIs and budget constraints.

Figure 7.2 gives an example of a marketing team's structure in which external outsourced support is included. You can see which team member is responsible for which area by following the lines linking the in-house marketing team with the outsourced one. Alongside this team is the sales team.

And in Figure 7.3 we can see the key responsibilities for the three core in-house team members.

When planning your marketing campaigns, I recommend grouping activity into core themes. If you're promoting a product, these themes should align to the key features that the product provides. For example:

- **insight** (explaining what the product does);
- **optimize** (explaining how the product can fit in with and enhance the customer's life); and
- **explore** (exploring the potential of the product).

These themes will ultimately lead to a rich and complete detailing of the product's core elements. Via themes like these, the entire topic can be

FIGURE 7.2   An example marketing and sales team structure with outsourced agency support

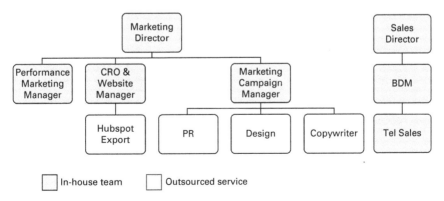

FIGURE 7.3   Example roles and responsibilities of a marketing team

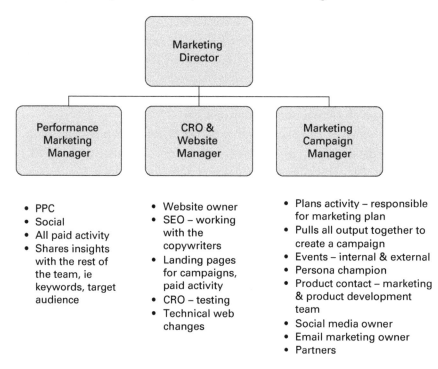

explored in the marketing activity, be that through a blog post on the website, in social media content, in email marketing, in research focus areas or in paid advertising activity (see Figure 7.4).

Forming an action plan

Laying down an action plan is vital if you're to roll out your tactics in an effective manner. Your action plan should include every single element and tactic of the marketing activity that is taking place. These elements and tactics should be aligned with:

- start and end dates;
- target personas;
- roles and responsibilities within the team.

Table 7.2 gives an example of what an action plan may look like. To the left of a plan like this you will usually find the individual team members who are responsible for each activity.

FIGURE 7.4 Example of how content themes inform multichannel marketing campaign activity

You can see that if the activity is an event (which will typically happen on a single day) the timing includes when the preparation activity needs to begin, and when to follow up the event by sending marketing communications to attendees.

The entire schedule for the marketers, from earliest research to prepping slides, gathering promotional assets, confirming speakers and all the way through to final follow-up emails is included. It is important to factor this level of detail into the plan in order to ensure that the resources required are assigned sufficient time, and that activity planning starts in time to hit the deadline date.

TABLE 7.2 Example action plan

					MONTHS				
ORGANIZER	Apr 2021	May 2021	June 2021	July 2021	Aug 2021	Sept 2021	Oct 2021	Nov 2021	Dec 2021
Marketing Director (oversees and approves the tasks below)		Webinar event		Press interview		Speaking at event		Podcast interview	
	Finalizing logistics for webinar event				Content theme 1 runs here				
Marketing Team member 1		Coordinate blog content following webinar & automated follow-up emails.			Research survey with PR and external research provider. Gathering results and key findings.				
			Website update/relaunch				Partners (1 Oct 2021–31 Dec 2021)		
			Marketing campaign running			Sponsored content running			
Marketing Team member 2		New product feature launching	Summer event	PR activity		PR The Drum - Martech (23 Sept 2021)			
					Target audience focus				
		Brief copywriters		Brief designers for next campaign					
					Q2 & Q4 marketing campaigns				

Project management

There are two main project management approaches. These are known as the **Agile** and the **Waterfall** methods.

Typically, these are used for managing the development of software projects but are equally useful to managing the implementation of marketing campaigns.

The Agile approach is one in which the ability to adapt to changes is vital to the success of the project. The plan is broken down into bi-weekly sprints and each sprint has a set of tasks that need to be completed. While this approach wouldn't be the most suitable for many marketing campaigns, the ability to respond to change is a principle that should feature heavily and be catered for.

Waterfall is in some respects more robust than Agile, in that there is a concrete plan with less opportunity for things to drop in and out. There is a clear process to follow, similar to that of defining a marketing strategy, and then there is a sprint-to-release process to follow. The downside is that there is little room to adjust the plan if a new requirement or a market change happens while the plan is underway. To include this in the plan, it would need to wait until the end, and by then it could be too late.

To manage a marketing campaign successfully, I recommend using a combination of both of these approaches. I suggest including clearly defined processes to follow when implementing each marketing tactic, clear briefing criteria, templates to ensure consistency, and a process for reporting to ensure that all activity is captured. This will then become business as usual (BAU) activity that happens constantly and consistently.

For reporting, it is important to create a marketing performance dashboard that clearly breaks down: each tactical activity; the audience that is being targeted; the objective; the date and time it took place; the budget spent; and the weekly/monthly target required to achieve the end goal.

Choosing your tactics

Of course, your action plan is going to need to be populated with tactics. We went into the history and nature of various channels in the last chapter. Now let's look at how you might implement them as tactics.

PPC (pay-per-click) ads

The vital thing to remember with PPC is that clicks don't necessarily mean conversions. It's still important to optimize every step of the customer journey from click onwards. Don't just tailor your content for clicks.

Google Ads (formerly known as Google AdWords) is the main advertising platform companies use when creating PPC ads. As Google is the world's predominant search engine, it makes sense to create ads which will appear on Google's own search pages (and other properties). But it is also worth not forgetting search engine Bing. Although a smaller proportion of searchers use Bing to find answers to their queries, PPC ads on Bing are achieving a 50 per cent higher average click-through rate (CTR, explained in more detail in Chapter 8) than Google (Irvine, 2020).

When creating ads in AdWords, marketers bid on 'keywords' relevant to their operation or campaign. For example, a company selling apples might select keywords like 'fresh', 'juicy', 'healthy' and so on. The more popular the keywords, the more expensive each click will be.

However, it can sometimes be worth stacking your ads with expensive keywords as these can bring in big conversions if they're relevant enough to what you're selling.

Social media

Social media is rich and fertile ground for marketers – but you have to know how to use it.

Julie Atherton (2019) recommends the ABC approach when planning social media activity. The three core elements of this approach are: Audience, Brand and Campaigns.

As we identified in Chapter 4, it's important to define who your audience is, the social media platforms they are using and engaging with and so on. The next step is to establish and develop a social media presence which will push your content in front of that audience. Just as your website can be discovered when someone uses a search engine, the right click or hashtag search will take a social media user to your brand.

The final step is to ensure that your campaigns meet your objectives. A social media presence requires a constantly-on approach. To fully achieve your objectives, a multichannel approach should be established to ensure that you retain a consistent message across all of the tactics that you use.

Direct mail

Direct mailing may appear old-school – but there's no reason why it can't be used in innovative ways. For example, the gold winner of the DMA Awards 2019 for the best use of direct mail was the brand Jaguar Land Rover, for their launch of the Range Rover Evoque. Jaguar Land Rover combined both digital and offline techniques and delivered a direct mail experience which worked for everyone (DMA, 2019).

The 'Triggering a Reaction' campaign worked like this.

In a world first, Jaguar Land Rover used WND Network and Sigfox technology within a direct mail format. Packs were sent out in the post to potential Evoque customers. These packages contained a replica button (and who doesn't want to push an enticing button?) that came equipped with radio transmission technology, which connected to Jaguar Land Rover's CRM system. By pressing this button, recipients of the mailshot were able to instantly book a test drive at their local Land Rover vendor.

Once the test drive was logged on the system, an SMS was triggered to the recipient's phone, confirming their booking and letting them know that the retailer would be in touch to arrange things further. All of this happened in real time, was GDPR-compliant and worked seamlessly. No sign-up was required, no pre-arrangements, no wifi connection or Bluetooth – just a physical 'button', some radio tech and a clever CRM.

The results were fantastic. The Evoque campaign received an enormous 44 per cent response rate – corresponding to over 2,000 test drive requests.

So, never underestimate the potential of seemingly 'old fashioned' channels! Combined with the right tactics, these channels still have a lot to offer (Brown, 2019).

Email

I consider there to be four key stages when implementing email marketing, outlined in Figure 7.5.

1. BE SEEN

The focus here is on your email marketing being seen by your customers. The first starting place is to ensure that the email has landed in the inbox. This may seem like a given as soon as you press send on your campaign, but several stages take place before your email enters the inbox. The reputation of your sending domain (the email address you are sending from) is one of

FIGURE 7.5   The four key stages of email marketing

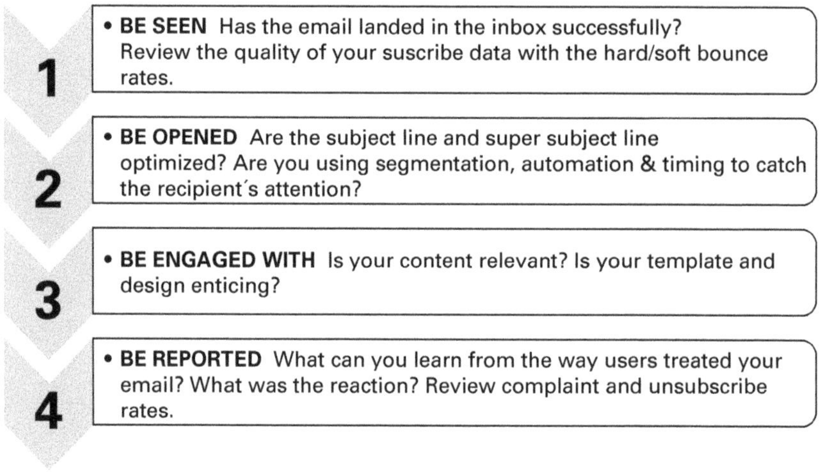

1
- **BE SEEN** Has the email landed in the inbox successfully? Review the quality of your suscribe data with the hard/soft bounce rates.

2
- **BE OPENED** Are the subject line and super subject line optimized? Are you using segmentation, automation & timing to catch the recipient's attention?

3
- **BE ENGAGED WITH** Is your content relevant? Is your template and design enticing?

4
- **BE REPORTED** What can you learn from the way users treated your email? What was the reaction? Review complaint and unsubscribe rates.

the most important as this is what the ISPs (such as Gmail, Yahoo and Outlook) will be checking along with many other variants as to whether your email lands into the inbox, and if it does, whether it ends up in the main inbox, promotions (for Gmail) or Spam.

The quality of the data that you're sending is equally as important. All of your subscribers should have consented to receive your marketing email. There may be varying sources of this subscriber data, such as events, webinars, your website and so on. There are tools available to validate the quality of your data to confirm that the email address does exist and is still receiving email. This is important because data that isn't reviewed or cleaned periodically could contain fake email addresses and potential spam traps, which if sent to could dramatically impact your email deliverability rate and being seen in the inbox.

2. BE OPENED

Driving action with your email marketing once it's landed in the inbox is crucial for the success of not only that individual campaign but also the overall performance of email. The key focus areas here are to ensure that the subject line and super subject lines (this appears underneath the subject line in the preview text) are optimized. Are they going to engage your subscribers to open the email? Testing different variants of subject lines is important to understand more about what engages your audience to drive action.

Segmenting your subscribers based on areas such as likes, dislikes and behaviour will help ensure that the campaigns sent are relevant to each segment, enabling you to tailor and personalize the content. It may also be that you have an international subscriber base. Optimizing the send time of when your email marketing campaign reaches your subscribers based on their time zone is a great starting point.

Automated email campaigns are a great way to instantly connect with your subscribers at the relevant point in time, such as when they first sign up to receive email marketing from you. Sending a welcome email journey to those subscribers to thank them for subscribing, setting expectations and describing your organization's USPs is a good way to start building a relationship with the recipients.

3. BE ENGAGED WITH

Driving repeat engagement with your email marketing is an important way to keep your subscribers active with your brand's communications. This links back to being seen, and the use of segmentation. If you're able to segment based on purchase behaviour, for example, you could tailor the content to include complementary products to your subscriber's recent purchase.

Testing here is also important to validate that your email template and design displays as intended on the devices that your subscribers use such as a laptop, a phone and a desktop computer. It's possible to see within your email service provider (ESP) or email sending platform the devices that your recipients use to open your emails.

Consider the customer journey and the stage that your subscriber may be at when building your email campaigns. If it's an order confirmation email, for example, the information a recipient will be expecting to receive will be different to a welcome email that is greeting the new subscriber.

4. BE REPORTED

Reporting the performance of your email marketing is vital to understanding what's working and what isn't within your email campaigns. It also enables you to better understand the behaviour of your subscribers which can inform future sends. The areas to focus your measurement are covered in Chapter 8, and the KPIs to use for email marketing are explained in detail in Chapter 9.

Creating content

The content with which you implement your tactics depends a lot on your own brand voice, tone, goals, vision, etc. The right content for you will depend ultimately on knowing your audience, using the right tone and voice, respecting your brand guidelines and so on. And a little bit of well-thought-out innovation that achieves your objectives always helps!

Storytelling

Storytelling is a common and very successful tactic, which you can even tie in with other tactics. Ultimately, for a strategy to be successful, it needs to be tied into a storyline. Humans are hard-wired to respond to stories. We engage with them like nothing else!

The key to engaging customers is through storytelling. It's important to identify and explain what the brand stands for and what it offers so that customers can relate to it. Tactics are the means you will use to get your story out there.

If the story is good and one that customers can relate to, it can evoke empathy and should address customer needs.

CASE STUDY
TOMS Shoes

A great example here is TOMS Shoes where they developed an initiative to donate a pair of shoes after every purchase.

'One Day Without Shoes' is their annual marketing campaign, encouraging people to not wear shoes for a day. The objective is to raise awareness for children's health and education in countries such as Peru and India. Social media is used to drive awareness and promote their campaign, using the main tactic of encouraging people taking part to tag their bare feet on Instagram. Every photo that is tagged results in TOMS donating a pair of shoes to children in developing countries. In 2017, 27,435 children received donated shoes in over 10 countries (DMI, 2017).

The personal approach

Personalized content is vital for implementing any campaign. It's how you grab and keep consumer attention.

What's more, people are increasingly expecting it. They won't bestow their precious attention upon anything that isn't personally relevant. So, I would always strongly recommend that your tactics have a personal element to them.

It's important to remember that the purpose of marketing is to build relationships by satisfying the needs and wants of consumers as highlighted in Chapter 1. Getting to know someone personally is vital when building a relationship with a friend, and the same applies for the relationship between an individual and a brand.

The Land Rover Evoque campaign I mentioned earlier is a perfect example of personalization. Through a seemingly identical mailshot, customers were sent texts directly to their own phones, offering a personal experience optimized for their own schedules, locations and so on.

As humans we enjoy feeling involved and personalization satisfies that joy. The more that people feel that content is speaking directly to them, the more involved they will feel with it. And the more involved they feel, the more likely they are to engage.

Personalization may seem difficult in this age when we're mostly communicating from behind screens. But, in fact, technology can help us get closer to our audiences than ever before.

A digital single-customer view provides marketers with the ability to view a customer's behaviour in its entirety. To do this, web analysis, CRM (customer relationship management) software and marketing automation are needed. And they have to work together. When linked, these will provide you with the full customer story. And you do have to know the full story. It's not enough to just address your customer by their first name. As Sara Meikle explains in the interview at the end of this chapter, automation was crucial to the success of their campaign, not only in effectively communicating with their subscribers but also in supporting the marketing team:

> Automation is essential to success. Having a system in place where I could create and send multiple elements of the campaign to hundreds of different people, whilst still personalizing each user's experience was a huge factor in the campaign running smoothly.

Personalization starts with a name (which is why Starbucks asks for your name when you order your coffee), but it shouldn't end there. Each stage of building a friendship for brands means more trust and more data. If you don't use what a customer has already told you about them, then you're not listening. Everyone wants to be listened to. But that's not all they want. Let's be honest, we're all human: there's an element of self-interest in any relationship. In a brand–consumer relationship, this element is heightened. To have a need fulfilled is, after all, the reason that most consumers come to a brand in the first place. So, the key thing that you're listening for is any indication that you're not adding as much value as you could to your customer's experience. Or ways in which you are exceeding expectations! Listen, respond as personally and individually as you can, and take any lessons on board.

Then there are the experiences that we share together within relationships. Personal experience brings people together – and there's no reason why people should not have personal experiences with a brand. The brand will become a better friend because of a good, shared experience. Shared experiences are a big part of how we build connections.

The most obvious 'shared experience' between an individual and a brand involves the provision of something at the time of need. If your customer needs something, and you deliver it, that's a connecting experience. Now all you need to do is build upon that experience to foster a personal relationship. If you can create this kind of relationship, you'll not only be rewarded by the relationship itself, you may also find that your customers become brand ambassadors.

The stand-out example of this kind of thing is, of course, the 'Share a Coke' campaign by Coca-Cola. If you're not familiar with it, the multiple results a quick online search provides will soon give you an idea!

Barriers to personalization

Personalization is fantastic if you can get it right. But remember – there is a fine line to walk between 'personalized' and 'stalkerish'. If you're going to use personalization as a tactic, you must continually refer back to your strategic resources to make sure you're not overstepping that line.

Here are a few areas to watch out for when personalizing your content.

DATA PRIVACY
Firstly, there's the data aspect. We covered this in more detail when we discussed the GDPR in Chapter 4, but for now let's just clarify that approaching customers or taking their information unsolicited will not come off as 'personalized'. It'll come over as creepy.

CREEPINESS
And, speaking of creepy, that line between 'personalized' and 'intrusive' is in a different place for everyone. You won't get it right 100 per cent of the time. For example, a lot of people like the Starbucks 'name on cup' thing, and

Starbucks clearly think it's a winner for them. But a lot of people find it annoying, and an unnecessary waste of time – especially when well-meaning staff members make mistakes!

COMING ON TOO STRONG WITH FIRST-TIME CUSTOMERS

Being too personal with 'strangers' is weird. How would you like it if a total stranger approached out of the blue, called you by your first name and seemed to know everything about you? You wouldn't. Yet sometimes this is forgotten in a marketing campaign and is particularly noticeable in the inbox. Here's an example of my inbox:

Email 1: *Subject line:* Jenna, was it something I said?

Email 2: *Subject line:* Hi there, Jenna, it's me again…

Email 3: *Subject line:* This is my third attempt to contact you, Jenna.

Email 4: *Subject line:* Jenna, I just can't seem to reach you.

Email 5: *Subject line:* Jenna, I know you're busy, but…

Email 6: *Subject line:* Jenna, I get the feeling this isn't a priority.

Email 7: *Subject line:* Jenna, should I wave the white flag?

As you can see, my name is included in the subject line, yet I don't know the person who has persistently emailed me or their company. If this was a scenario in real life it would be considered stalking. As marketers, it's important we always remember the end customer, recipient, user. The person we are marketing to and their experience.

NOT PUTTING THE WORK IN

Build personal relationships – the keyword here being 'build'. Good personal relationships develop over time – and it's two-way. Let customers offer information freely. That successful Coke campaign was brilliant because it simultaneously was and was not intensively targeted. Customers could choose their level of engagement, could choose to accept or reject a personal relationship with the brand. And millions of them decided to, because it didn't feel forced, or intrusive, or like Coke had been stalking them!

ONLY BASIC ELEMENTS INCLUDED

On the other end of the scale, only including basic elements creates a barrier to personalization. While personalization should not be creepily intrusive, it should make an effort to give your audience content that's timely and relevant. Just sticking a first name in the subject line and setting up some tracking-based automations is not enough, as the earlier examples demonstrate.

We have a considerable amount of resources available to us, but we still have a long way to go to make our marketing methods as sophisticated and as useful to the consumer as they could be. Displaying an ad to a recent customer promoting the item they have purchased is a waste of marketing budget and not an enhanced experience for that person.

Unleash your tactics – strategically!

So, you've come up with some great, targeted tactics based on your understanding of your customers and tied into your strategic goals. Fantastic! Now it's time to unleash them upon your public – but when, and how?

This is where the customer journey comes in

Let's say a consumer has a problem. Their car has broken, they need a new one. They search the internet, and they come across a company. They sign up to receive emails. They compare various companies, and then they make their decision. They have just followed a basic customer journey.

In this example, a timely email or push notification could have an impact at almost every stage of the decision-making process. Remember that the information a consumer will have and the information a consumer will want will differ at each stage in this process. And consumers will, of course, drop in and out of the process. So, a lot of strategic thought needs to go into any marketing scheme.

Relevancy is vital here. The more comprehensively you've mapped out your customer journey, the more relevant and timelier you can make your tactics. Where is the customer in their decision-making journey with you? How can you improve that experience based on the context that the consumer finds themselves in during each stage? At each stage the consumer will need different information from you to progress on their journey.

A useful model to plan out the customer journey and to map the different messaging at each stage is the AIDA model. I have adapted this model to include an additional stage named 'Educate', for organizations that are either a start-up or have an innovative offering in the marketplace. In this scenario the marketplace may need to be educated about the benefit that the offering provides; for example, if it is a new type of technology that provides unique functionality that wasn't possible before. The last stage I've also added called 'Loyalty' which is about focusing on ensuring your customers return.

The EAIDAL model is illustrated in Figure 7.6.

FIGURE 7.6   The EAIDAL model

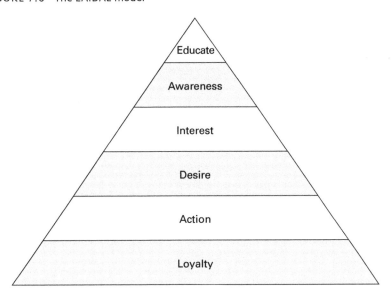

Let's look at the breakdown of what's included in each stage and the relevant KPIs (Table 7.3).

TABLE 7.3   The detail for each stage in the EAIDAL model

	Marketing tactics	KPIs (detail about each KPI available in Chapter 9)
Educate	This is where you're educating your target audience on your offering and effectively 'pulling' them to your brand. This is known as pull marketing. Videos, guides, content, events, webinars, exhibitions to explain the benefits and the offering at an informational level.	• Website visits • Video views
Awareness	The focus here is in driving more awareness about your offering. Landing page, email newsletter, YouTube video, providing useful whitepapers, guides, templates and guides that offer visitors valuable content aligned to the offering.	• Email marketing subscribers • Content downloads

(continued)

TABLE 7.3 (Continued)

	Marketing tactics	KPIs (detail about each KPI available in Chapter 9)
Interest	Product description on the website, photos, video demos of the product, but this can be in more detail than the educate video that is to continue to pique the interest of your potential new customer.	• Unique visitors • Audience share
Desire	What are your USPs, and why should a prospect purchase from you ahead of the competition? This is the key element to focus on for this stage.	• Bounce rate • Pages per visit
Action	Push marketing would be used here with the goal of quickly moving the customer to making a purchase. For e-commerce websites, this would be the online shopping process which leads to a conversion. There should be CTAs (call to actions) to encourage a conversion. Reviews, testimonials and displaying elements that promote that you're trustworthy for a new customer.	• Conversions • Conversion rate
Loyalty	Encouraging customers to return is important for the success of a business. Loyalty schemes providing incentives to return can be an effective tactic to use. Keeping communications with your customers via email marketing and social media are also valuable approaches to take.	• Returning visitors • Churn rate of customers

The EAIDAL should also be aligned to the marketing objectives.

TASK

Over to you, to fill in the EAIDAL in Table 7.4.

TABLE 7.4   Your EAIDAL model template

	Marketing tactics	KPIs *(detail about each KPI available in Chapter 9)*
Educate		
Awareness		
Interest		
Desire		
Action		
Loyalty		

CASE STUDY
iamproperty Group

The iamproperty Group offers end-to-end services to estate agents. In this example, they had the objective to raise awareness of a key challenge that their target audience (estate agents) face. Research identified that many estate agents relied 'on their gut instincts and their experience to highlight any concerns in a purchase or sale'. And, while 80 per cent of estate agents felt they understood the anti-money laundering (AML) regulations, many did not think their agency met HMRC requirements.

The responsibility to prevent money laundering during a property purchase is a complex issue. If a mistake is made the estate agents risk hefty fines. Add technology into that mix during the purchase process and it can get even more difficult to spot. To highlight the findings of this research, iamproperty launched their 'Smell the Difference' campaign to 'raise awareness of the need for a behaviour change from estate agents.' To stop using their gut instinct when trying to prevent money laundering. This was also an opportunity to promote their new compliance service

FIGURE 7.7 'Smell the Difference' campaign

Reproduced with the kind permission of iamproperty (2020)

which was developed to help overcome these challenges and to support their target customers.

This marketing campaign included a billboard campaign with the headline 'Can you smell the difference?' with money stuck to the billboard (Figure 7.7). The scent of money was created by a perfumer and infused on the £20 notes (Bottle PR, 2020). Passers-by were asked to sniff the money to determine which was 'freshly laundered' and which was 'clean' money.

This highlighted that it's not possible to identify if money has been laundered by sniffing it, and that using 'gut instinct' isn't a robust approach.

This marketing activity with the new research findings received lots of press coverage (Renshaw, 2020; Manchester, 2020), helping to increase awareness. Tips and advice were shared with estate agents to provide support in overcoming this challenge and promote iamproperty's new compliance service. The campaign also included branded videos, infographics highlighting the research findings, a whitepaper including tips, and custom aroma diffuser bottles that were branded, filled with the money scent, and sent to specific estate agents (Bottle PR, 2020).

View the full campaign at www.iamproperty.com/services/compliance/smell-the-difference/.

TABLE 7.5 Example implementation plan

CAMPAIGN TYPE	OWNER	PROJECT GOALS	TARGET AUDIENCE	CLICKS / VISITS	COMMENT	WEIGHT	PROJECTED COST	ACTUAL COST
Display Marketing Media								
Display Ads Google		Example...	Women 18–25, city, +25k	2,000 unique		10%	£21,235	£11,342
Display Ads Bing								
Display Ads others								
Local Marketing Display Media								
Local portals web ads								
Register for local events								
Public Relations								
Sponsorships								
Press releases								
Webinars								
Social Media Ads								
Twitter								
Facebook								
Instagram								
Google+								
LinkedIn								
Other specific niche SM								
Digital Media								
Google AdWords								
Bing Ads								

MARKETING INVESTMENT

The implementation plan

There are key questions to ask during the implementation plan phase, including:

- What are the essential tasks?
- How will the marketer allocate the resources?
- What responsibilities will marketers give?
- What are the training requirements?
- Who will project manage the overall plan?
- Who is accountable for the success of the plan?

This would include a Gantt chart, the evaluation of the results, a contingency built into the plan and be in a written format. An example is provided in Table 7.5.

To explore a real-life strategy which went through each of the STRATEGY framework stages and uncover the decisions made and results achieved, in 2020 I interviewed Sara Meikle, Senior Loyalty Officer at Action for Children.

Interview: Sara Meikle

Sara Meikle is Senior Loyalty Office for Action for Children, a UK children's charity that helps vulnerable children and young people, and their families.

JT: *Tell us about yourself, your marketing background, what you do, who you work for and your passion.*

SM: My role encompasses digital marketing communication with existing supporters or event participants via email and SMS. I use a CRM marketing system (dotdigital) to send campaign emails/SMS and create complex automated journeys for supporters post-donation or after signing up to an event. I also manage our monthly communications which include e-newsletters and fundraising appeals.

I have a BA Honours degree in Event and Business Management from The University of Winchester (graduated in 2015). In the second and third year of my university course, we had the option to choose some of our modules. I chose marketing-focused subjects rather than events-focused and my dissertation topic ended up being: 'The future of traditional marketing methods: Exploration of the marketing preferences for student-based events within Winchester.' In my last year of studying I realized my passion for marketing, specifically digital marketing and I knew I wanted a career in the industry.

After leaving university I went straight into a marketing role in a small embroidery company and worked there for 10 months. My next role was as a marketing assistant (in a team of two, including myself) for a large national chain of private day nurseries – I covered all areas of marketing in this role from website management and social media management to event marketing and email communications. I was in this role for two and half years. When I joined the company we had 19 nurseries, but when I left we had 42. I was constantly learning on the job and scaling up all areas of my work and my own skills to meet demand.

I moved to London and joined Action for Children in January 2019 as a Loyalty Officer and was promoted to Senior Loyalty Officer in April 2020 due to my expertise in the digital side of business development and retention team (aka Loyalty) that I had developed in the time I had been with the organization. My focus is mostly on email marketing.

JT: *What are the objective(s) of the campaign and what activities do you undertake?*

SM: Action for Children is a UK children's charity. We protect and support children and young people, providing practical and emotional care. We ensure the voices of the most vulnerable are heard and we campaign to bring lasting improvements to their lives. Last year, we supported more than 368,648 children and families across the UK.

'Byte Night' is Action for Children's flagship sleep-out event for the corporate sector, taking place every October as a series of simultaneous sleep-out events at multiple locations across the UK. Since 1997 it's raised over £12.5 million. However, given the onset of the coronavirus pandemic and the uncertainty surrounding the length and severity of its impact, we realized in April that it wouldn't be feasible to deliver our usual event this year.

With 40 per cent of the charity's fundraising income at risk, the question posed to fundraising teams was: How could we still generate vital income in the challenging circumstances? As a result, we developed a new virtual sleep-out event that could raise funds and appeal to our previous Byte Night participants, whilst also attracting a completely new audience and acting as a test product for future activity: Boycott your Bed.

The event was launched via email in June to previous Byte Night participants, warm Action for Children supporters and on organic social media channels. In July, we went live with paid ads on Facebook and Instagram and encouraged all staff across the organization to get involved.

It was imperative that as a new event, the registration process and following communication up until the big day was well thought out, with the supporter at the centre of the whole journey. The communications we sent needed to be completely automated due to the fast-paced changes that were happening internally whilst the event day progressed. As a virtual event, the information participants would receive would only be via online channels, mainly email and SMS.

On Friday 21 August, households from across the UK ditched their duvets, banished their blankets and slept in the most unusual spot around their homes or gardens. Over 4,500 families, friends and colleagues took part and boycotted their beds to raise an incredible £314,000 (and counting!) for Action for Children.

JT: *What were the challenges and risks and what approaches did you take to overcome them?*

SM: In the charity sector, it's natural to be risk adverse because if income or a strong ROI can't be guaranteed, you are potentially 'wasting' money that could be used elsewhere to support the beneficiaries of your organization.

We approached the decision to pivot to a virtual event with great caution but in a time when unrestricted income was critical, with 40 per cent of our income at risk due to the coronavirus pandemic, we knew we had to push forward with a version of an event. However, we were working to an extremely tight deadline in a time where staff members were on furlough and expenditure had to stay low. We knew that it would be a full team effort to pull off the high-quality, engaging event we envisioned.

We also couldn't be sure that pivoting to a virtual event, for a mass fundraising audience, was something people wanted to do. During a time where thousands of charities were pivoting to virtual events...

how were we going to get cut-through in an already overcrowded market? How were we going to sustain interest and financial support until August without fatiguing supporters?

JT: *What were the details of the campaign: the channels, activities and so on?*

SM: I used dotdigital to create three different registration forms which were then embedded into an iFrame on our website. It was decided that it was best to do this through dotdigital as it then meant any emails or SMS communications would all be sent from the same place, in the same style and everything was completely automated without any delays. We needed three different registration forms as we were capturing three different types of audiences: organizations who were taking part as colleagues; families who were taking part with children; and individuals who were adults taking part solo or with friends/housemates/partners, etc.

We captured different information in these forms which we used to tailor content in the ongoing stewardship journeys. I also created a drop-out form which was signposted in all emails which, if a participant filled out their details, they would be removed from the ongoing communications after receiving an email confirming they can no longer take part.

After completing a registration form, a participant would receive a confirmation email and an SMS. [Please see Tables 7.6 and 7.7 for examples of some of the communications sent.] After this, participants were entered into a stewardship journey where they would receive regular emails on the lead-up to the event. Depending on when a person signed up, it altered their ongoing journey and how many emails they would receive. For example, if someone signed up to the event on the day we launched, they received six emails over a seven-week period which included lots of fundraising ideas, information about our work and announcements as our event developed. But, if someone signed up a week before the event, they received 1–2 emails with just the key need-to-know information.

The data people provided in the registration form was used to make some of the emails feel very personalized for the user (Table 7.6).

TABLE 7.6 Email marketing for type of subscriber

CAMPAIGN – FAMILIES STEWARDSHIP	VIEW THE EMAIL
Families confirmation	Preview https://actionforchildren-email.org.uk/t/3WYU-156UH-19ZIK0ZJ87/cr.aspx
Dropout confirmation	Preview https://actionforchildren-email.org.uk/t/3WYU-1591K-19ZIK0ZJ87/cr.aspx
Families JustGiving	Preview https://actionforchildren-email.org.uk/t/3WYU-159H8-19ZIK0ZJ87/cr.aspx
Families recruitment/social sharing	Preview https://actionforchildren-email.org.uk/t/3WYU-15A2X-19ZIK0ZJ87/cr.aspx
Families fundraising ideas	Preview https://actionforchildren-email.org.uk/t/3WYU-15DT0-19ZIK0ZJ87/cr.aspx
Families fundraising with UGC examples	Preview https://actionforchildren-email.org.uk/t/3WYU-15E0B-19ZIK0ZJ87/cr.aspx
Families superstar fundraisers	Preview https://actionforchildren-email.org.uk/t/3WYU-15HIM-19ZIK0ZJ87/cr.aspx
Families impact on services	Preview https://actionforchildren-email.org.uk/t/3WYU-15HSO-19ZIK0ZJ87/cr.aspx
Families getting ready for the night	Preview https://actionforchildren-email.org.uk/t/3WYU-15HWP-19ZIK0ZJ87/cr.aspx
Families event week	Preview https://actionforchildren-email.org.uk/t/3WYU-15TSU-729011E72225D1E5ZIK0ZJ471E80379DB0D9C7/cr.aspx

Reproduced with the kind permission of Sara Meikle at Action for Children.

For example, if a participant registered as an organization but was taking part with their family, the fundraising ideas we provided to them would be a mix of work/colleague-based ideas and family-orientated ideas.

As the event content was developing at such speed, I used SMS to send participants 'breaking news' information. I chose to do this as each participant was on different time delays between emails; if the announcement was sent as an email, it posed the risk of someone receiving two emails in the same day. As the use of SMS was already proving to be successful, I decided to integrate it as a channel for our event day communications.

I created an integrated event day communications plan which combined email reminders to send the broadcast joining details with SMS reminders for timings. This was also supported by our social media channels too (we were even top trending in the UK on Twitter!). SMS was sent in tandem with activities that participants were watching on screen. An example of this: after an Action for Children beneficiary film has been shown to the audience, we sent an SMS reminder of how to text to donate (Table 7.7).

Using one CRM system to communicate with these supporters meant everything was branded the same, everything was automated and no manual manipulation or sending was required, therefore minimizing any human error/mistakes.

TABLE 7.7 All event and post-event communications

CAMPAIGN: ALL EVENT AND POST-EVENT COMMUNICATIONS	VIEW THE EMAIL
Silent auction live: single campaign send	Preview https://actionforchildren-email.org.uk/t/3WYU-163N1-729011E72225D1E5ZIK0ZJ471E80379DB0D9C7/cr.aspx
Late sign-ups confirmation	Preview https://actionforchildren-email.org.uk/t/3WYU-164N9-729011E72225D1E5ZIK0ZJ471E80379DB0D9C7/cr.aspx
Final streaming information	Preview https://actionforchildren-email.org.uk/t/3WYU-164MY-729011E72225D1E5ZIK0ZJ471E80379DB0D9C7/cr.aspx
Post-event thank you (Saturday AM)	Preview https://actionforchildren-email.org.uk/t/3WYU-1663H-729011E72225D1E5ZIK0ZJ471E80379DB0D9C7/cr.aspx
Feedback survey	Preview https://actionforchildren-email.org.uk/t/3WYU-1663J-729011E72225D1E5ZIK0ZJ471E80379DB0D9C7/cr.aspx
Second thank you: survey reminder, paying-in reminder	Preview https://actionforchildren-email.org.uk/t/3WYU-1663M-729011E72225D1E5ZIK0ZJ471E80379DB0D9C7/cr.aspx

Reproduced with the kind permission of Sara Meikle at Action for Children.

TABLE 7.8 Campaign results

Activity	Result
Fundraising income to date	£314,000+
Average email open rate	40%
Charity sector average for 2020	*25%*
Average email unsubscribe rate	0.16%
Charity sector average for 2020	*0.20%*
Average CTR%	13.73%
Charity sector average for 2020	*2.6%*
Average CTOR%	30.32%
Charity sector average for 2020	*10.3%*
Average SMS click-to-delivered rate	25%
Email opt-in rate	79%
SMS opt-in rate	33%
Phone opt-in rate	12%
Post opt-in rate	28%

JT: *What were the results for the organization and the audience response?*

SM: As a brand new event, there weren't too many KPIs set. However, the results exceeded all expectations and we smashed our predicted ROI for the overall campaign (Table 7.8).

With such high opt-in rates, this allows us to continue communicating with people on these channels, opening up opportunities for cross-selling areas of support, both financial and non-financial. And, as we gained so much insight about these supporters from the information they supplied when registering, we are able to make intelligent decisions and offer 'products' that are relevant to them. For example, asking a family participant when they signed up how old their children are so that we can promote a specific age-related child-led or family product.

From a feedback survey sent post-event, participants were overwhelmingly positive about the registration process and the communications:

- 'The registration process was quick and easy': 88 per cent strongly agree/agree.
- 'The emails before the event had all the information I needed': 95 per cent strongly agree/agree.

- 'I was happy with the volume of communication I received in the run-up to the event': 91 per cent strongly agree/agree.

Comments from the feedback survey from participants:

'Thank you for organizing such an amazing fundraising challenge where all the family can get involved. It definitely brought us closer as a family! We looked forward to each email and how involved we felt with the charity.'

'As a staff member, I've always wanted to take part in the Byte Night sleep-out but find the minimum sponsorship too much. It was great to be able to take part and raise funds without there being a minimum amount to raise.'

We had 111 Action for Children staff sign up to take part; it created great internal engagement.

JT: *What was the long-term impact?*

SM: There are two main areas that the success of this event has impacted for Action for Children as an organization.

1 It has shown that we *can* run virtual events that appeal to a mass audience and we don't have to put pressure on ourselves to run physical events to close the gap between a high-value audience and the mass audience. Historically, as a charity, our large fundraising events are aimed at high-value supporters rather than a mass audience. The success of Boycott your Bed has shown we do have capability to reach new types of supporters who we would typically struggle to communicate with prior to 2020. This leads into the second point.

2 With our paid ads bringing in a whole new pool of family-focused supporters, we as an organization are now developing new products, events and challenges that specifically appeal to parents and families. As a children's charity, being able to tap into this newer audience is going to align very well with our vision and mission.

When we quickly realized it was not feasible to deliver our usual sleep-out in October given the pandemic, we knew it wouldn't be easy, but every challenge brings with it an opportunity. This pivot created an incredible chance for teams to work closely together and create a new virtual event that could help us reach supporters that we wouldn't typically be able to reach. We can now develop the lifetime value of these new donors and make intelligent decisions when we cross-sell as we collected so much useful insight when they first registered for the event.

The success of the campaign showed that we can tackle a challenge collaboratively, passionately and quickly.

JT: *What advice would you give marketers who face the challenge of pivoting at short notice?*

SM: My main advice would be, once a senior decision has been made and you've been given the go-ahead, you need to gather together your key deliverable and operational stakeholders to create a plan for your minimal viable product (MVP). Together, what is the minimum you can achieve in the timelines you've been given, that you would be happy to take to market?

Once you've got an MVP plan, you will find that some people can achieve more than originally planned. They shouldn't be discouraged or slowed down as they could be essential components for developing your idea/event into something further than your MVP.

It's all about empowering people to make their own decisions, and have ownership of their work, and giving them space to grow in their role by providing new opportunities to learn outside of their comfort zone. Sometimes, you need time-pressured projects to do this – in the long term, it's not only beneficial to your organization but also for individuals' personal career progression and confidence in their role.

JT: *What are your main marketing takeaways from this experience?*

SM: Automation is essential to success. Having a system in place where I could create and send multiple elements of the campaign to hundreds of different people, whilst still personalizing each user's experience, was a huge factor in the campaign running smoothly. We planned and developed the event concept so quickly that if I couldn't have relied on our systems, I'm not sure I could have been as intelligent with tailoring content. A lot of my time could have been taken up with manual processes which makes room for human error – this campaign had very important stakeholders who would not have been impressed with anything going wrong with the communications in the lead-up to the event.

JT: *Do you typically see a difference between marketers' perception of what engages consumers in comparison to consumers' preference?*

SM: In the charity sector, there is a lot of context around supporters and types of supporters. At Action for Children, we were guilty of putting a supporter in a box – they did one action/challenge/event for us; therefore, we should only offer that same thing to them again year on year. This isn't profitable long term and, in a time where income is vital, we cannot go on like this.

As an organization, we are putting a lot of work into breaking this ideology down as our supporters can surprise us. We are actively trying to learn more about them through subtle surveying and lots of testing – we can't assume we know what our supporters want. We do, however, often see that people will tell us one thing and then do something different. It's not something we can control, but if we have more to offer, by giving people choice we can start to see patterns in behaviour and motivations. The more you learn about a supporter/consumer on their first entrance 'through your door' to your company, you can make intelligent decisions about their potential lifetime value.

Summary

In this chapter, you have:

- Identified the importance of a brand's tone of voice when conveying a consistent message.
- Learned how to structure brand guidelines that everyone in the business can implement throughout all of the customers' touchpoints.
- Recognized the need for roles and responsibilities within the marketing team when implementing varying tactics.
- Learned how to determine the focus areas when implementing your marketing tactics.
- Explored the brilliant multichannel marketing campaign example from Action for Children who had a clear challenge to overcome and they used strategy to achieve results.

References

Atherton, J (2019) *Social Media Strategy: A practical guide to social media marketing and customer engagement*, Kogan Page, London

Bottle PR (2020) iamproperty – Smell the Difference Campaign [Online], We are Bottle PR, available at: www.wearebottle.com/iamproperty (archived at https://perma.cc/3WLC-DVGE)

Brown, T (2019) Re-inventing direct mail: Edit and Jaguar Landover bring home the DMA Gold [Online], Edit, available at: edit.co.uk/blog/dma-award-win-direct-mail/ (archived at https://perma.cc/8J73-PND3)

Cannon, J (2020) Mailchimp claims over 60% share of email industry in latest report [Online], Marketing Land, available at: marketingland.com/mailchimp-claims-over-60-share-of-email-industry-in-latest-report-273926#:~:text=Mailchimp%20has%20released%20its%20first,comes%20in%20at%20only%209.52%25 (archived at https://perma.cc/ZL4Y-NTL6)

DMA (2019) 2019 Gold Best Use of Mail [Online], Edit, available at: edit.co.uk/blog/dma-award-win-direct-mail/ (archived at https://perma.cc/8J73-PND3)

DMI (2017) Content Marketing: 6 examples of successful digital strategies [Online], Digital Marketing Institute, available at: digitalmarketinginstitute.com/en-us/blog/content-marketing-6-digital-campaigns-to-learn-from (archived at https://perma.cc/4P54-8MFY)

Irvine, M (2020) Bing ads benchmarks for your industry [Online], The WordStream blog, available at: www.wordstream.com/blog/ws/2017/11/06/bing-ads-performance-benchmarks (archived at https://perma.cc/7UYB-YT67)

Lewis, A (2020) Marketing Director at Mailchimp [Interview] 2 October 2020

Manchester, S (2020) Agents warned over dangers of relying on 'gut feel' to spot AML criminals [Online], The Negotiator, available at: thenegotiator.co.uk/agents-warned-over-dangers-of-relying-on-gut-feel-to-spot-aml-criminals/ (archived at https://perma.cc/SYK2-QD6S)

Meikle, S (2020) Senior Loyalty Officer at Action for Children [Interview] 24 September 2020

Renshaw, R (2020) Nine in ten agents 'rely on their own instincts' to sniff out money laundering [Online], *Property Industry Eye*, available at: propertyindustryeye.com/nine-in-ten-agents-rely-on-their-own-instincts-to-sniff-out-money-laundering/ (archived at https://perma.cc/RLM5-3YVB)

Russon, M (2020) M&S: Five reasons the retailer is struggling [Online], BBC, available at: www.bbc.com/news/business-53478403 (archived at https://perma.cc/RST4-FKDS)

Statista (2020) Coca-Cola's brand value from 2006 to 2020 [Online], available at: www.statista.com/statistics/326065/coca-cola-brand-value/ (archived at https://perma.cc/6TZ6-C7GY)

08

Generate

Tracking the results

This chapter covers:

- How to track marketing performance.
- How to measure results and response.

Once you've launched your implementation plan (as discussed in Chapter 7), it's essential to keep track of the results.

The starting point when measuring and analysing your performance is to align the marketing objectives set with defined metrics.

Returning to your goals and objectives

Before you start measuring, remind yourself of what you want to achieve with your marketing. Many times, it's a case of getting a campaign live – but what if you took a step back and thought not only about the reasons why you're creating the marketing campaign, but also what you are trying to achieve: the action you're trying to provoke? Are you aiming to increase visits to your website or more downloads of your latest guide? Whatever the objective is, make sure that the KPIs you set can be tracked throughout your campaign.

Your strategic marketing goals should, needless to say, be tied in with your overall business strategy. Think back to that vision!

The value a customer brings

As well as making your objectives measurable, you also need to ensure that you have a way of measuring your customers' level of interest, potential for conversion and position within the sales funnel – their 'lead value'. Which means that you need to determine how you, as an organization, define a lead.

This is particularly relevant for B2B companies. Do you consider someone a lead when they enter their email address on your site? When they download a whitepaper? Book a demo? The way (and the point at which) you categorize your leads will differ depending on your operation — but it is vital that you do categorize them in order to measure your performance successfully.

If you're not sure how to establish lead values, start by determining your average sale value and the value number of sales per customer. It would be good also to identify your average profit margin, the target cost per acquired customer and, if possible, the projected lifetime value of a customer (this will help you to determine the incremental value each customer brings to the organization as a result of your campaigns).

Doing this will not only help you to align specific lead measurements to your marketing campaign – it will also give you the kind of results that senior leadership teams understand and are interested in.

Turning data into insights

When conducting your analysis, you will find yourself presented with an awful lot of data.

Data is hugely important to marketing. At this point, I'm going to talk to you about how you can turn your data into actionable analytical insights.

For example, the ability to track the performance across all marketing tactics is incredibly useful when allocating marketing budgets and in measuring engagement with the target audience. In order to achieve this action from the data in front of you, it's important to review several metrics, not just the traffic that an individual tactic has generated.

While it's great if a tactic and/or channel is generating a lot of traffic, it's vital to analyse the quality of that traffic in order to ensure that you're allocating the right resources to the right areas. There are a few ways to assess the quality:

- Does the traffic spend a long time on your website or is the bounce rate high? (anything above 40 per cent should be investigated).

- Does the traffic typically visit more than one page on your website or just the homepage and then they leave? For an e-commerce website this would demonstrate that there is little interest in your products/offering.

- Is it a consistently high percentage of new visitors that doesn't appear to be translating into return visitors (when reviewing weeks and months of data)?

The decisions made about how to split the marketing budget across the tactics and activity can then be informed based on more than performance insights. This is important. When I've consulted with brands, I've often found marketers that are just looking at the vanity metrics (opens and clicks) for their digital performance. Marketing has much more to offer than a click.

For example, my marketing agency previously advised a B2B financial organization who told me that they were drowning in data. Their problem was not that they had the wrong data – every part of the conversion journey was tracked. Their problem was the analysis that followed.

To provide some context, their sales process is typical of many B2B brands: when a prospect expresses an interest via their website, their sales consultant will then have a 1:1 conversation with them. The prospect then revisits the website to research products and gather more information. As the conversion journey is online, the new customer starts their application process. The customer is then provided with a dedicated account manager.

So, there is a mix of online and offline engagement constantly throughout this process. The human interaction is key to keep the lead warm. As a result, some of the data gathered during the offline portion of the journey was entered manually.

In order to bring their data into line and start transforming it into useful insights, I took four steps. Let me share them with you:

Step 1 – Define your benchmark. These become your check-in points.

Step 2 – Set non-subjective KPIs to measure performance. These should be quantifiable such as conversion rate, engagement score, click-through rate, top traffic sources, new vs returning visitors.

Step 3 – Consistency is critical. The approach taken to measure performance should be consistent across time to enable fair comparisons; if changes are made to the measurement method, document the difference.

Step 4 – Align to objectives. There are hundreds if not thousands of data points to measure, but if they are misaligned to your objectives, they are not going to highlight anything relevant. This will ensure you're spending time and effort on the right areas that are going to provide valuable insights.

In less than a day using the methods above, we could determine the channels that were driving the highest volume of traffic and those which didn't. This was also in comparison to the channels which drove the most conversions.

In this case, we discovered that the channels which drove high volumes of traffic did not provide quality traffic. Prospects arriving from these channels left the website immediately after joining.

Channels which drove less traffic had historically been viewed as unnecessary for budget allocation. Yet the strategic insights demonstrated that these channels consistently drove the highest amount of conversions.

Following our restructuring of their data-gathering and measuring process, the company was able to use these insights to their advantage, focusing their efforts on the channels giving the greatest return on investment (ROI), and enhancing the tactics used for channels which were falling behind.

Methods and tools for tracking marketing performance

Of course, you can't start drawing insights from data until you've extracted it!

As a general rule, customer behaviour over digital channels is measured via tracking pixels. These are pieces of code embedded in a customer's digital 'signature', which gather data on their online behaviour and feed that data back to algorithms and analytics dashboards.

When using tracking pixels, be sure that you do so with full transparency and consent.

Here are a few common ways to track and draw out the data from your digital campaigns.

Website analytics

By tracking your website performance, you can measure visits to your website, the marketing tactic which drew them there and the location from which they're visiting. Website analytics should also tell you how long your visitors are spending on your website, the pages they've visited and the products they've purchased (for e-commerce sites). This will give you considerable insight into the tactics that are driving the most visits, clicks and purchases on your website – enabling you to optimize your campaigns around the highest-performing tactics.

There are many tools available to help you gather and draw insights from website analytics. One of the most popular is Google Analytics (GA). It's free to use and easy to configure by adding a single tracking script to your website. GA works by collecting data from visits and provides detailed reports about a website's performance – including bounce rates, time on site and if goals have converted.

Paid advertising

To measure the success of paid advertising from PPC and paid social activity, there are individual tracking platforms within the ad managers themselves. Facebook Ad Manager, Google Ads, Bing's Ad Manager and Twitter Advertising all come with analytics embedded as standard. Each of these tools are focused specifically on each particular advert, so it's important to constantly monitor these accounts, set budget limits and include the results within your overall marketing campaign performance report.

Email marketing

Most email marketing platforms offer a sophisticated array of analytical tools. You should be able to tell with a glance at your dashboard how your open rates are doing, whether click-throughs are going up or down and so on. The trick is to understand what those numbers indicate in the real world.

For example, if your average open rate is high, your subject lines are engaging your recipients and they are engaged enough to open your emails. If the click rate is also high then the content is interesting enough to keep reading more on your website. However, if you achieve a high open rate and a low click-through rate, it may mean that the content of your email didn't match the promise of the subject line, or that the content in the email isn't relevant to your subscribers and people dropped off before reaching your call to action (CTA).

If a single campaign receives a high unsubscribe rate, the content has definitely not engaged the audience and also raises questions about the quality of your email list. It is also possible to report on the number of conversions on your website which came from email by combining email with website analytics.

Social media

Campaign-specific hashtags are a great way to not only raise awareness of your marketing across social media, but also to measure mentions, engagement and sentiment of users. Keywords can also be assigned to help track campaigns as well as specific locations, languages and pages. There are tools available such as Mention that will collate all of the conversations that have taken place with specified criteria – for example, brand name mentions, use of your hashtags, mentions of your product or service and so on. This is also useful for reacting in real time to prospects and potential customers, and to joining in conversations related to your keywords.

Tracking offline activity

If you're including offline marketing tactics such as print, direct mail, TV and radio, there are still ways to track whether these channels brought people to your website.

One way is to use a unique URL which is campaign and marketing tactic specific. For example, you may have a specific web landing page for your campaign or a product page that you're sending visitors to. A unique URL can be created that is used solely on your direct mail activity. That URL will then redirect all prospects arriving by direct mail to that same landing page. The key here is that in using this unique URL, you're able to see the visits, how long they spend on the website, pages viewed and all the rest of those important findings – along with the fact that these customers were sent to your website by print, direct mail, etc.

There are distinct urchin tracking module (UTM) parameters that can be added to a URL to track every piece of your marketing campaign. I like to think of them as unique items to add to a tracking URL. Within the URL builder you can add the campaign source, medium and so on to track specific campaign activity in GA. With the right settings the majority of tools (such as your email platform) will add these parameters for you, but where this is not possible, using a URL builder enables you to add that customized tracking.

Call tracking is also very useful. Even if you're an e-commerce business, some of your marketing activity will generate phone calls. With call tracking, different phone numbers can be used for each tactical activity (eg one phone number for print, another for radio ads, etc). With phone tracking software, any calls received to those specific numbers are then tracked and the cost per sale can also be calculated for any conversions made over the phone.

Customer relationship management (CRM)

A customer relationship management (CRM) system is very useful for tracking, storing, sorting and analysing customer data.

A CRM system like HubSpot securely stores data on all of your leads, prospects, customers and subscribers. Within this software, you'll be able to find reports on the stage of the conversion funnel that your leads have reached (blog.hubspot.com/service/how-to-calculate-customer-lifetime-value). You can also see the lead source to determine where the lead originally came from.

For example, a B2B sales funnel may look like this:

MQL > SQL > SQL demo held > Proposal > Contract > Customer

Performance reporting

To keep your finger on the pulse of your campaign, I recommend implementing performance reports. Depending on the number of moving parts (and therefore how fast things are likely to change) in your campaign, these should be monthly or weekly. During crucial times (for example, when you're holding an event), you could even ask for daily reports.

Performance reports should include all marketing tactics and detail the traffic each source is bringing to the website. It's useful to include last year's performance stats as a comparison (if possible), and to identify any particular trends, peaks or troughs during the year. Include the bounce rates by channel to help determine the quality of the traffic. Include ad spend for any PPC and paid advertising spend (such as paid social), clicks, click-through rate, cost per visit and total conversion. This will help you to start measuring the ROI of your marketing campaign. This is important for organizations and as the example with charitable organization Action for Children details in Chapter 7, it's an important metric to predict to avoid wasting investment:

> In the charity sector, it's natural to be risk adverse because if income or a strong ROI can't be guaranteed, you are potentially 'wasting' money that could be used elsewhere to support the beneficiaries of your organization.
>
> Sara Meikle, 2020

Year-on-year (YOY) comparisons

Comparing your marketing performance from year to year should, in theory, quickly highlight whether it's going in the right direction. However, if you've implemented a brand new marketing strategy this year, take a comparison with a pinch of salt. A complete change in direction will have a short-term impact on your marketing performance.

Creating a reporting dashboard to measure performance each month will help you keep an eye on performance against any targets and KPIs you've set. Don't worry if your performance isn't quite where you expected – drill down into an analysis of each channel to see if there is a glaringly obvious reason for the difference in comparison to last year. For example, there may have been more marketing budget spent on Facebook-sponsored ads in 2019 and nothing spent in 2020. Consequently, awareness has dipped with your Facebook audience, and they're not heading to your site any more.

Analysing both traffic and conversions is key to ensuring that high-quality, relevant traffic is landing on your website. My top tip is not to try and include everything that you are tracking in every marketing report. This is where the alignment to your marketing objectives is important. The secret to success is determining what to measure linking back to objectives and not try to track everything.

There will be a lot of analysis gathered by implementing and using the methods and tools I've mentioned above. When compiling these into a report, it's important to be clear on what is useful to know about for the live campaign, future campaigns and the wider business. For example, you may learn that a particular web page is receiving the most visits, and that those visitors are spending on average a much longer time on that page than on the rest of the website. This would highlight that this page's content is of interest to those visitors. This information is useful for other areas of the business (for example, the product development team) to understand, as it can inform future product iterations and enhancements.

Summary

In this chapter, you have learned about:

- The importance of returning to your goals and objectives and using them as regular check-in points when measuring a live campaign and at the end of marketing activity.

- Turning data into insights to assist the development of future campaigns and to learn more about your target audience.

- The different ways to track the progress of each channel used and the benefit doing so provides.

- The key elements to include in a performance report and the value of using a PCA (post-campaign analysis) when presenting findings to the rest of the business.

09

Yield

Analysing your strategy's success

In this chapter we'll cover:

- The importance of analysing marketing strategies and campaigns.
- The meaning of statistical significance.
- Key performance indicators (KPIs) for marketing and specific tactical channels (SEO, PPC, social media, direct mail and email marketing).
- What a post-campaign analysis (PCA) is, what it looks like and how to create one.

Why is analysis important?

Allow me to relate the cautionary tale of British Gas and the Twitter War.

British Gas once ran an infamous Twitter event. The idea was for customers to ask the Customer Services Director questions about their recent 9.2 per cent price rise using the hashtag #askBG.

And ask they did. Over 11,500 tweets were sent using the hashtag – approximately 160 every minute (Macleod, 2013). Pretty much all of them were negative. The price rise was hugely unpopular, not to mention controversial within the industry. Customers took full advantage of the opportunity to tell BG how they felt. In public, on Twitter, for all to see.

This Twitter event went from bad to worse for British Gas, so much so that experts have called it 'one of the worst PR disasters' ever on social media (Macalister and Rankin, 2013). There was a fundamental lack of understanding on the part of British Gas about their customers. A simple review of the audience's historical reaction to similar price rise news would have provided the British Gas team with a robust prediction on the outcome of this marketing activity.

It's always tricky to find the right marketing approach when communicating unpopular decisions, but it's essential to make sure that the strategy uses online channels to soften the blow, not make it even harder to receive the news.

The starting point is to assess which marketing channels are driving the largest number of visits to your website. Next is to dig deeper into this to understand the best performing landing pages. Compare this with your top exit pages to identify content which needs improvement. There are some pages such as your blog content that would naturally have higher bounce rates, but the goal for those pages should be to increase the read rate and encourage your visitors to read other pages during their time on your website. We touched on this in the last chapter, but it's worth getting into a little deeper here.

There is an excellent content journey visualization tree in Google Analytics that will display where your customers' journeys start on your website and where the drop-off points occur throughout those journeys. Similarly, your email marketing activity data will tell you a lot about your subscribers, such as the subject lines which drive a high open rate and those which don't engage your audience. The same is relevant for the content in your emails. Analytics will show you the content that receives the most clicks (if that is the main call to action) and the click-free content which doesn't engage your subscribers.

Over time, trends can be generated from this data analysis by digging deeper into interests and behaviours of your subscribers. These learnings can then inform segmentation for future email marketing activity. Analysing the search terms, keywords and content driving traffic to your website by the SEO and PPC activity can also highlight potential gaps and areas for improvement. Combining that analysis with your email marketing data will present a very insightful picture about your prospect and customer base.

Social media analysis can seem relatively limited by focusing only on likes and shares. It does enable you to determine over a set period of time (ideally one month) the optimal times when your social media activity receives the most interaction and impressions. Many marketers miss out on painting a fuller picture of what engages their audiences by not mapping all your digital marketing channels analysis together. You may find that one audience engages more with a particular topic than another and identify learnings that other marketing channels and tactics can also adopt. Use this insight to inform your future strategy and marketing activity.

Statistical significance

Before you draw any conclusions from your data analysis, it's essential to ensure that the data you're analysing is statistically significant. To do this, I recommend comparing performance across 12 months (although if you have lots of data you can reduce this time period).

What you are looking for are trends in your data. Often, these trends won't be evident from a small snapshot, but comparison over an extended time period makes them much clearer. For example, you should be able to easily spot peak months, which helps a lot when forecasting your marketing spend.

Once you've identified trends and established a statistically significant dataset, you can start to review your performance. Dig deep into everything and scrutinize it hard to see where you sit in the marketplace, and what you need to improve upon.

Without this strategic approach, you could find yourself fixing things that aren't broken, missing opportunities or creating more significant gaps for your competitors to swoop in.

Map data against goals

Earlier on, you undertook the task of creating measurable goals. This is the point when we see how well you succeeded!

Performance tracking has to be aligned to the objectives and goals set for your marketing strategy. For example, if your goal was to achieve an increase in website traffic from SEO, then this is what needs to be measured and analysed.

Control systems tell you what's working and what's not. They help you to determine what data you will look at each day, week, month and quarter, and the objectives that need to be measured and monitored.

Data insights: how to get them and how to use them

The first step towards gleaning those all-important insights from your data is reminding yourself of what you wanted to achieve with your campaign. This will determine the metrics you need to focus on in your analysis. You can give yourself a helping hand with this by setting and analysing KPIs.

Key performance indicators (KPIs)

Key performance indicators, otherwise known as KPIs, are the performance metrics that highlight whether the specific activity you're measuring is achieving the goals set.

KPIs immediately indicate if a marketing campaign has been a success and whether the tactics at play are achieving the desired results. These insights should be a snapshot. They should be easily identifiable, specific to your business and the marketing campaign, and aligned to your objectives. To determine your KPIs, go back to your SCALE objectives and determine how you would measure whether you have achieved them or not.

KPIs are not vague or unclear; they should be actionable and quantifiable. Each KPI must be capable of being measured, be transparent in its results and be numerical. They should also have an exact alignment to marketing objectives and targets, and not be merely exciting metrics. KPIs need to provide tangible and actionable outcomes.

It's important not to measure everything, as this will waste time and effort, as well as diluting your focus, which could potentially derail your marketing efforts, as mentioned in Chapter 7. If a KPI isn't adding direct value to your insights, you don't need it. There is a wealth of data available, and it can be all too easy to measure everything – but in doing so, you'll reduce the amount of concrete (and useful) conclusions you can draw.

Focusing on 'interesting' rather than useful KPIs is known as measuring 'vanity' metrics. For example, measuring social media 'likes' instead of social media engagement or referrals to your website is a vanity metric. You could have 20,000 people liking your social media post, but not a single one visiting your website. Yet your objective is to increase website visits from social media fans/followers. While for the vanity metric the campaign has been in some part successful, the actionable metric (website visits) that should be the KPI tells a very different (and much more insightful) story, as Victoria Peppiatt explains:

Marketing teams are always looking to quantify the effectiveness of their work and improve KPIs, but not at any cost. The key is to improve metrics without resorting to cheap clickbait tactics, and ensure the improvement lasts not just today, but tomorrow as well.

Consistency in the application of your chosen KPIs is crucial. Throughout the business, if the same KPI is being used, it must be measured in the same way. This is the same when comparing marketing campaigns. Otherwise, you'll end up comparing apples with pears and could draw incomplete or incorrect conclusions.

Let's go through the common KPIs.

Marketing KPIs

Marketing KPIs involve interactions (or additional data) from outside your content itself. They can be a bit more complicated to work out, but are essential to indicate how well each channel is contributing to the brand's overall marketing and business objectives. For example, if email drives visitors to your website, and plenty of those visitors convert, this would indicate that email is performing well – even though the KPI figures are drawn primarily from outside the email itself.

CONVERSION RATE (CR)

Any piece of campaign content has a goal. The conversion rate indicates the extent to which it achieves its goal. For example, if the goal is to get customers to click through to the website, a high click-through rate will double as a high conversion rate. Making a purchase is a common goal for marketing content, particularly for e-commerce companies. To understand the CR for this goal, marketers need to look to website statistics. The CR here would be the number of impressions (people who have seen the content) divided by the number of users who have 'converted' by making a purchase.

RETURN ON INVESTMENT (ROI)

Return on investment measures how cost effective a particular channel was in a campaign. It is a useful metric when comparing each channel's performance, but it's not always relevant. For example, social media activity may not provide any immediate financial gains to the business but could be aligned to the objective of raising awareness of the company's brand and offering. Therefore there are times where ROI isn't relevant to measure, depending on the objectives set. There is also the criticism that ROI is too short-termist and ignores the value created by generating brand and customer equality, which are longer term in achievability and perspective (Rogers, 2019).

Nonetheless, if profit is part of a campaign's aim, calculating ROI is simply a case of working out how much revenue has come in as a result of the said campaign and comparing this to the campaign's costs.

CUSTOMER LIFETIME VALUE (CLTV)

Customer lifetime value measures the value a customer brings for the duration of them being a customer. The calculation is based on the average purchase value, the average frequency of their purchases from the brand, and their average customer value.

If the average 'lifetime' during which a customer purchases from the brand is five years, their 'lifetime value' is calculated based on the average predicted purchase, frequency and amount of their purchase across the five years. Predictions are based on averaging data.

COST PER ACQUISITION (CPA)

Cost per acquisition determines how much it costs the company to acquire a new customer. It measures both marketing costs, which may be your email marketing costs, and sales costs:

$$\frac{Marketing\ costs + Sales\ costs}{No.\ of\ conversions} = CPA$$

CLOSE RATE (CR)

The close rate measures the number of prospects that become customers in comparison to the number of leads in the pipeline:

$$\frac{Customers\ generated}{Leads\ in\ pipeline} = CR$$

This can be determined for each channel and be used as a comparison for each one too.

CUSTOMER RETENTION RATE (CRR)

This KPI measures the percentage of customers that are retained for a specific time period; for example, a YOY measurement could be made with the timing set at 12 months:

$$\frac{No.\ of\ customers\ at\ end\ of\ the\ year - No.\ of\ new\ customers\ during\ the\ year}{No.\ of\ customers\ at\ start\ of\ the\ year} \times 100 = CRR$$

This is important to understand because if this KPI is low, it would highlight an issue in retaining customers and demonstrate a high churn rate.

Channel-specific KPIs: Websites

When measuring the performance of channels, you're aiming to discover if that tactic is achieving what it was designed for and delivering the desired results.

Ways of measuring the performance of a website will differ depending on the objective set and the type of business. For e-commerce websites, the following will be useful KPIs:

CONVERSION RATE (CR)

The *conversion rate* (CR) measures the percentage of visitors that land on the website and then place an order. This is a useful metric when used with the others below. However, it paints little in the way of a picture of what else is happening, so it's important to include other metrics to support this one.

BASKET/CART ABANDONMENT

Measuring the number of people who showed a desire to purchase by adding items to their basket but then didn't complete their order is known as measuring *basket/cart abandonment*. It's a useful KPI for several reasons. If this percentage is high, it could highlight an issue with the check-out process. If the website is correctly tracking activity, you may identify a particular stage or page with the highest abandonment rate. This is where further investigation would be needed. It may also highlight that the delivery price is higher than expected, potential issues shipping to specific countries or other problems. Other channels can also be activated here to help support a reduction in this rate, such as including an email marketing campaign to encourage the potential new customer to complete their order.

AVERAGE ORDER VALUE (AOV)

Average order value (AOV) is the total number of sales divided by the total number of orders. You may have a target in mind for this to benchmark against, and it's an important metric when gauging profit margins. If your company also provides offline ordering options, you could compare online and offline AOVs.

REFERRAL SOURCE

Identifying which referral channel is converting at the highest rate is a handy metric for marketing planning, adjusting campaigns if needed and potentially budgets too if there is a particular channel or tactic that is outperforming others. This is known as the *CR by referral source.*

For B2B websites that are focused on generating leads, there are slightly different KPIs.

CONTENT DOWNLOADS

Content downloads is a useful KPI for understanding the number of downloads of whitepapers, guides, videos and so on. A download demonstrates that the visitor is engaged with the company and that the content is resonating well with them. A high download rate indicates that your content and targeting are landing well with your audience.

LEAD FORM ABANDONMENT RATE

Lead form abandonment rate helps to identify how many visitors start a form but don't finish completing it. If the metric is high, it may be that the form has too many fields to complete, or isn't working correctly. It certainly sheds light on an area for further exploration. This can be a tricky metric to measure though and relies on effective tracking to identify the number of visitors landing on the form and then bouncing off.

GOAL CONVERSION RATE

Goal conversion rate is tailored to the company and the objective. A goal could be completing a form, subscribing to the email marketing newsletter, watching a demo video on the website or many other things. Measurement here is focused on the percentage of visitors that go on to complete the goal.

Channel-specific KPIs: PPC

Let's follow PPC KPIs through the customer journey.

IMPRESSION SHARE (IS)

First, your ad appears in a search result. This is called an 'impression'. To measure how many impressions your ads are generating, you can use a metric called *impression share* (IS). This metric should be used with caution because, while it is a useful metric to understand how many times your ad has appeared, it doesn't highlight whether the ad has been successful. After all, it doesn't measure engagement with the ad. Your ad appearing in search results doesn't always mean it was seen.

QUALITY SCORE (QS)

However, you can determine the impression share you have for a particular keyword(s). For example, you may own 50 per cent of the search impression space available for a keyword. The remaining 50 per cent is your competitors and, if you increase your share further, that's fewer times that your competitors' ads are shown. However, to increase cost per thousand impressions (CPM) and make more bids, you'll also need to increase your budget. To assess how relevant your ad content is to the keywords you're bidding on, there's *quality score* (QS). This is measured by the search engines and includes expected CTR, the landing page experience and so on.

For example, if your bounce rate is high, this would indicate that the ad didn't correctly set expectations or that there's a disconnect with the landing page. Perhaps the ads aren't relevant to the landing page, or the format doesn't inspire click-throughs. Whatever the problem is, this disconnect will lower your quality score.

The bad news is that the lower your quality score, the more expensive it will be to advertise. You could also be penalized if your QS is very low, as the goal of the search engine is to only present results that are relevant to the search query. If an ad is trying to position itself using an irrelevant keyword, then the searcher's experience is damaged. QS is important as it will determine the cost of each click and can impact cost per click (CPC) and cost per acquisition (CPA).

AVERAGE POSITION (AP)

Now, how prominently can the customer see your ad? Where does it appear in the search feed? Position 1, 2 or 3? To measure this, you can use the *average position* (AP). To calculate this score, multiply QC with max CPM. Even with a higher budget than your competitors, your ads won't be position 1 all of the time. The search engines use several factors to determine the position of an ad and are unlikely to keep a single advertiser at position 1 permanently. Being position 1 also doesn't always guarantee results either. You may find that positions 2, 3 or 4 achieve better results for your ads.

CLICK RATE

Moving on – after your ad has run through all these processes and achieved a position in search results, a searcher/viewer may click your ad. The first way to identify whether or not your PPC ads are performing is to assess how many viewers have clicked the ad. A click demonstrates that the content in the ad is driving interest, curiosity and intrigue enough for the viewer to want to click the ad and find out more. From your *click rate,* you can analyse how many clicks a month are being generated, how many per ad campaign, and if certain ads are driving more clicks than others. The entire performance of your PPC activity shouldn't be determined purely from the number of clicks, but it is a good starting point.

CLICK-THROUGH RATE (CTR)

Click-through rate (CTR) can be used to analyse the performance of a marketing campaign. It analyses the number of clicks an ad campaign has generated. This shows whether or not your campaign is heading in the right direction. If you have previous data to compare against, you can use this as benchmarks to strive towards. To measure CTR, start by dividing the total number of clicks your ad campaign achieved in the time frame you're reporting on (ie a month) by total impressions. You'll then uncover a percentage for your CTR based on the number of times your ad was displayed (impressions).

COST PER CLICK (CPC)

The next step from here is to understand the cost of each click using the *cost per click* (CPC) metric. You'll have a budget assigned to your PPC activity, so it's essential to understand how much each click is costing and whether it is affordable within your budget. Depending on the competitiveness for those specific search terms, the quality of your ads and the targeting applied will all impact the cost of each click. A bid budget will be determined within your paid advertising account, but that doesn't mean that this will be the final cost. A maximum you're willing to pay will have been configured based on the budget available, and if the term is incredibly competitive, it may cost more than your maximum.

Think of it as an auction. The more buyers available within the advertising space, and the more bids that are received, the higher the price goes – the fewer the bids, the lower the price. The CPC determines the price paid for each click. This can be measured by dividing the total cost of a campaign by the number of times the ad was clicked.

COST PER CONVERSION/ACQUISITION (CPA)

The next part is to analyse the *cost per conversion/acquisition* (CPA). This is the average price advertisers pay for every new customer acquired. To calculate your CPA, divide the total cost of conversion by the number of conversions. Your QS influences your CPA, which is why QS is an important metric. The CPA you achieve will depend a lot on the product/service you're promoting. If it's a high-value item, you might be willing to spend more budget on advertising it than you might for a lower-priced item with lower profit margins. A high CPA will very quickly eat away at your budget if the targeting, ad copy, QS and search terms you're targeting aren't optimized.

TARGETED CPA

There is an additional option available to advertisers called *targeted CPA*. This enables advertisers to set automatic bids to achieve as many conversions as possible, based on the CPA aligned to the budget. Conversion tracking, a minimum of 30 conversions in the last 30 days and an understanding of different bidding strategies are needed to make the most of targeted CPA.

CONVERSION RATE (CR)

The next metric to consider is the *conversion rate* (CR). This tells you how many conversions your PPC has generated. Typically, performance managers will optimize ads for clicks, but they'll still have a keen awareness of the number of conversions generated. For some companies, measuring the CR can be challenging. There needs to have been a minimum of 15 conversions in the last 30 days for this metric to work. If your sales cycle is months or years down the line, attribution can be tricky. This is why utilizing a combination of all the metrics described here is useful. It helps to paint a full picture of the health of your PPC advertising.

CUSTOMER LIFETIME VALUE (CLTV)

Similar to the marketing KPIs above, *customer lifetime value* (CLTV) can also be measured for PPC activity. This can be complex to achieve, as the attribution needs to be aligned to PPC, but if it is manageable within your company, it is a useful metric to determine which tactics are driving CLTV, especially when choosing budget splits.

BUDGET ATTAINMENT (BA)

Then there is *budget attainment* (BA). This isn't a metric that all marketers use, but it can be particularly useful when assessing how well campaigns are being managed. If there is an agency operating your PPC activity, this metric is suitable for indicating how close they came to achieving the budget they set out to use. If there is a big difference or maybe a vast overspend, this might merit further investigation.

Channel-specific KPIs: SEO

For visitors to find your website, you must appear in organic search results. A potential prospect is looking for a particular solution. Up pops a link to a blog post on your website. The searcher clicks it, and voila! They are now on your website, engaging with your content. Which is exactly where you want them to be.

ORGANIC TRAFFIC

To measure how many visitors come to your website from organic search, you can see traffic by the source in Google Analytics (GA). This is also a useful comparison to other traffic sources such as paid search (PPC), email marketing, social media and so on. This KPI is called *organic traffic*. You'll be able to see the health of this traffic, their duration on your website, whether they leave straight away (bounce rate) or stay on your site viewing a few pages (average pageviews).

SEARCH RANKING

Search ranking is important as it measures where your website appears in the results, and also the keywords/search terms. There are tools available to help you monitor the search position for specific keywords you're targeting and those that are relevant to your company. It's important to regularly watch your search ranking to uncover any changes taking place. It's also possible to see competitors domains and to spot any gaps in rankings that maybe your website could fill. It's useful to feed this analysis into your content strategy, so you can plug those gaps or adapt existing content to improve your rankings.

SEARCH VISIBILITY

Search visibility measures how many times your domain has shown in the search results for the keywords the site is ranking for. Google Search Console is a tool that will report how many impressions your website is receiving and is generally a very useful tool to use when monitoring your website's search performance and if there are any 'crawl errors' where

Google is struggling to 'read' your website. This is useful to understand as this could be hindering your search performance.

ORGANIC SESSIONS

Organic sessions are useful to monitor. An increase in relevant impressions should increase the organic sessions and in turn, result in more traffic to turn into conversions. The relevancy is important here. If there are lots of impressions, but these are for irrelevant search queries to your business and offer then this would demonstrate a high bounce rate in your website analytics. The key area when analysing organic sessions is to retain the context of seasonality. When making comparisons, make sure that year on year is being compared rather than month on month as this could fluctuate based on the time of the year.

BRAND VS NON-BRANDED TRAFFIC

It's useful to understand the *brand vs non-branded traffic* that is being driven from search. Branded traffic demonstrates that the searcher has previous awareness about your organization and offering. Non-branded traffic represents searchers that are looking for services or products similar to your offering, and if you have received this type of traffic, this demonstrates that you are ranking within the search results in the SERPs for those queries. There is a wide range of tools available to analyse this split between the brand and non-branded search traffic; SEMrush is one example.

BACKLINKS

One of Google's top-ranking factors includes *backlinks*, and while there are constant changes to what Google is monitoring, this remains a constant. This isn't about getting as many backlinks as possible. This is definitely a case of quality over quantity. The metrics to measure are: the total number of backlinks; how many referring domains does your website have; number of links lost; number of links earned; and any toxic links that could be potentially damaging your website's search performance. To provide context to the analysis compare with the performance of your competitors' domains to see how your website compares.

PAGE SPEED

Page speed can have an impact on your search performance. If it takes too long to load a page on your website, you will be penalized as it's providing a poor experience to searchers who land on your site. An increase in the time it takes for a page load can happen for several reasons, and there are tools available that can identify issues such as Google's free PageSpeed Insights tool (developers.google.com/speed/pagespeed/insights/). It may be due to the size of an image that is taking a long time to load. Once the issues have been identified, it's important to try to resolve them as quickly as possible, not only to improve your search performance but also for any visitors that are exploring your site.

Channel-specific KPIs: Social media

To what extent did your social media activity reach your audience? These are the specific KPIs to measure that.

IMPRESSIONS

Impressions measure how many times your post or ad appeared in a person's timeline view. This doesn't measure engagement with your social media post or ad, so this metric shouldn't be used alone. It doesn't provide the full picture.

AUDIENCE GROWTH

Audience growth is a useful KPI if an objective is to increase your social media following. This can be measured on a weekly, monthly, quarterly and annual basis. The total number of new followers are counted for the specified time period, eg a month, then divided by the entire audience to understand the growth rate. Multiply by 100 and compare to the previous time frame, eg the last month, to discover trends.

POST REACH

For your organic social media posts, you can measure the reach of that post. This KPI is called *post reach*. The results of this metric highlight the content that is resonating well with your following and driving engagement. It will also show you the days/times performance improves and declines. The 'reach' part is identified by measuring the number of people that viewed your post. This is then divided by the total number of followers and multiplied by 100. Again, this can be compared to other posts for the same campaign, time frame or audience, and the results will highlight content that is engaging and disengaging your audience.

SOCIAL SHARE OF VOICE (SSoV)

Comparing how many people mentioned your brand name in comparison to the competition is a useful KPI to measure. This is known as *social share of voice* (SSoV). The same can also be measured to identify if your product/ service or the campaign hashtag is being mentioned on social media. I could use this to count every time the name of my book is mentioned on social media, and compare it to an existing marketing book to see which one is receiving the most mentions.

There are various social media reporting tools which can help you to gather this information. Hootsuite is a well-known example. Firstly, you need to identify the reporting period; week, month, campaign, etc. Then, measure every mention of the brand both directly and indirectly. Do the same for competitors and add the two together to get the total mentions. Multiply by 100 to get a percentage and compare them.

Engagement KPIs

Measuring engagement on social media is vital to identify how many people are interacting or not engaging with your posts. These are the KPIs to do that.

AVERAGE ENGAGEMENT RATE (AER)

Average engagement rate (AER) measures how many likes, comments and shares your social media activity is getting relevant to your total number of followers. For this metric, you're looking for a high rate – the higher it is, the better the engagement rate. The results of this KPI should be used to guide future content.

AMPLIFICATION RATE (AR)

Amplification rate (AR) measures the shares, retweets, repins and regrams your following has given your social media activity. Again, a high rate is a good sign that your followers are sharing your content with their network and are happy to associate themselves with your brand.

VIRALITY RATE (VR)

Virality rate (VR) isn't to be the one and only KPI you use to measure social media success, because having a goal of going viral might not be strategic if it does not link to your objective (as covered in Chapter 3). However, it can be a useful KPI if you want to increase exposure, awareness and engagement. To measure VR, calculate the shares of a particular post, time frame or campaign and then divide that by impressions (with matching criteria), and multiply by 100. This will then provide your VR percentage.

Measuring conversions

Now on to measuring conversions from social media activity.

CR/CTR

CR and CTR cover all channel and tactical activity and are measured in the same way each time, making them consistent metrics to use when comparing results. For social media, these should be divided by impressions. You can then understand what the CTR could have been if everyone who saw your content on their timeline had clicked through. Achievement goals can also be set for both of these KPIs against which to benchmark your performance.

BOUNCE RATE

To measure whether the traffic being sent from social media is of the right target audience, there is the *bounce rate*. This is a KPI that can be measured across all channels and tactical activity and is a valuable metric to determine the quality of the traffic being sent to your website or specific landing page. The goal for this KPI is to keep the results low.

COMMENT CONVERSION RATE (CCR)

Comment conversion rate (CCR) is a useful metric for understanding how many of your followers comment after reading your post. Of course, it's also important to add context here as not every comment is positive. A slew of negative comments will require further investigation. But it is useful to know what you're posting that is sparking conversation with your audience; after all social media is a 'social' medium.

COST PER CLICK (CPC)

For social media advertising, also known as 'paid activity', it's crucial to understand how much you're paying for engagement and placement of each social media ad. This is the same KPI and measurement as PPC, with *cost per click* (CPC). This is an important KPI to keep an eye on to know if the budget is spent is efficient or being wasteful.

COST PER THOUSAND IMPRESSIONS (CPM)

Cost per thousand impressions (CPM) is the amount that is paid after 1,000 people scroll past your sponsored content. This is not a useful metric for measuring how effective an ad is, so shouldn't be used in isolation. But it is helpful to understand in advance the costs of the sponsored post and projected costs for new campaigns. It also gives you an idea of how many people will see your ads, and how many new customers could be exposed to your brand and offering.

CR

Conversion rate is also a KPI that can be used for paid as well as organic advertising. There are then additional KPIs for customer support if your social media activity is used to help customers too. This includes measuring the number of customer testimonials, *customer satisfaction score* (CSat) of your product/service and *net promoter score* (NPS) to identify how many people would recommend the company/ product/service.

Direct mail KPIs

There are key elements within the content of the DM that can be tracked, such as a unique telephone number that is related to that specific campaign, a dedicated URL to measure how many visits it has received following the DM landing, and tailored discount/coupon codes that relate back to the campaign.

RESPONSE RATE (RR)

Response rate calculates the percentage of a mailing list who responded to the DM through any tracked methods; that could be by calling the phone number, using the specific URL or discount/coupon code that are unique for the campaign:

$$\frac{No \ of \ Responses}{No \ of \ DMs \ sent} = RR$$

CONVERSION RATE (CR)

How many people that received your DM purchased the item advertised? For items that are more impulse-led products (such as a takeaway) the response rate and CR may happen at the same time. For items that have a longer sales cycle the conversion rate will be important to measure as the response rate may seem initially low during a longer sales cycle.

COST PER ACQUISITION (CPA)

CPA is the same across channels. As it is the same calculation, this means you can compare the CPA of your DM campaigns with other channels such as PPC to determine which one is most cost effective. But when doing so, do remember to consider the whole picture and review engagement, acquisition and retention performance metrics too and not just cost:

$$\frac{Campaign\ cost}{No\ of\ orders} = CPA$$

AVERAGE ORDER SIZE

This KPI determines the amount of revenue earned for each sale that DM has generated.

Email marketing KPIs

Email KPIs are metrics which are tracked within the email itself. They're measured by email marketing platforms and presented to marketers as easily comprehensible data.

DELIVERY RATE

Delivery rate – this measures the number of emails that have successfully reached the inbox of your recipients. Any that don't reach the inbox have been potentially blocked by ISPs (internet service providers). This is calculated by dividing the number of emails delivered by the total number of emails sent. This is an important metric to keep a close eye on, if this is low, it could signal an issue with the quality of your email list and your sender reputation.

OPEN RATES

Open rates – the open rate metric measures how many recipients opened your email in comparison to the total number delivered. It's worth noting that simple open trackers often count re-opens as well as initial opens, meaning that a recipient can open the same email multiple times and each click will be counted as an 'open'. So, while it's a useful metric, bear in mind that the 'real' results are likely to be slightly lower than the data appears to show (depending on the email service provider you're using).

A/B testing different subject line content provides insight into what engages your audience to open your email campaigns and what doesn't. But use this metric with caution as not opening your email doesn't necessarily mean that a recipient hasn't seen your email or brand name pop up in their inbox. If it's unclear to your subscribers that they will be tracked in this way, anonymize all data derived from these tests.

CLICKS

Clicks – the usefulness of this metric depends on the number (if any) of clickable links within an email. When a recipient clicks on content within an email, that demonstrates an interest in that particular content, making it a useful metric for measuring engagement. By A/B testing this metric, marketers can also improve click-through rates in real-time.

BOUNCES

Bounces – bounce rates are useful for keeping lists clean and for tracking deliverability. When an email is undelivered, it has 'bounced'. If a high number of emails bounce it could lower your sender reputation and highlight an issue in the quality of the database. There are two types of bounces: a hard bounce or a soft bounce. A hard bounce is flagging that there is a permanent reason the email could not be delivered (perhaps the email address doesn't exist, for example). A soft bounce is highlighting that there is a temporary reason that the email cannot be delivered. The inbox may be full, for example.

UNSUBSCRIBES

Unsubscribes – tracking subscription rates is important for understanding how well a brand's reputation is doing, and how good that brand is at maintaining relationships with customers. There are lots of reasons for unsubscribing to email marketing, but a peak indicates that there is an issue that needs to be resolved. Meanwhile, troughs show when content is resonating well with subscribers. This makes it an important metric to keep an eye on, especially to monitor deliverability. After all, if your emails aren't being delivered they won't reach your subscribers.

CLICK-TO-OPEN RATE (CTOR)

Click-to-open rate (CTOR) – the CTOR metric is potentially the most useful for measuring subscriber interactions. It tracks clicks in tandem with opens. So, for example, the CTOR metric can tell marketers how many readers close an email immediately after opening it, how many continue to read, how many click-throughs and so on. It's great for assessing engagement at a glance. This can also start to highlight the content that your recipients are interested in by monitoring their engagement.

DEVICE STATS

Device stats – knowing the devices upon which users are reading their emails is beneficial. Content will be displayed differently in each device, so it's important to optimize content based on the devices used by your recipients. For example, if you discover a high proportion of your audience is opening your email marketing on a smartphone, then the content and design should be built with that at the forefront.

SPAM SCORE

Spam score – not to be confused with the bounce rate, a campaign's spam score will indicate just how much value customers are getting from the campaign content. A high spam score shows that they're not impressed with what they're receiving and are flagging your email as spam. This then sends a signal to the internet service providers (ISPs) such as Gmail or Outlook, 'Hey those subscribers are not interested in receiving emails from your brand'. If you continue to send to subscribers that don't engage with your emails this can start to impact your sender reputation, which, in turn, impacts how many of your emails end up in the inbox measured by your deliverability rate.

Turning measurements into action

The analysis conducted shouldn't hide away in a spreadsheet but should be used to inform change and future marketing activity. The value from evaluations comes from drawing insights that aid development and learnings. For example, if you find when comparing device use that a high proportion of subscribers open your emails using a desktop, but a higher proportion click through on mobile, it may be that your templates have a problem. It's easy to optimize each template for the appropriate device, but it's still worth knowing about this issue early.

If you have a good marketing platform, a lot of the work of gathering and reporting metrics will be done for you. All you have to do is notice trends (for example, dips in engagement) and work out what's going on. You can do this by comparing with other metrics, looking at the wider context and coming to an informed understanding of the issue based on what you've learned.

The bottom line is this: the more able you are to measure your success, the better your campaigns will be in both the long and short terms. You need to weave measurability into every stage of your marketing strategy. This is the only way to learn, grow and improve.

Post-campaign analysis

Post-campaign analysis (PCA) is vital to understanding what worked and what didn't, to inform future marketing campaigns. Your PCA will also help to assess whether the strategy was a success by analysing if it achieved the objectives set. The place to start when conducting a PCA is actually at the start of your campaign. The objectives are set, and the tactics are being added to your action plan. Include details of the date of when the activity begins, and details on who, when and where, as we covered earlier.

The purpose of a PCA is also to present/share your results with the rest of the business and key stakeholders, so it needs to include the detail that many outside of the marketing team wouldn't be aware of. In your PCA, include visual examples of the content and advertising that has been published as part of the marketing campaign. For example, screenshots of email marketing sent, online banner display ads and secured press coverage. This is also a very effective way to document past campaigns to revisit at a later date.

When your campaign is over, you can return to your PCA. The next part is to analyse the performance of the activity against the objective(s). If the objective was to increase website traffic from new visits, did the campaign do that? Did engagement levels rise? Did orders increase? Were there any sales conversations following the activity, increase in live chat enquiries and so on? By utilizing a dedicated landing page and/or UTM tracking (as detailed in Chapter 8) you'll be able to uncover these insights.

As part of this analysis, be critical. We all want to end on a high note, but it's important to ask yourself what went wrong. What didn't work? What could have been better or more efficient? Consider: if you were to repeat this activity, what would you change, improve or keep the same? The way to progress and improve in marketing is through critique. In doing so, you take away key learnings that can be used in the future activity, always pushing your marketing further.

If campaigns are repeated like for like over and over again you'll not only get the same results; you'll also see a decline, as fatigue starts to set in from targeting the same audience repeatedly with the same unchanged message. So, be brutally honest with yourself! The best way to do this is to document the next steps by answering these three key questions:

- What are you going to repeat?
- What are you going to change?
- What are you going to stop?

Suppose you found yourself adjusting the planned activity during the campaign, including that in the PCA. Document your rationale as to why. This will be important to come back to when planning your next campaign, and it's easy as time passes to forget these nuggets of information. The PCA is an effective way of documenting the campaign activity as and when team members change.

Depending on your business set-up and communication channels, your PCA can be created in a presentation format or PDF that can then be widely shared across the company. This is important to keep the rest of the business informed and engaged in the marketing activity, but it also works as a self-promotion for the marketing department.

On reflection, what would you change?

As you reflect on your marketing performance, remember that a successful marketing strategy is one that can adapt to changing environments and situations. Use your PCA to reaffirm any assumptions made and adjust any areas that have since changed. For example – customer comprehension. Do you know your customers? Do you have an understanding of what they're interested in, what they like to read, what they don't want to receive from your organization, the products they are most likely to purchase and how many times a customer visits your website before making a purchase or enquiry? Customer needs are likely to change quite quickly in response to a fluctuating market, personal circumstances, world events, etc. Reviewing these questions will help you to identify where your comprehension is dropping off and how you can get back in touch.

To find out how a company determines their vision in a way to encourage growth, I interviewed Ade Lewis, Marketing Director at all-in-one integrated marketing platform, Mailchimp.

Interview: Ade Lewis

Ade Lewis is a Marketing Director for Mailchimp. He has a background in web design and coding, but since 2005 he's been heavily involved in the SEO and Digital Marketing industry with a fanatical addiction to finding what strategies really work to make a business successful online. Over the years Ade has helped many enterprise-level companies, but his true passion is helping small and medium-sized businesses achieve their dreams.

JT: *What do you think are the key ingredients that should be included in a marketing strategy?*

AL:

- **define** what your **business goals** are;
- **define** what your **marketing goals** are;
- **understand** who your target customer is;
- **segment** your market/audience and prioritize on the best ROI opportunities;
- **measure** your successes and failures;
- **learn** from your mistakes;
- **reiterate** and **improve** your strategy.

JT: *Describe what a marketing strategy is in one sentence.*

AL: Defining and shaping all marketing goals, activities and outcomes towards a single overarching business marketing plan.

JT: *From your experience, what do you think are the key challenges to implementing a marketing strategy?*

AL: Very often it can be the strategy itself (or lack of one). You would be surprised how many marketing planning sessions take place without taking the overall business goals into account. The impacts are different but this is relevant for any size of business from a solopreneur start-up to an enterprise-level company.

A strategy doesn't have to be complicated, and often the most simple strategies are the most effective. Make sure you understand the business goal, ensure that the strategy can achieve that goal with as few moving parts as possible and you should face the least number of challenges.

Small businesses almost always have very small marketing budgets (if any at all). They are always short on time and fairly often have little marketing experience. There is a tendency for small businesses to jump straight into action without thinking about how each action is going to help them get to where they want to be. This can result in a marketing campaign being mistaken for a marketing strategy and money being wasted without achieving anything concrete for the business.

For larger businesses, one of the key challenges is poor communication which can lead to a lack of buy-in and support from key stakeholders and business leaders. A marketing plan that doesn't have the support of the business as a whole is, at best, going to be a hard slog to implement. Any marketing strategy should start by stating the goals of the business. Every campaign, initiative or tactic should cascade upward into achieving those goals and should include a succinct narrative of how each element will be achieved, along with predicted outcomes of success. If you can clearly communicate your strategy in this way and get everyone on board before you start on delivering any of the elements then you can hopefully reduce the number of challenges that you'll face.

JT: *What common pitfalls do you see marketers falling into when they are creating a marketing strategy?*

AL: **Failing to understand the customer.** It is very easy to make assumptions about your customers. You started your business because you liked a thing and so the majority of customers (and potential customers) look just like you, right? Some of those customers might look just like you but you can guarantee that a lot of them won't. If you don't know and understand your customers then how do you know where they hang out? What marketing channels, platforms, mediums and content are best for getting in front of them?

A lot of marketers make the mistake of starting campaigns without truly knowing who the audience are, and whilst individual campaigns can see positive results they can also hide the missed opportunity. Understanding your customers is one of the key elements of a successful strategy.

Not identifying when your strategy isn't working. There is a common military saying that 'no plan survives contact with the enemy'. It is now very much seen as a cliché but it doesn't mean that it isn't still very true. A marketing strategy is based on everything that you think you know and the experience that you have before you start delivery. After that point anything from public opinion, economic and social factors to internet regulation and unforeseen business circumstances can change. The important thing is that you give every campaign within your strategy a predicted outcome before you start, and that you measure, learn and adjust your strategy if needed.

JT: *Do you think marketing can be effective without a strategy?*

AL: If success means that your marketing efforts earn more money than you spend then I think that marketing can be somewhat successful without a strategy but this is not the same thing as being effective.

To be effective you need to know what marketing activities you are going to undertake to achieve your marketing goals, why you are carrying out those particular activities over other marketing options, how they all complement each other and what the predicted outcomes for each activity are. This gives you the best chance of maximizing your return on investment rather than just covering your costs. I don't see this as being possible without a considered strategy.

JT: *Are there any stand-out marketing strategies that you have seen? What made that particular marketing strategy stand out?*

AL: The best answer that I can give here is Mailchimp.

Mailchimp grew from being a side project for a small web design company, to a global all-in-one marketing platform with a beloved brand. This didn't happen by accident. There was a very clear marketing strategy that broke the mould for how a tech company could connect with customers. There were many facets to the overall strategy, but they pretty much all boiled down to one key element: understanding and connecting with customers.

The founders, Ben Chestnut and Dan Kurzius, started Mailchimp for one simple reason: to help their small business customers. At a time when 70–95 per cent of all emails being sent were spam, and the email marketing landscape consisted of bland corporate solutions, they created a brand and a product that not only resonated with their target small business market, but that turned sending an email campaign from a boring chore into an enjoyable experience.

During a time when the vast majority of brands projected a formal and corporate tone, Mailchimp created a point of difference in its brand with the now iconic Freddie logo, and a sense of fun and playfulness that small business owners connected with. This brand identity worked because it was more than just a fun mascot. It truly represents Mailchimp as a company, and it represents some of the values that Mailchimp believes in: creativity, independence, humility and making work fun.

This sense of fun was seamlessly worked into the Mailchimp product. Mailchimp demonstrated that it understood its customers in clever ways by including fun gifs showing a sweating hand just about to press the send button on a new email campaign. And an animated Freddie high-five gif encapsulating the sense of relief and achievement that a business owner feels once the campaign was sent. And, not only is its platform fun, it's effective and powerful for small businesses as well as easy to use.

Creating this brand was a key element in connecting with customers, but it walked a very thin line between the fun vs the silly. Mailchimp made this fine balance seem easy and natural, but there was a lot of work that went into getting it right. You can see just how much effort they put into it within the Mailchimp voice and tone guide (styleguide. mailchimp.com/voice-and-tone/).

FIGURE 9.1   Freddie high-five gif

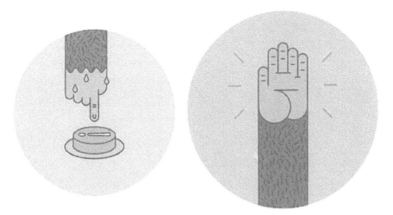

Reproduced with the kind permission of Mailchimp (2020)

Already a successful company, the master-stroke of Mailchimp's marketing strategy for driving customer adoption came with the introduction of free accounts. Not just free for a while or free but with less functionality, completely free for life until you reach a generous level of contacts in your account. This suddenly gave every small business (pretty much world-wide) access to an email marketing solution that was easy to use and that they felt was built for them. Every email sent via a free account included a clickable Freddie image in the footer that linked back to the Mailchimp website. Every customer with a free account was helping to spread the word, and ultimately helping to do Mailchimp's marketing job for them.

Most businesses would have stopped there and congratulated themselves on a job well done, but Mailchimp's marketing goal wasn't just to successfully build a huge pool of customers. It was to build a huge pool of customers who loved them. One of Mailchimp's paths to achieving this was simply by making people happy. They gave away gifts including T-shirts, Freddie figures, even hand-knitted Freddie hats for cats. There was no ROI agenda to this, the only goal was to make their customer smile and love them a little bit more. And who doesn't love a picture of a cat on a social media account wearing a knitted Freddie hat?

JT: *Are there any key marketing models, theories or concepts that you'd recommend marketers utilize when creating a marketing strategy?*

AL: My passion for marketing has always been for small to medium-sized businesses. It is where I get my satisfaction and where you can see real change and make a difference on a personal level. The vast majority of marketing models/concepts that I have seen or attempted either don't align with this level of business or add a much higher level of process than is actually needed. The only exception to this is AIDAR (Awareness, Interest, Desire, Action/Purchase, Retention). For me, this pretty much holds true for any type of marketing for any business.

JT: *Do you think AI has a role in a marketing strategy?*

AL: Definitely. AI coupled with machine learning is transforming (and will continue to transform) the way in which we market to customers.

Machine learning can be used to process large sets of data and offer insights into customer behaviour that previously would have taken either too long to be viable or too complex to be understood. Marketing automation can drive the decisions around the types of website or ad content that work best with customers on an individual level, rather than broad customer segments. This saves time and also allows us to achieve the highest conversion rates.

AI can replicate ever increasing levels of interaction with consumers. Again, saving time and directing consumers on the best path to becoming customers.

JT: *Do you have any tips to share on creating a successful marketing strategy?*

AL: **Keep your strategy as simple as possible.** For smaller businesses this is easily achieved by having simple goals. This could be as basic as increasing the customer base by 10 per cent and conversion rate from 1.8 to 2 per cent. Your marketing efforts roll up directly into your strategy for achieving your goals.

For bigger businesses this approach probably isn't a viable option. In this case you introduce marketing initiatives to achieve your goals. Your marketing campaigns roll up into achieving your marketing initiatives which roll up into achieving your strategy.

Start Small. Test each marketing effort/campaign by starting small, investing a small amount of resource/budget. Only scale when you have confirmed that your chance of success is high.

Fail quickly. Don't let marketing tests drag on and on. If they don't work then recognize this as quickly as possible. Rethink your approach and come up with a better idea.

Keep an open mind. Don't discount an idea as being bad without at least considering it. You might be surprised. Similarly, don't fall in love with one of your own ideas and cling on to a failing campaign beyond the point that you should have thrown in the towel.

Accept failure and learn from it. Some of your marketing efforts will fail. The only thing worse than failing is failing to learn. When you do fail, try not to do it with all of your marketing budget. Test first before you go all-in.

Don't be boring. I always tell my kids that 'only boring people get bored'. If you are creating your marketing strategy then make sure that it isn't boring; you'll be setting yourself up for either poor results or a long, hard slog. Either you will be delivering your own marketing plan and regretting every day of it. Or your team members will be regretting the day they took the job.

JT: *What do you think the future of marketing holds?*

AL: Personalization and regulation. We have already seen some of the power of machine learning and AI and we are really only at the start of what could be possible when it comes to personalized targeting and marketing.

Tech companies are collecting huge amounts of data about us. Some of this data is at the level expected by most people, such as age, gender and our basic preferences. This is nothing new, marketers have been using consumer data for years to improve their marketing efforts. But at the time of writing this it has just been revealed that Amazon keeps records of every motion detected by its Ring doorbells, as well as the exact time they are logged down to the millisecond and images of the people who visit your home. 'Smart Home' devices know pretty much everything about your personal life at home, your phone tracks you away from home and everyone is trying to track your online habits.

The volume of data being collected about us is mind-boggling and historically there has been too much data collected to feasibly process. This is changing. Supercomputers utilizing parallel processing now have the power to process these gigantic datasets, to understand what we like, what we don't like, who we socialize with, where we will be at what time and what we are most likely to buy.

There are genuine benefits for us from this understanding of our data. We are magically recommended the things we like, just when we didn't even realize that we needed them. The perfect film, blog post, handbag, pizza or holiday. But we have definitely reached the point where increasing numbers of people feel that the use of our personal data has gone too far and global privacy regulators and law-makers seem to agree with them. Around the world, regulators have been slow to recognize the privacy risks and have had a hard time catching up with the privacy and security challenges of big data. The European Union's General Data Protection Regulation (GDPR) has had a major influence on the global privacy landscape with many other markets already following suit.

Many tech businesses have been enjoying extremely high conversion rates based off of personalized data which has bolstered revenue and stock prices. Over the coming years, I think that we are likely to see a cat and mouse game of technology vs regulation and legislation. I can't see how this can fail to hit the bottom line for these bigger companies and it might mean that there is a glimmer of hope for smaller companies trying to market their products and businesses.

JT: *What are your tips for identifying a target market?*

AL: Learn as much as you can about your existing customers. Use both demographics (age, location, gender, etc) and psychographics (hobbies, values, attitudes, etc) to create several potential customer segments then discover where these segments hangout [Note: see Chapter 4]. Test the engagement from these segments via low-level paid social advertising or PPC advertising.

  Analyse your main competitors to see where they are spending their advertising budget. You don't have to go head-to-head with these competitors but you might spot some gaps that you can fill.

  Look out for niche opportunities. As an example… Rather than selling just running gear you could focus solely on women's performance running gear. If this niche is big enough to support your business then it could laser focus your marketing efforts, reduce your competition levels and greatly reduce marketing effort/spend.

JT: *Do you have any tips on creating effective marketing objectives?*

AL: Start with the basics. For almost all types of business, there will be tried and tested channels that will shift the revenue needle the most. Using e-commerce sales as an example, you could try organic social media marketing, paid social advertising, print advertising or affiliate referral schemes but it is well documented by a great many studies that email marketing and abandoned basket retargeting will likely produce the highest levels of conversions and ROI. This doesn't mean that you should only engage in email marketing but you should cover this base as a first step.

  Market via multiple channels. Almost any marketing effort will be amplified by using multiple marketing channels. As a first step, pick two or three channels with the highest ROI opportunities and completely nail those before expanding into other channels.

  Use marketing automation. One of your most precious marketing resources is your time. Using an integrated marketing platform to automate marketing efforts across channels can be very cost effective and allow you to scale your marketing efforts without needing to invest lots of time.

  Stay focused. It is easy to sometimes get side-tracked with the possibilities of different channels and to end up down a rabbit-hole where you are spending a lot of time without much gain. Remember that marketing objectives exist for the sole purpose of delivering your marketing strategy. It is really helpful to step back from what you are doing on a regular basis and to review how your objectives are aligning with your strategy. There is nothing wrong with adjusting your objectives to make your strategy more effective.

JT: *What are your tips for creating experiences using digital marketing?*

AL: For me this returns back to the repeating topic of truly understanding your customer. You may have heard many times that digital marketing is all about delivering the right content, to the right person at the right time in the buying cycle, but the only way to know what that content needs to be is to understand your customer.

Understand what their needs are and why. What pain points do they have in their businesses or their lives that your product or service can solve? Where do they interact online? What channels are best for getting in front of them and what messaging works best to bring them into your funnel?

Ensure that you have a consistent narrative for your acquisition funnel so that when your marketing efforts bring a potential customer to your content/product/service, that content aligns with your original messaging and the conversion element becomes a continuation of the same journey rather than a completely new journey.

JT: *From your experience, are there particular marketing techniques that drive customer loyalty?*

AL: Marketing is the doorway, but for me it is the honesty and integrity of your brand that ultimately drives customer loyalty. Your brand styling, the voice and tone that you use in your messaging and what you say to your customers is the promise. The ethos of your business as a whole and your brand values are what will shape loyalty. It is delivering your product, your after-sales service, how your team shows up for your customers when things go wrong that makes the difference.

We spend time and make new friends with people that we like. We buy from people that we like. We don't stay friends with people who lie to us and who promise us one thing but then give us something different. Always deliver on your marketing promises.

I once gave a presentation about leveraging your brand to drive organic traffic to your website and for that talk I asked some friends what their definition of a brand was…

> Brands are companies you give a s**t about. So whatever they did to make you give a s**t, that's branding.
>
> Oli Gardner, Unbounce

A brand is what gives people the warm fuzzies. Or makes them vomit in
their mouth a bit when they hear the name of a company.

Greg Gifford, SearchLab

JT: *What are your go-to measurement metrics when analysing the success
of a marketing campaign?*

AL: Measurement and metrics is an area that can define the success of a
strategy or that can be the cause of its downfall. The problem for me
with metrics is that they are very often seen as the north-star goal for
someone owning an objective, which can easily drive the wrong
behaviour. This is a topic that could fill a book so all I'll say here is that
metrics should always be viewed collectively, never in isolation.

If your business goal is to increase revenue by 10 per cent then your
north-star metric should be revenue. Any metrics that you use to measure against objectives should be dictated by your strategy.

JT: *Mailchimp is widely known for email marketing. Why do you think
email as a channel remains a favourite with consumers?*

AL: As online consumers, we live and breathe via email. We may spend half
of our lives trawling through social channels, keeping up to date with
trends, friends and the latest gossip but the first thing that we all do as
soon as we make an online purchase is to open our email app to make
sure that our purchase went through ok and that our receipt arrived via
email. This is because, for retailers, email is by far the most reliable and
effective way of communicating with customers at scale.

For me, the truth is that there simply isn't a viable alternative to using
email that encompasses all of the transactional requirements associated
with buying and selling online. (By transactional, I mean the emails that
you receive and respond to for setting up an account, resetting your pass-
word, making a purchase, etc). This reliance on email for consumers
buying online means that it is also the best performing marketing channel for most businesses selling online... so long as you follow the rules.

With the advent and growth of data protection and privacy laws
around the world, most of us have woken up to permission-based
marketing and the benefits associated with it. When you provide someone with the opportunity to sign up to receive your newsletter or
product promotions and they accept, then it means that they genuinely
want to hear from you. They have made a conscious choice to receive
your emails and so their interaction with your brand will be closer and
conversion rates will be higher.

For consumers it is becoming increasingly less acceptable to receive unsolicited marketing emails promoting brands and products that they didn't sign up for. When this happens it can have a large negative impact on the sender's brand, spam reports go up and deliverability rates go down. As well as the fact that this practice is now illegal in a lot of countries it also violates the terms of use for almost all marketing email providers (such as Mailchimp) and your account with them will be quickly banned.

Whilst data privacy was initially seen by many as the end of our ability to effectively market via email to consumers, for the brands doing it the right way, the result has actually been the opposite. Yes, email marketing lists are smaller but they are also much more effective because messages are being delivered to people who want to read them. This fact alone accounts for why email remains a favourite channel for consumers.

It is worth a reminder here that whilst email is likely the best converting channel for most businesses selling online, Mailchimp research and analysis shows that your marketing efforts will be much more successful if you utilize multiple marketing channels. Email should be your base layer but you can effectively increase conversions via other channels such as Google remarking or social retargeting.

JT: *What excites you most about marketing?*

AL: My marketing buzz has always come from making a discernible difference to someone's business. This is the reason that I enjoy working with smaller businesses so much. Marketing for small businesses comes with a unique set of challenges that can sometimes be frustrating but the trade-off is that you get to see the direct results of the work that you do in the feedback you get from the business owner. The business was struggling but now they are hiring new staff. That is what defines success for me and it means so much more than meeting a KPI.

Summary

In this chapter:

- You learned that, before drawing any conclusions from data analysis, you must ensure that it is statistically significant.
- You defined what data insights are, how to get them and how to use them.

- You identified KPIs related to your marketing objectives and specific channels.

- We explored the importance of relating measurements back to objectives to ensure that you are choosing the most relevant ones.

- You discovered that measurement is a good approach, but the value is in being able to use those insights to inform change and future marketing activity.

- We identified that conducting PCA should be part of your strategic process to determine the overall success of the strategy, what worked well and what didn't work as intended.

References

Lewis, A (2020) Marketing Director at Mailchimp [Interview] 2 October 2020

Macalister, T and Rankin, J (2013) British Gas: energy bills price hike turns into PR disaster [Online], *The Guardian*, available at: www.theguardian.com/money/2013/oct/17/british-gas-backlash-price-hike-energy-bills (archived at https://perma.cc/85E7-Z7HS)

Macleod, I (2013) British Gas on #askBG Twitter Q&A: it's important we're there for customers to talk to and it was the right thing to do [Online], The Drum, available at: www.thedrum.com/news/2013/10/17/british-gas-askbg-twitter-qa-it-s-important-we-re-there-customers-talk-and-it-was (archived at https://perma.cc/JVE2-KYM6)

Mailchimp (2020) How to measure your email marketing success [Online], available at: mailchimp.com/resources/how-to-measure-your-email-marketing-success/ (archived at https://perma.cc/P8XV-ZBYT)

Peppiatt, V (2020) COO and co-founder at Phrasee [Interview] 20 October 2020

Rogers, C (2019) Why chasing ROI could kill your business [Online], *Marketing Week*, available at: www.marketingweek.com/dangers-marketers-chasing-roi/ (archived at https://perma.cc/CY3T-3ZUU)

10

Common pitfalls
in marketing strategy

This chapter covers:

- The 10 most common pitfalls that marketers face.

- Tips on how to overcome them.

- Examples of how to recognize each pitfall in the future.

We're all human, and the world is an unpredictable place and more so now than ever! Even the best-laid plans can run into trouble. Here, I'll run through some of the most common pitfalls: a) to help you avoid them; and b) to provide tips on how to overcome them if you do happen to fall into any of them.

These tips will also help if you find yourself running into something less predictable. Understanding how to prepare yourself for common pitfalls can give you the tools and knowledge to deal with the unexpected, as well.

So, let's dive in.

Pitfall 1: No clarity of vision

A strategy needs to contain focus, a clear direction to take the company where it wants to get to. This is where the vision comes in. A vision should clearly articulate what the business is aiming to achieve, as covered in Chapter 1. The challenge comes when a vision is unclear, when it's difficult to understand or the ambitions of the business are constantly changing. There may be moments when there is a change in the direction of a company but that shouldn't be a regular occurrence. Everyone within the organization should be clear on where the business is trying to get to, what it is trying to achieve and who it is targeting. If none of that is clear, there's a problem either with the way in which the vision has been articulated, the communication of it or that it hasn't been defined in a concrete way.

Trying to define and establish a marketing strategy without a vision or one that isn't clear will ultimately mean that the strategy may miss the mark and not achieve the desires of the organization. A vision that is clearly communicated throughout the organization and one that everyone is working together to achieve will help the business achieve its goal. This provides a clear brief for the marketing strategy which is then filtered into the key actions that need to take place in the marketing plan to achieve that vision. Without it, the marketing strategy may be effective in engaging the audience, but may not deliver anything related to fulfilling the vision of the company.

Pitfall 2: Too much complexity

There is an art to keeping the very complicated simple. Many times, I have worked with companies who have brilliant technology, products and services but who over-complicate their marketing message to the point that no one truly understands what the organization does.

As the saying goes, less is definitely more. Creating a 200-page document detailing what makes your organization different is a long-winded way of getting to the point. Simplicity should be the byword throughout the entire organization. Processes should be simple. Communication should be to the point and tailored to the recipient. This links back to understanding more about the customer – what does simple look like to them? Do they really need to know the ins and outs of how your technology works before they've even seen it?

Providing too much and being overly complicated will alienate and turn away many prospects. Being clear and concise is a way of winning business and retaining customers. If it takes more than three lines to explain what your organization provides then it's already too long and overly complicated.

A good way to start the process of simplicity is to describe what your organization does within one line. Can you do it, or do you try to explain every intricate detail? As time and attention becomes more limited, the more important this becomes. Why have three paragraphs explaining your service when this could have been condensed to its core essence within a couple of sentences? Capture the attention. Talk about it in the same way as you would when meeting someone for the first time. You introduce yourself by saying your name and the other person does the same. 'It's good to meet you, I'm Jenna,' 'Likewise, I'm Melissa.' You wouldn't then start reciting your entire life's story because, well, let's be honest, Melissa probably wouldn't be so keen on chatting to you after all that inappropriate oversharing! Yet in a business context, companies do this every day. State their brand name, potentially the name of the product and then start reeling off everything about themselves without even coming up for air. That's intimidating to a first-time visitor (who maybe wanted to find out more about what the company does and what it's offering – but in their own time!)

The rule of simplicity also applies to your wording. Complicated words have their place – but people need to be able to easily understand what you're saying.

The same applies to processes. Are they over-complicated and could they be shorter, clearer, with fewer steps? There's a misconception that by making things simple it's 'dumbing things down' but that's not the case at all. Simplicity is the key to keeping everyone on the same page, working towards the same goal in an efficient manner and in delivering results.

Pitfall 3: Unstructured processes

An area that can be easily overlooked is the structure of a marketing team. A structure can make or break the effectiveness of a marketing strategy. It can hinder communication, reduce efficiency, limit people and demotivate teams.

A structure that was fit for purpose a year ago may no longer be the case today. And that purpose is dependent on the goals that need to be achieved. A structure needs to elevate and support the marketing team. There need to be clear lines of responsibility, ownership and accountability. Any blurring of lines in roles and responsibilities can cause leaks in the structure where key tasks or areas of focus are slipping through the cracks without anyone noticing. This could also result in areas of tasks which fall outside anyone's responsibility, leaving it deserted.

Tim Watson, EOS Implementer at Traction Six, highlights below how a marketing strategy can fail due to the wrong structure being place:

> Strategy fails when structure is wrong. All businesses know that they need to have a clear strategy, yet often underestimate the importance of company and team structure. Little effort is made to crystalize the right functional structure, the seats and roles for which each person is accountable. Right structure is as necessary as right strategy because if they aren't aligned structure prevails. What happens will be determined by the company structure and not the strategy.

Reviewing your structure doesn't always result in the restructure of a team or department. It may simply be the case that there aren't clear reporting lines for team members. This can then be re-defined so that it becomes clear who reports to whom, and who are the escalation points should any issues arise.

The crux of getting the structure right starts with the vision, understanding the marketing environment from the findings in the situational analysis and defining the objectives. Then the structure has clear goals to achieve, clear targets to steer by and a good understanding of skill sets needed, the experience and the people to achieve those milestones. As Sara Meikle explains below, empowerment is also crucial to enable people to fulfil their roles and responsibilities (more detail on this interview can be found in Chapter 7):

> It's all about empowering people to make their own decisions, have ownership of their work and giving them space to grow in their role by providing new opportunities to learn outside of their comfort zone. Sometimes, you need time-pressured projects to do this – in the long term, it's not only beneficial to your organization but also for individuals' personal career progression and confidence in their role.

Unclear and unstructured processes

There have been many times when I have been contacted by a brand to help them with their marketing efforts. The brand could be struggling with output, or with delivering results, or unsure where to start or where to focus.

When I work with these brands, it quickly becomes apparent that there is a lack of process and templates. Without a defined marketing process and any templates, everything is created from scratch, each time. Can you imagine starting your day-to-day job from the very beginning, every day? That's effectively what is happening without any templates to help guide you on the information that is needed. Pitfall 2 of keeping things simple still applies here. The templates created should be for repetitive tasks such as briefing templates for copywriters, sharing regular event speaker information, all of which are stored in the same sharable folder: email marketing templates, sales outreach templates, all to increase efficiency and allow more time for strategic thinking, rather than repeating the same tasks over and over again. Initially this requires an investment of time and effort but it is worth it when you free up the head space to start testing campaigns, optimize landing pages and conduct research, time that without templates and processes would have been used repeating the same task over and over again.

In terms of processes, if everyone and their dog wants to approve every piece of marketing activity, the business isn't going anywhere fast. Does the CEO of the organization really need to approve the new Facebook ad? Potentially if it includes a quote or image where they are featured, but ultimately approval processes need to be as lean as possible to enable a marketing team to be reactive when needed, to capitalize on opportunities and to engage the audience. What may appeal to the audience may not appeal to the CEO, but that's the point. The marketing isn't trying to engage the CEO, it's trying to engage a different demographic. It's important to remove personal biases as much as possible when conducting approvals.

The best way to reduce approval processes is to have involvement from key stakeholders at the very beginning, present the marketing strategy to them, talk them through the thought process, consider any points that are raised and then agree on the approval process for the first piece of activity. Once that trust has been developed, the number of people involved in that approval should reduce. The last thing a marketing team wants to be doing is spending hours on end going through discussions about a particular colour that has been used because one stakeholder doesn't like it. This is unproductive, wastes time, effort and resources – the key emphasis here is that those discussions are costing the business money and time that can't be redeemed. Consistency in elements such as brand guidelines as detailed below in Pitfall 4 and defined processes of who has clear ownership as discussed in Pitfall 3 will assist overcoming this challenge.

Lack of consistent decisive decision-making

This is the scenario that I mentioned in the Introduction – the one that every strategist and marketing manager dreads. That call into the director's office, to be told that there haven't been enough sales, and that the marketing for the channels for which you are responsible needs to be cut in favour of short-term profit. Ultimately you find yourself being asked to go against the marketing strategy and plan.

So, what do you do in this scenario? Well, you have three options:

A You protest that any short-term tactical activity will damage the long-term strategic plan you have in place. You argue your case to keep the faith and continue as planned.

B You do exactly as directed and don't question it.

C You implement a mixture of both. You retain the long-term planned activity and add in an additional tactical, short-term campaign. You hope that the short-term campaign will complement future plans but also drive immediate revenue to keep the director off your back.

OUTCOME IF YOU GO WITH OPTION A

The director isn't going to see the immediate sales uplift and is going to keep demanding for more. You stay firm, develop and share convincing performance analysis to show the upward trend and share forecasts of when the results are expected.

LONG-TERM RESULT OF OPTION A

There is a lot of value to be gained from sticking to the plan, but unexpected things may arise which mean that you need to adjust your plan at a tactical level. It is possible to do this without ruining the long-term marketing effectiveness of a well-thought-through, well-researched and strategic marketing plan. In the long term, the brand will be stronger for choosing Option A – but it's worth remembering that the strategy must complement the business's goals. If the business's plans change drastically, the strategy does have to change with them. If that isn't the case and this is just a short-sighted moment of 'we need more leads!' then continually chopping and changing your marketing strategy and activity last minute isn't just going to confuse the target audience. It is also going to cause burn-out very quickly and demotivate the marketing team.

OUTCOME IF YOU GO WITH OPTION B

You create the short-term tactical activity and bring in the desired revenue.

LONG-TERM RESULT OF OPTION B

You continue this approach for the next 10 years of your marketing career. For a decade, you reinvent the same offer with tweaked straplines. You see the effect of this campaign steadily decline. You become jaded and wonder why you ever joined marketing. Where's the creativity in producing the same offer or promotional campaign over and over again? Where's the fun? Where's the profit?

OUTCOME IF YOU GO WITH OPTION C

Both yourself and the director are aligned. There is a long-term marketing plan at play, and a short-term unplanned tactical campaign is live too. By utilizing this approach, you're able to fulfil the immediate revenue and sales needs in a way that will complement the plan.

LONG-TERM RESULT OF OPTION C

The tactical campaign will deliver in the short term alongside the marketing plan providing results in the long term. This is the best of both worlds. The critical thing here is to ensure that the tactical campaign doesn't disrupt the plan and is aligned with the overall marketing strategy. If it goes off on a tangent, it could undermine previous and future efforts, so it needs to be aligned and consistent in approach.

There will be the odd time when a marketer will win this debate, and I have worked with a few that have fought the long, hard battle and come out the other side smiling.

My advice to you is: always focus on the long term and create that compelling case. When organizations constantly move from offer to offer and create an 'offer-cycle' this undermines marketing. Work on these kinds of campaigns, and you'll become an agent of your demise. You'll eventually be put out of a job as the department becomes redundant.

Pitfall 4: Inconsistent messaging

If you're interested in a product, you'll probably get into it by searching on Google, which will take you to the brand's website. You could then sign up to receive the brand's email marketing and check them out on social media.

That's a lot of channels. For the customer to develop a sense of brand consistency (crucial to building brand/customer relationships) it's important to maintain the same branding, ToV, goals and so on across all your channels. For this, you need a decent strategy.

Consistency is surprisingly hard for some brands to nail. The reason for this is usually that a lot of marketing teams are working in silos. Different channels work separately, or the content team never talks to the budget team – you know how it goes! It's understandable – but it does make for a lot of inefficiencies.

A common example is sales and marketing not communicating well enough. Sales have amazing insights into customers that marketing could benefit from, and vice versa. This is usually because the departmental model is stuck in the post-war era. Break out of that era, if you can! Sharing insights makes for much better, more consistent campaigns and (crucially) a more consistent customer experience. This applies across all departments and sub-departments. Social media has a lot to learn from email, and everyone can benefit from the wisdom of the customer service team. Remember, the customer doesn't know that you're separate departments. From their perspective, they're dealing with the brand as a whole. So – work as a whole!

So – and I cannot stress this enough – remember that your colleagues are not your competitors. Your colleagues on other channels are creating content all the time. You could be using that content. And they could be using yours. It's not a competition – you're all ultimately working for the benefit of the customer. Marketing channels should share and complement one another's efforts. Share ideas and plan together.

I strongly suggest planning monthly meetings in which channel representatives meet to share insights, discuss goals and coordinate efforts. Team collaboration is key when it comes to brand consistency – and it makes for a much nicer work environment, too!

Inconsistent branding and messaging

As covered in Chapter 6, inconsistent branding and messaging can be a real problem. If your branding is inconsistent, your target audience won't be clear on what the company provides, what the product/service offers, or how it will benefit them.

This confusion makes it harder to engage the target audience and will hinder revenues. To remedy this, you need to work out why the inconsistency exists. What's the reasoning behind it? For example, is it due to a lack of clear direction from the organization? Is the benefit the product/service provides unclear or challenging to explain? Is it unclear who the target audience is? Is there a lack of a clear marketing plan? Does the marketing activity tend to be created in an ad hoc, knee-jerk way without any clear direction? Are there documented brand guidelines for everyone to follow? Or it may be that there aren't any clearly defined roles, responsibilities and ownership in the marketing team, causing blurred lines across the marketing mix. Who approves or confirms that the brand is being correctly represented? If nobody – who could or should?

If any of this is unclear, there will be inconsistencies across the business which will quickly translate to its messaging. Review Chapter 6 to revisit the approaches to take to ensure that branding and messaging is consistent.

Pitfall 5: Communication failures

Meetings can be incredibly useful for progressing essential decisions, but can also very quickly zap time. In March 2020, when many businesses began working from home, the switch from office to online meetings was instant. The challenge was in the heightened disruptive nature of online meetings in comparison to an office setting. In an office, you can see if the person you'd like to discuss something with is currently busy. In an 'online' environment, it's not as easy to see if that same person is busy before you dial them online. This is the same for telephone calls, which can be highly disruptive to creative ideas and progressing with tasks on a to-do list. Pre-scheduling meetings is a way to combat this unless it is a very urgent matter. There can be exceptions, but those exceptions shouldn't become standard practice.

There is also the number of communication channels now available, increasing the chances of over-communicating. There's email, telephone, Slack, Hangout, Skype, online video and WhatsApp to name a few and believe me, I have worked with clients who have used all of these channels simultaneously! The key questions to ask here are:

- Does everyone included need to know about that particular communication? For example, does an entire team need to be all dialled into the same online meeting, or can there be a key representative? If every member of the team is dialled in, then nothing will be progressing during that time.

- Is there one core communication channel that is used across the business? It may be that there is a particular departmental Slack group, so it's vital that only that channel is used consistently.

- What action do you want attendees of the meeting to take either before, during or after the meeting? What is required of them?

The time spent communicating should be considered as a cost to a business in both time and money because time is taken to send that email or join that Zoom call, distracting that person from their key tasks. This costs the business money. Communication is important but only when done in an efficient way.

The danger businesses are now facing with the increasing reliance on and use of online video meetings is fatigue. Fatigue of being in meetings online all day and then trying to catch up on deliverables that are expected. In an face-to-face environment, the atmosphere will feel more relaxed due to what is likely to be a conference room setting, with snacks and beverages and comfortable seating. Switch that to online, and there aren't any beverages and snacks unless the attendees make their own – which means they need to leave the screen, they're unlikely to be sitting in a comfy chair and they may have other family members close by. This is an entirely different environment. The like-for-like switch from offline to online in this context doesn't work and will lead to employee burn-out. This is important to consider because time spent away from the day-to-day responsibilities if the meeting doesn't cover those areas can cause unproductivity in a team.

Ask your attendees after each meeting (using a feedback mechanism such as a survey) if they found the session useful: was it a good use of their time, did they feel they needed to be there? If the answer is no, there are warning signs of over-communicating, which is as damaging as under-communicating.

It's a good idea to have policies in place. These don't have to be lengthy but do need to be communicated to all staff. Policy areas can include the channels that will be used to communicate (and for which purposes), meeting agendas and action points.

Pitfall 6: Not recognizing the value of marketing

Sometimes, the rest of your organization doesn't understand the value of marketing.

This can be a tricky one, especially if the rest of the business thinks that marketing is something that 'just happens'. The primary cause of this pitfall is the learnings and successes within the marketing activity not being communicated to the wider business. It can also be from bad experience of poor performing marketing activities (which usually result from not defining an effective marketing strategy).

If the rest of the business isn't informed of the value that the marketing activity is bringing to the organization, then it will be looked at in terms of cost. Typically, marketing and sales have the highest costs in a business – making a cost-based judgement dangerous!

While the two departments may have the highest cost to the company, they also provide a return on that investment. To communicate the value that the marketing strategy is bringing to the organization, results and learnings need to be aligned with the company's ambition and vision. If the vision remains unclear and not succinct, then marketing may well be delivering – but not delivering what the business wants. Clearly define a company vision and align the marketing strategy to it, and develop objectives which will include measurements of success. Break down those goals if needed from the long-term view to a quarterly, monthly and weekly view. Have regular check-in points to assess if those goals have been achieved, and provide the key metrics to communicate success and the value that is being delivered with the rest of the business. This may include ROI and many other metrics as uncovered in Chapter 7, the definition of which is dependent on the objectives and goals set.

If you're not doing so already, create marketing performance reports which measure each part of the marketing mix that is currently being used and the impact it's had on the business as a whole. Also consider the interests of the different stakeholders – what is going to pique their interest? What value does marketing bring their team or department? This could be insights into the customer such as direct feedback or engagement levels with various types of content. This level of insight would be particularly useful for a product team who are working on developing the next feature. Tailor the communication in a way that will engage the internal stakeholders – consider them another customer target group and tailor content as you would for prospect audiences.

There will also be an educational element to the rest of the business, to share and explain all of the different aspects that go into a marketing strategy. Explaining and running through the STRATEGY framework would be a great starting point.

The same frequent discussion that arises is when a particular channel is performing well when compared to the objectives and KPIs set (as covered in Chapters 3 and 9). There can then be the temptation to switch all of the marketing budget to this channel to the detriment of the others. This decision needs to be thoroughly analysed. There will be multiple touchpoints for consumers when engaging and purchasing with a brand in their journey, so while this channel might be performing well in increasing awareness, other channels may be better at converting. Switching off one channel could therefore have a negative impact to the overall success of the marketing strategy.

Pitfall 7: Ignoring the customer

Unclear target audience: 'let's target everyone!'

It may sound like a great idea great to target everybody, but, in reality, not every single person on the planet will want, like or need your product/service. If the target market for your product/service is unclear or unfocused, you'll very quickly burn into your marketing budget unnecessarily. This is where STP (segmentation, targeting and positioning) come in, as covered in Chapter 4.

It may be that a broad target audience will benefit, like and want your product/service. If that is the case, it's best to segment that large audience into smaller portions so that your marketing efforts can be focused on delivering the results outlined in your objectives. With a defined target audience, the entire business can work together. Which brings me back to my previous point about branding and messaging in Pitfall 4 – this will be consistent and focused on the needs of each segment/persona. This is also important in ensuring that the marketing tactics you are using are where that target audience is too. Remember – the focus should always be on the customer.

There are tools available such as automation to help support the marketing and sales teams effort, to increase efficiency. The time spent creating those automated journeys saves hours in the future and ultimately, by sending the message to the right person at the optimal time, achieves better results than if it was sent manually.

Pitfall 8: Failure to plan

The challenge of going from ad hoc marketing to a strategically planned approach

There are several challenges to overcome when adjusting from an ad hoc reactive marketing approach to a strategically planned one. This switch doesn't necessarily mean that you can't react at short notice. The switch is in the approach to clear objectives and outcomes. When marketing is constantly ad hoc and doesn't contain any overarching long-term focus or any form of plan, objectives or focus, the results of success and even what resembles success become very unclear. Communication between the marketing team and the rest of the business typically starts to wear down. It can appear externally that the marketing activity is veering off on its own and is not connected to the rest of the business. And I'll be honest: it can wear a marketing team out, not sure what the next day will bring, not having any form of a plan or roadmap as guidance. The constant day-to-day instant 'launches' mean that inconsistencies start to creep in as time is cut shorter and shorter. I've also witnessed it cause inefficiencies as there will typically be a lack of process, a lack of clear steps to follow. When more and more people are added to that mix, it becomes chaotic, unstructured, with unclear responsibilities. This all leads to a leaking bucket where multiple areas are either not focused on at all or forgotten in the constant cycle of ad hoc activity.

Ad hoc marketing activity often occurs when a director in the organization has an idea and insists that the marketing team see it through. The request is to do so quickly, regardless of what else is taking place. The more of this that takes place the more and more ad hoc the marketing activity becomes.

Thankfully, I'm here to help you overcome this challenge! Many times, I have been tasked as a consultant with the brief to 'fix marketing'. This can mean many things, but in the most part it is where the team is seen by the rest of the business to be underperforming, so I immediately seek to uncover the root of the problem. Nine times out of 10, it is because there is a lack of strategic planning. If each day the task you're being asked to do is new, different, unstructured and uninformed, it will start to have an impact. Of course, as marketers, it's our role to seek new ways to engage an audience, but that should be done in an informed manner as we have explored throughout this book. It may be that the direction of the organization has changed and that could impact the long-term marketing plans, but it shouldn't be affecting every day and every week because if it does, then that means marketing has gone from one having a plan to not having one at all.

The first step to overcoming changes to the direction of the organization or a difference in the target market is to determine what in the marketing activity is no longer going to be fit for that new purpose. Do the objectives set need to be adjusted? They most likely will require a tweak, and if is a complete change to what the organization now provides then this may need a complete overhaul. Either way, it doesn't mean objectives are no longer required, because they remain vital.

How to introduce and create a plan

It won't be possible to start strategizing straight away; there may not be the team structure to support the change, and the most significant barrier of all will be the initial lack of buy-in when transitioning.

Start by adding a structure and action plan around the current ad hoc activity by pinning down themes for the marketing activity. This will start to bring in structure and planning. For example, if you already know what is engaging your audience from the current ad hoc activity, is there a particular topic that is resonating the most? Use that as the stimulus to build a theme around, as covered in Chapter 7.

Develop a plan even if that initially means progressing from a daily to a weekly schedule – that is a big step forward! Once there is a weekly plan of activity in place, translate it into a two-week plan and then develop that into a month-long programme. As everyone in the marketing team is actioning the new longer plan, there will be processes that will need to be defined to increase efficiency and maintain consistency.

Map out how to communicate with external agencies. Is there, for example, a central place where all documents are stored, such as a system on the cloud?

How do you brief copywriters, designers, event organizations, internal teams and so on? Are these tasks repeated regularly? If they are, consider creating a briefing template. This will not only save time; it will ensure you receive all of the information you need in the correct formats consistently each time. This reduces the need for 'last-minute' items because there's time to plan in the development of the template.

The other area to try to streamline is communication. There are a vast number of platforms to use for communication now and sending the same message across all is time-consuming, especially if that same communication needs to be repeated to various teams and suppliers. Can a group channel be created or a group email address to keep everyone that needs to be updated in the loop?

Once the above is actioned, you'll start to very quickly see the efficiency in marketing increase. This then frees up time to start with the S in STRATEGY. As you move through the situational analysis, conduct a SWOT on the internal organization and another on the marketing team and activity itself. Identify the strengths that are helping you succeed, and the weaknesses that are holding the activity and the team back. What opportunities are there to improve, do more, test or continue with, and what are the threats that are or could impact marketing's success?

This is useful for everyone in the marketing department. A great way to build a case to the rest of the business to support the changes being made.

The rest of S-TRATEGY can then be progressed through, each part building a more strategically focused marketing plan and activity. If there are findings and discoveries in each section, these can be implemented but remember to plan this in. This is how you start to build a long-term plan shifting from a day-to-day to an ad hoc one.

This will take some time to transition. From my experience, it can take between five and eight months depending on the internal stakeholder's buy-in and whether there are structural team changes needed. But it will be worth it! It will improve the performance and efficiency of your marketing activity almost instantly, along with the value it brings your company.

The tactics are defined: we have our strategy

During my time in marketing, I have repeatedly faced this challenge. When I worked in the marketing team for brands, I wouldn't be briefed on the broader strategic picture but only on the tactical activity. There is value in understanding the overarching objectives, the ambitions of the business. Based on that information, there may have been recommendations I could have made.

I've also experienced this as a consultant. I've often received a brief that didn't contain much detail in the way of objectives and strategic planning but a lot in the way particular tactics should be used, and this links back to

Mark Ritson's experience as detailed at the beginning of this book. This has been the primary stimulus for writing this book – to help marketers, business owners and students in identifying when the strategic element is missing and providing a framework to build strategy in a straightforward way. As we've uncovered from Chapters 1 to 9, the tactical part of a marketing strategy has a place, but it is one part; there are seven other parts and four elements before tactics that should inform the decisions made when approaching that fifth stage.

What can you do to overcome this particular challenge? You may likely find yourself in this position when the copy and design for an email campaign are completed, but there aren't any clear objectives to identify why the campaign was being created in the first place. That's not to say that sending that email campaign isn't the right tactic to use, it may well be, but how can you be sure if there aren't any clear goals? This starts to become a sticking point when the campaign has been sent, and you're reviewing the results. Without an objective, how can success be determined? Was it good or bad? Without a reference point to refer back to, it's anyone's guess. This then relies heavily on benchmark data and past performance. Both of these provide guidance, but when it comes to the next round of budgetary conversations, how can tactics without clear goals be driving value to the business? Throughout this book, each stage is clearly determined: identifying the situation the organization is operating in, its vision, the personalities of the target customer and then the tactics that are going to not only engage that audience but also perform, and in this way the organization's objectives can be achieved. Jumping straight to tactics is the No 1 reason many marketers campaigns fail. They become ill-informed, untargeted and unfocused.

How can you determine that the other steps in STRATEGY are missing? Review if there are clear objectives – not ones that are individual goals for each tactic but the overall activity. Is there an identified plan? Do you have information about the target persona and industry insights to understand the full context that the activity would be operating in? What are the performance metrics and targets? If any of these parts are missing, part of STRATEGY is missing. Each element has a vital role to play and, just like a jigsaw puzzle, the full image isn't visible without all of the pieces in place.

If you find yourself in this position, take a step back and question the value that particular tactical activity is going to bring. It may be that you find yourself short on time, but there is still an opportunity to research the audience. While it may not be a full strategy, some research and insights can inform the tactical activity even if it's at short notice. Communicate those learnings with the broader business as there will be value in those discoveries which will, in turn, help others to see the value a strategic approach has not only to marketing but also to the rest of the company. To avoid this for future campaigns, review the approach from Pitfall 9 as the likelihood is that this is heavily ad hoc activity too.

Pitfall 9: Missing milestones

You have a strategy but with no clear goals

Well, I'm sorry to say it, but that isn't a strategy. If you think you have a strategy, but it's one that doesn't include any milestones or objectives and isn't aligned to your business objectives as a whole, it's merely an indicative plan. Let's not forget the first T in STRATEGY, which means Target. This is where the desired destination, ambition is defined in the objectives that are set. If this stage is missed, then you're missing that T in strategy.

Creating a plan is a great start but, without aligning it to your organization's objectives, you can trot along your planned path as much as you want, but it's unlikely to achieve anything. Your objectives are essential because they will outline how you can achieve the goals you've set your sights on. Remember – SCALE objectives: Strategic, Considered, Audience, Leverage and End.

It's important to be clear within your objectives, so that everyone in the organization understands their overall purpose and how their input feeds towards that purpose. This retains enthusiasm and motivation, ensuring that everyone within the company is working together in the same direction.

Pitfall 10: Poor people management

The right strategy is in place, but the wrong people are executing it. People are featured in the 7Ps, an essential element of the marketing mix and one that can complement or hinder the success of a marketing strategy. Let's explore why.

The people executing the marketing strategy must be motivated. Motivation can suffer due to Pitfalls 1 and 2. There is also the importance of the structure that supports People, as covered in Pitfall 3. But the wrong people in the wrong jobs can be a pitfall in its own right. I've experienced this on several occasions in situations where the direction of the business has changed but people have not changed with it. There is also the challenge of potentially unmotivated team members if an ad hoc plan has been in play as covered in Pitfall 8. Unmotivated team members can very quickly erode the company's culture.

The starting point here would be to conduct a SWOT (as covered in Chapter 2) of the team members. What are the strengths, weaknesses, opportunities and threats within the team? Within the threats, gaps could highlight that a particular skill set or experience is missing. This would indicate training requirements, or a need to use an external agency to fill those gaps. Or it could be that roles and responsibilities need to change entirely to fulfil the structure (both existing and new) depending on the changes taking place within the organization. If the company is moving from an ad hoc plan to a strategic one, more experienced team members may be required to steer the company in the new direction. Budgets also play an essential part.

The energy to pursue and keep learning is a vital one in marketing. It's important to keep up to date and stay ahead in the latest trends and techniques, and to be continually researching and aligning efforts to the change in consumers' expectations. Marketers who keep their finger on the pulse by researching, exploring, investigating and discussing new and existing topics in marketing are those that will become experienced and leant on in their organization. There never becomes a moment to stop learning, because to do so will quickly mean that person soon becomes out of touch. Experience is important, but the willingness to learn is an attitude that will overcome any gaps in knowledge because that person will fill those gaps quickly. This attitude is also contagious to other team members who will be inspired.

Summary

- We've identified the 10 most common pitfalls that marketers face.
- We've explored the approaches to take to overcome the pitfalls.
- We've discovered examples of how to recognize each pitfall in the future so you have the awareness and techniques at hand.

Closing thought

As I write my closing statement in conclusion of our journey together in this book, I think about how you, the reader, can have an impact on the future of marketing where strategy is at the very heart of every campaign.

In this future, strategy always comes first. It informs every decision made. Ideas are embraced with open arms but always with the core focus on satisfying the needs and wants of the target consumer.

I also think about your potential to inspire your community, company, classroom or organization with what you have learned. Sharing your expertise with stakeholders, peers, colleagues, friends, family and anyone else with a keen ear to overcome the misconceptions around strategy vs tactics.

If you have successfully completed the tasks throughout the book then you will be aware of the environment in which your organization operates, and its internal situation that has been analysed. The ability to overcome competitors has also been assessed. You've defined marketing objectives aligned with the organization's vision and goals. You now understand the needs and wants of your target customer. You've used this information to identify appropriate tactics, and set KPIs to measure your performance. Finally, you are armed with the 10 most common pitfalls facing marketers, and you know how to overcome them and avoid them. You are equipped with the knowledge and frameworks you need to create award-winning strategies in the future.

Writing this book has been a passion of mine. The lack of focus on strategy and increasing focus on quick-win tactics without a clear plan in the world of marketing has been a constant battle throughout my career and I highly suspect it will be the same for you. My goal in writing this book was to provide a framework that marketers, students and business owners can use to create new and review existing marketing strategies for the better.

For any tips when creating your next strategy or to discuss training or speaking opportunities, reach out to me using the details in the 'About the Author' section.

I hope this book serves you well at all times as you march into the battle of the marketing world. May it be a great source of inspiration on your future marketing journey.

Reference

Watson, T (2020) EOS Implementer, Traction Six [Interview] 9 October 2020

GLOSSARY

4Cs: An alternative method to the 4Ps created by Lauterborn in 1990. The focus is on targeting niches in a similar way to segmentation, rather than mass markets. The 4Cs focus on understanding what the consumer truly wants from a product or service, and consist of: **Customer, Cost, Communication** and **Convenience.**

4Ps: The original marketing mix: **Price, Place, Promotion** and **Product.**

7Ps: The extended marketing mix from the 4Ps: **Price, Place, Promotion, Product, People, Process** and **Physical Evidence.**

A/B testing: Also known as split testing, this is where two variations of the same thing are tested, eg a website landing page. Option A is tested against option B to see which one performs better based on the goals set.

Above-the-line (ATL): This uses mass media methods. The advantage of using this type of promotion is that it attracts a large audience. The disadvantage is that anyone and everyone would be exposed to marketing, not just the target customer.

Affiliate marketing: Affiliate marketing is based on performance in which an external partner receives a reward, typically a commission for delivering a specific result to a merchant or advertiser. The affiliate searches for a product related to their website/offering, then promotes that product and receives a commission from each sale. The tracking of sales from one website to another takes place through specific links that are created for each affiliate.

Agile project management: The Agile approach is one in which the ability to adapt to changes is vital to the success of the project. The plan is broken down into bi-weekly sprints and each sprint has a set of tasks that need to be completed. While this approach would not be the most suitable for many marketing campaigns, the ability to respond to change is a principle that should feature heavily and be catered for.

AIDA model: A useful model to plan out the customer journey and to map the different messaging at each stage. AIDA stands for **Attention, Interest, Desire** and **Action.**

Amplification rate (AR): Measures the shares, retweets, repins and regrams your following has given your social media activity.

Artificial intelligence (AI): The theory and development of computer systems able to perform tasks that normally require human intelligence, eg visual perception or language processing.

Audience growth: A useful KPI if an objective is to increase your social media following. This can be measured on a weekly, monthly, quarterly and annual basis. The total number of new followers are counted for the specified time period.

Augmented product model: Breaks down a product into three levels. Each 'level' provides marketers with an opportunity to identify the core benefits customers would gain. This model is particularly useful to ensure that product design focuses not only on practical elements but also on the benefits to the customer.

Automation: This is where technology fulfils a task without human intervention. For example, an order confirmation email is automatically sent after an order has been made using automation technology.

Average engagement rate (AER): Measures how many likes, comments and shares your social media activity is getting relevant to your total number of followers.

Average order value (AOV): The total number of sales divided by the total number of orders. You may have a target in mind for this to benchmark against, and it's an important metric when gauging profit margins. If your company also provides offline ordering options, you could compare online and offline AOVs.

Average position (AP): Measures how prominently the customer sees your ad, and its position in the search feed.

Basket/cart abandonment rate: Measures the number of people who showed a desire to purchase by adding items to their basket but then didn't complete their order.

Below-the-line (BTL): Promotion methods the company can control, eg in-store offers and direct selling. Smaller audiences are reached through targeted advertising. The advantage of using BTL promotion is that the company has more control and can target specific groups of customers. This enables marketers to be more efficient in the budget being spent.

Bounces: Bounce rates are useful for keeping lists clean and for tracking deliverability. When an email is undelivered, it has 'bounced'. If a high number of emails bounce it could lower your sender reputation and highlight an issue in the quality of the database. There are two types of bounces: a hard bounce or a soft bounce.

Brand audit: To determine the health of your brand, a brand audit is a useful exercise. The brand audit can identify where brands may need more support, brands that aren't adding any value or those that require changes to be made in areas such as positioning or to suit changing customer preferences.

Brand guidelines: Documents like this are hugely useful for keeping all marketers and contractors on the same page. Creating comprehensive and consistent brand guidelines should involve all stakeholders. You need your instructions to cover everything from your voice to the way you represent your products/services, and the visual 'feel' of your brand. This will include the colour representation of your brand with pantone numbers.

Brand: A brand is how a person perceives and identifies an organization or person (if it's their personal brand). This perception can be influenced with branding elements, such as logos, a specific slogan/strapline, designs, symbols and (most importantly) the feelings which the products or services evoke. A brand is more than a product or service; it is the combination of all of these elements. Together, branding elements portray the core message of the company.

Budget attainment (BA): A particularly useful metric when assessing how well campaigns are being managed. If there is an agency operating your pay-per-click (PPC) activity, this metric is suitable for indicating how close they came to achieving the budget they set out to use. If there is a big difference or maybe a vast overspend, this might merit further investigation.

Business-to-business (B2B): Transactions made between businesses.

Business-to-consumer (B2C): The business sells directly to the consumer.

California Consumer Privacy Act (CCPA): This legislation provides consumers with more control over the personal information that businesses collect.

Call tracking: Different phone numbers are used for each tactical activity (eg one phone number for print, another for radio ads, etc). With phone tracking software, any calls received to those specific numbers are then tracked and the cost per sale can also be calculated for any conversions made over the phone.

Chartered Institute of Marketing (CIM): Marketing body.

Clicks: The usefulness of this metric depends on the number (if any) of clickable links within an email. When a recipient clicks on content within an email, that demonstrates an interest in that particular content, making it a useful metric for measuring engagement.

Click-through rate (CTR): Used to analyse the performance of a marketing campaign. It analyses the number of clicks an ad campaign has generated. This shows whether or not your campaign is heading in the right direction. If you have previous data to compare against, you can use this as benchmarks to strive towards.

Click-to-open rate (CTOR): Potentially the most useful metric for measuring subscriber interactions. It tracks clicks in tandem with opens. The CTOR metric can tell marketers how many readers close an email immediately after opening it, how many continue to read, how many click-throughs and so on. It's good for assessing engagement at a glance.

Close rate (CR): Measuring the number of prospects that become customers in comparison to the number of leads in the pipeline.

Comment conversion rate (CCR): A useful metric for understanding how many followers comment after reading a post. It's also important to add context here as not every comment is positive.

COMPETE framework: When analysing competitors, COMPETE provides a structure that ensures all the bases are covered. Focusing on **Current operators, Offering, Market share, Price, Expertise, Target** and **Employees.** The analysis included in COMPETE provides a complete overview of your competitors and the marketplace that you're competing in. By analysing your competitors' offering and the marketplace, you'll be more aware of your organization's challenges, the opportunities in the marketplace and competitors to keep a close eye on.

Competitive advantage: Where a company outperforms its competitors and in doing so gains an advantage.

Consumer-to-consumer (C2C): Sales from customers to customers, eg eBay.

Content downloads: A useful KPI for understanding the number of downloads of whitepapers, guides, videos, etc. A download demonstrates that the visitor is engaged with the company and that the content is resonating well with them. A high download rate indicates that your content and targeting are landing well with your audience.

Content marketing: Content can take many forms such as videos, blogs, infographics, podcasts, whitepapers, leaflets, emails, books, press releases and much more. Content marketing has evolved from traditionally printed content to digital marketing and electronic formats. Used across all marketing channels and tactics, it's an important area to optimize.

Conversion rate (CR): Any piece of campaign content has a goal. The conversion rate indicates the extent to which it achieves its goal; eg if the goal is to get customers to click through to the website, a high click-through rate will double as a high conversion rate.

Cost per acquisition (CPA): Cost per acquisition measures the marketing costs (which may be your email marketing costs) + sales costs / number of conversions. This determines how much it costs the company to acquire a new customer.

Cost per click (CPC): A metric to understand the cost of each click. You'll have a budget assigned to your PPC activity, so it's essential to understand how much each click is costing and whether it is affordable within your budget. Depending on the competitiveness for those specific search terms, the quality of your ads and the targeting applied will all impact the cost of each click. A bid budget will be determined within your paid advertising account, but that doesn't mean that this will be the final cost.

Cost per thousand impressions (CPM): The amount that is paid after 1,000 people scroll past your sponsored content. This is not a useful metric for measuring how effective an ad is, so should not be used in isolation.

CR by referral source: Identifying which referral channel is converting at the highest rate is a handy metric for marketing planning, adjusting campaigns and budgets if there is a particular channel or tactic that is outperforming others.

Customer journey: The stages a customer goes through on their journey with a brand/organization, from awareness of the offering to the stages to making a purchase.

Customer lifetime value (CLTV): Measures the value a customer brings for the duration of them being a customer. The calculation is based on the average purchase value, the average frequency of their purchases from the brand and their average customer value.

Customer persona: Creating profiles/personas is a widely used method of getting to know your customers. A customer profile defines your ideal (or targeted) customer by establishing their likes, dislikes, habits, behaviour, where they work, income, etc. They can be known as customer personas or buyer personas (depending on where they are being used in the business) and will add value throughout all departments, not just marketing. Customer personas should be based on market research and insights gathered from existing customers.

Customer relationship management (CRM): A CRM suite is useful for tracking, storing, sorting and analysing customer data. A CRM system securely stores data on all of your leads, prospects, customers and potentially subscribers. Within the software are reports on the stage of the conversion funnel that your leads have reached.

Customer retention rate (CRR): This KPI measures the percentage of customers that are retained for a specific time period, eg a YOY measurement could be made with the timing set at 12 months.

Customer satisfaction score (CSat): This measures the satisfaction a customer has with a business, purchase or interaction.

Data & Marketing Association (DMA): Marketing body.

Delivery rate: This measures the number of emails that have successfully reached the inbox of your recipients. Any that don't reach the inbox have been potentially blocked by ISPs (internet service providers). This is calculated by dividing the number of emails delivered by the total number of emails sent.

Device stats: Knowing the devices upon which users are reading their emails is beneficial. Content will be displayed differently in each device, so it's important to optimize content based on the devices used by your recipients.

Direct mail (DM): Refers to physically printed and posted promotional messages. Direct mailing may involve a 'door drop' campaign in which content is sent directly to the target customers' door. Direct mailing can take several forms, including leaflets, brochures, letters and postcards. Many charities rely on this method of communication if an email address isn't available.

Distribution channels: This is how your offering is made available to your customer, eg direct to the consumer from the producer, indirect from producer to wholesaler to retailer to consumer.

DMA Code of Practice: Sets the standards for the industry to which all DMA members must adhere, in addition to all legal requirements. The Code is an agreement and commitment to always be fair and respectful to customers, understanding that this will also cultivate a profitable and successful commercial ecosystem.

EAIDAL model: Adaptation of the AIDA model with two additional stages: 1) 'Educate', for organizations that are either start-ups or have a new offering in the marketplace. In this scenario the marketplace may need to be educated about the benefit that the offering provides, eg if it is a new type of technology that provides unique functionality that wasn't possible before; 2) 'Loyalty' which is about focusing on ensuring your customers return.

E-commerce: The ability to buy and sell products on the internet. To enable businesses to provide this online service to its customers, an e-commerce store is used. This enables organizations to handle both online marketing and sales activities as well as logistics and fulfilment functions that are required to make an e-commerce store operational.

Email marketing: An electronic method of communicating to an audience known as 'subscribers'. Subscribers can be made up of both customers and non-customers, but both groups will have an interest in the company, the brand and/or its product or service. The term 'email marketing' describes commercial emails that are sent from a company to a prospect or customer. All email marketing should be sent to people who have provided their consent.

General Data Protection Regulation 2018 (GDPR): Legislation on how data can be collected, stored and used.

Goal conversion rate: This is tailored to the company and the objective. A goal could be completing a form, subscribing to the email marketing newsletter, watching a demo video on the website or many other things. Measurement here is focused on the percentage of visitors that go on to complete the goal.

Google Analytics (GA): Online analytical tool.

Hard bounce: A hard bounce is flagging that there is a permanent reason the email could not be delivered (eg the email address doesn't exist).

Impression share (IS): To measure how many impressions your ads are generating.

Impression: When an ad appears in a search or on a social media timeline, this is called an 'impression'.

Internet service providers (ISPs): Such as Gmail, Outlook, Hey mailboxes.

Key performance indicators (KPIs): Metrics that highlight whether the specific activity you're measuring is achieving the goals set. KPIs immediately indicate if a marketing campaign has been a success and whether the tactics at play are achieving the desired results. These insights should be a snapshot. They should be easily identifiable, specific to your business and the marketing campaign, and aligned to your objectives.

Lead form abandonment rate: A KPI which identifies how many visitors start a form but don't finish completing it. If the metric is high, it may be that the form has too many fields to complete or isn't working correctly.

Lead scoring: Lead scoring involves allocating a score based upon activities which the lead/prospect has fulfilled. For example, if a prospect completed a form online, that may equate to a score of 2. If that customer also then subscribed to your email marketing, they receive a score of 3, making it a total of 5. This method enables you to understand more about how your customers 'behave'.

Machine learning (ML): A form of AI where computer-generated outcomes and rules such as recommendations are created based on previous interactions.

Macro factors: External environmental factors that consist of all the outside forces and influences that could affect the organization, eg the economy or current events.

Market research: A useful way to gather information about your target audience and prospects. It will help you to develop customer personas, as well as giving some insights into how successfully your product or service fits your targets' needs. Market research can also help identify who your prospects and customers go to first for information, for more options or to make a purchase.

Marketing channel: The main route taken to promote your offering such as social media and SEO. The way that channel is implemented is the tactical element.

Marketing environment: Made up of the macro (external) and micro (internal) factors in which an organization operates.

Marketing KPIs: These involve interactions (or additional data) from outside your content itself. They can be more complicated to work out, but are essential to indicate how well each channel is contributing to the brand's overall marketing and business objectives.

Marketing mix: An excellent model to use to ensure that your marketing strategy is equally weighted and not overly focused on one area: otherwise known as the 4Ps or the 7Ps.

Marketing plan: A marketing plan is part of a strategy, but is not the whole thing. A marketing plan, rather than being a road map, is an assessment of the terrain you'll be covering. Marketing planning involves looking at the wider context in which your strategy will be operating. A good marketing plan informs the strategist about the state of the market, the competition, what resources are available and how the consumers are feeling.

Marketing qualified lead (MQL): A lead that has been qualified based on specific criteria by marketing as a valuable lead for the organization.

Maslow's Hierarchy of Needs: A five-tiered triangle which demonstrates the position and relative urgency of human needs. The requirements at each level must be satisfied before the person moves up a tier.

Micro factors: Internal environmental factors that directly impact an organization. The micro marketing environment consists of the factors which affect an organization internally, and the resources which help them to respond to these factors, eg team skills, patents, financial stability, reputation or supplier relationships.

Net promoter score (NPS): This measures the likelihood of customers recommending an organization or product.

Objectives: Objectives give a sense of **purpose** and **direction**. They help departments direct their activities towards the same goals in a consistent way. Objectives **motivate** staff to achieve them, particularly if they are tied into performance measures. Objectives give a **benchmark for control** so organizations can assess whether they are meeting the set objectives.

Open rates: The open rate metric measures how many recipients opened your email in comparison to the total number delivered. It's worth noting that simple open trackers often count re-opens as well as initial opens, meaning that a recipient can open the same email multiple times and each click will be counted as an 'open'.

Out-of-home (OOH): Out-of-home advertising is any form of advertising that is promoted to customers outside of their home, such as ad wraps on transport, on benches and billboards. Billboards are the most common form of OOH advertising, and come in many forms, from a traditional poster to ever-changing digital formats, and can be found at roadsides, sides of buildings, shopping centres and bus shelters. The aim of billboards is to grab attention, and due to their size, they can be seen by many, especially in areas of high population.

Pay-per-click (PPC): When you are using a search engine (such as Google or Bing), ads appear at the top of the results and on the right-hand side: this is PPC in action. Brands pay for their ad to appear in search results based on a range of criteria such as specific keywords, location, time of day, day of the week, device and much more.

People: The People factor was added to the extended marketing mix of the 7Ps during the rise of the services industry. It has since become one of the most important elements of the marketing mix. People includes everyone who is involved, either directly or indirectly, in the product or service. Not all of these people will be in contact with customers, but these people all have a role to play in the production, marketing, distribution and delivery of the products or services to the customer.

Perceptual/Positioning map: Used to determine your organization's product or brand positioning is by using a perceptual or positioning map. A perceptual map illustrates consumer perception of the products in your market. This enables you to identify how competitors are positioned in comparison to yourself and allows you to identify any opportunities in the marketplace.

Personal Information Protection and Electronic Documents Act (PIPEDA): Canadian law focused on data privacy.

Personal selling: Personal selling is where the business has representatives who sell directly to consumers. They aim to inform the customer and persuade them to purchase. Typically, personal selling is conducted by sales representatives who communicate the benefits of the product or service to the customer and, while receiving instant feedback, can adapt their approach specifically to their unique prospect.

Personalization: Personalization often starts with the inclusion of a customer's name but it does not end there. As humans we enjoy feeling involved and personalization satisfies that joy. The more that people feel that content is speaking directly to them, the more involved they will feel with it. And the more involved they feel, the more likely they are to engage.

PESTLE: An analytical framework used for understanding the external factors that could impact an organization. It stands for **Political, Economic, Social, Technological, Legal** and **Environmental.**

Physical evidence: The marketing mix is a blend of both physical and psychological factors. For services, don't forget to consider the physical elements. For a hotel, for example, this would include the building, the hotel rooms, the décor, etc. The atmosphere and general feeling when experiencing the service can also contribute towards physical evidence.

Place: The Place factor concerns where or how your product is bought. There is a variety of ways in which a product can be sold, including through intermediaries such as distributors, wholesalers, retailers, or direct to the consumer via your website. Placement is vital to ensure that your product reaches the right target audience at the right time.

Positioning: The approach taken by an organization to market its product or service. When establishing positioning, the image or identity of a brand or product is created for consumers to view it in a certain way. A product or brand's 'position' is the place it occupies in the consumers' minds relative to competitors. It is influenced by the way in which the product is defined by consumers according to important attributes.

Positioning statement: Once you've identified your market and product positioning, a statement can be created to communicate this across the organization. This positioning statement will detail how you want the brand to be perceived by consumers succinctly.

Post reach: For organic social media posts, you can measure the reach of that post.

Post-campaign analysis (PCA): This is vital to understanding what worked and what didn't, to inform future marketing campaigns. A PCA will also help to assess whether the strategy was a success by analysing if it achieved the objectives set.

Price: Pricing should reflect the product's positioning and business objectives. The pricing method used can be influenced by where the product is in its life cycle.

Primary research: First-hand information directly from the target customer. This can be gathered by conducting interviews and surveys where an organization can ask specific questions.

Process: Process is focused on the systems and processes that deliver a product to a customer. It could include the process of making transactions on your website, website design, the process of providing customer service support to your customers.

Product life cycle: The product's life cycle is broken down into four key stages: **Introduction, Growth, Maturity** and **Decline.** Each stage will require a different marketing approach. The price may change as the introductory offer ends and demand grows, the place in which the item is being sold may expand as the product begins to mature in the market and the promotional channels used can vary at each stage too.

Product: The focus here is on creating a product that will satisfy the needs and wants of your target market.

Promotion: Focused on advertising and communicating your product or service to let your target customer know what you're offering.

Public relations (PR): A form of using communications to inform, raise awareness, influence and maintain a positive reputation of an organization. This can be focused on the company, the products/services, employees or showcasing customer success stories.

Quality score (QS): This assesses how relevant your ad content is to the keywords you're bidding on. It is measured by the search engines and includes expected CTR, the landing page experience and so on.

Radio advertising: The promotion of a brand's offering on the radio during the break in broadcasting or as a sponsored partnership with a particular show.

Response rate (RR): Calculates the percentage of a mailing list who responded to the direct mail through any tracked methods, either by calling the phone number, using the specific URL or discount/coupon code that are unique for the campaign.

Return on investment (ROI): Measures how cost-effective a particular channel was in a campaign. It is a useful metric when comparing each channel's performance, but may not always be relevant.

Sales qualified lead (SQL): This type of lead has been qualified by the sales team as a valuable prospect that fits the profile of the target customer.

SCALE framework: An acronym that describes each aspect of an objective. SCALE objectives include all of the key elements which help you to align your marketing objectives to your organization's goals: **Strategic, Considered, Audience, Lift** and **End.**

Search engine optimization (SEO): The focus of SEO is to ensure that the content on your website is optimized to appear in the results when relevant search terms are entered into a search engine.

Search ranking: Measures where your website appears in the results, and also the keywords/search terms.

Search visibility: Measures how many times your domain has shown in the search results for the keywords the site is ranking for.

Secondary research: Public record information such as trend reports, sales data available within your organization and industry content. This research is useful when analysing competitors.

Segmentation, targeting and positioning (STP): *See individual items*

Segmentation: A useful way of splitting up a broad target audience into smaller groups with similarities, such as segments in an orange. Each segment is separate from the others, but they are all part of the whole, and are all suitable prospects for your product/service.

Social media: A way to connect with your audience to build your brand, increase sales and drive website traffic. Content is published in a variety of formats on the social media platforms to engage audiences, and discussions take place to listen to and to partake in. Advertisements can also be promoted on the platforms and results of both organic and paid-for content can be analysed.

Social share of voice (SSoV): Comparing how many people mentioned your brand name in comparison to the competition is a useful KPI. The same can also be measured to identify if your product/service or the campaign hashtag is being mentioned on social media.

Soft bounce: Highlighting that there is a temporary reason that the email cannot be delivered, eg the inbox may be full.

Software as a service (SaaS): A software licensing and delivery model in which software is licensed on a subscription basis and is centrally hosted. It is sometimes referred to as 'on-demand software'.

SOSTAC®: A planning model developed by PR Smith which breaks down the six key stages in marketing planning.

Spam score: Not to be confused with the bounce rate, a campaign's spam score will indicate just how much value customers are getting from the campaign content. A high spam score shows that they're not impressed with what they're receiving and are flagging your email as spam.

Statistical significance: This is important when determining a result based on the amount of data available and its reliability in that same result being repeated.

Strapline: Straplines should embody your brand's voice while clearly summarizing what you do.

STRATEGY framework: A way to break down all of the key components that are included in a marketing strategy. Those parts are: **Scenario, Targets, Reach, Awareness, Tactics, Execution, Generate** and **Yield.**

Strategy: The map which takes you to your destination. Strategy is the 'who, what, where, when and why'. A strategy is an overarching plan by which you hope to achieve your vision.

SWOT: A simple but useful framework for analysing an organization's **strengths** and **weaknesses,** as well as the **opportunities** and **threats** that it faces. It helps focus on strengths, minimize threats and take the greatest possible advantage of opportunities available.

SWOTELL: Adds the marketing-specific focus to the SWOT. While the SWOT focuses on the situation as it is in the present, when combined with the SWOTELL the focus is more action-based. This model is useful to add further actionable areas when assessing where the business needs to make strategic preparations. The ELL are purely marketing focused and remain aligned to the specific organization but also incorporate external perception, such as engagement, to determine what's currently **effective,** the **limitations** being faced and what is available to **leverage** and enhance further.

Tactics: Work hand in hand with strategy. Tactics determine the 'how' of a campaign. The 'how' should never be established before the who, what, when, where and why. The tactics are the vehicles you use to get to the destination of your strategy.

Targeting: Once customer segments have been defined, the next step is targeting. The purpose here is to not target 'everyone' with the same message but to define the target group by identifying and understanding a particular niche. It's by understanding more about target customers that they can be targeted with relevant content, messaging and advertising that will appeal to them.

Tone of voice (ToV): 'Voice' and 'tone' are closely related but different concepts. In everyday life, you generally use the same 'voice' which sounds roughly the same all the time, and which is recognizable and unique to you. 'Tone' will differ, depending on the circumstances.

Trade shows/Exhibitions: Trade shows and exhibitions (also known as Expos) provide excellent opportunities for brands to showcase their product or service offering within a specific industry. Typically, they are more prominently used in B2B industries where attendees are within a particular industry and are ideally at the point of purchasing or searching for a new product/service. They are an opportunity for a company to showcase their expertise and knowledge about a particular topic, with stages available for speakers to present their ideas.

TV advertising: Advertising on television is typically for a slot of 30 seconds, but can be anything between 10 to 60 seconds or longer. They feature within the 'break' of a television programme or before/after the start of the next showing.

Uniform resource locator (URL): A web address.

Unsubscribes: Tracking subscription rates is important for understanding how well a brand's reputation is doing, and how good that brand is at maintaining relationships with customers. There are lots of reasons for unsubscribing to email marketing, but a peak indicates that there is an issue that needs to be resolved.

Urchin tracking module (UTM): Distinct parameters that can be added to a URL to track every piece of your marketing campaign. Within the URL builder you can add the campaign source, medium, etc to track specific campaign activity in Google Analytics (GA).

Virality rate (VR): A KPI that measures the rate at which social media posts go viral. This KPI should not be the only one measured, as it might not have a strategic objective linked to it.

Vision: A strategy needs to contain focus, have a clear direction to take the company where it wants to get to. This is where the vision comes in. A vision should clearly articulate what the business is aiming to achieve.

VRIO framework: A model that helps to ensure that the strategy you have created actually can be implemented. VRIO stands for: **Value, Rarity, Imitability** and **Organization.** The VRIO framework can be applied across the organization or to individual departments. It provides a solid perspective on each area of the business and how it should position itself in the marketplace. Capabilities and resources change over time, so the framework should be used regularly.

Waterfall project management: Waterfall is more robust than Agile, in that there is a concrete plan with less opportunity for things to drop in and out. There is a clear process to follow, similar to that of defining a marketing strategy, and then there is a sprint-to-release process to follow. The downside is that there is little room to adjust the plan if a new requirement or a market change happens while the plan is underway. To include this in the plan, it would need to wait until the end, and by then it could be too late.

Website analytics: By tracking your website performance, you can measure visits to your website, the marketing tactic which drew them there, the location from which they're visiting, how long your visitors are spending on your website, the pages they've visited and the products they've purchased. This will give you considerable insight into the tactics that are driving the most visits, clicks and purchases on your website: enabling you to optimize your campaigns around the highest-performing tactics.

FURTHER RESOURCES

In addition to the tools and resources mentioned throughout this book, here are further marketing resources, Twitter accounts, books and research sources to be explored.

Marketing associations

American Marketing Association (AMA): www.ama.org
Chartered Institute of Marketing (CIM): exchange.cim.co.uk/blog/
Data & Marketing Association (DMA): dma.org.uk/
Interactive Advertising Bureau (IAB) Europe: iabeurope.eu
Information Commissioner's Office (ICO): ico.org.uk
Internet Advertising Bureau (IAB): www.iabuk.com
Institute for Public Relations (IPR): instituteforpr.org
Institute for Direct and Digital Marketing (IDM): www.theidm.com
Institute for Practitioners in Advertising (IPA): ipa.co.uk

Marketing resources

Advertising Age: adage.com
Digital Doughnut: www.digitaldoughnut.com
Econsultancy: econsultancy.com
Let'sTalk Strategy: www.letstalkstrategy.co.uk
Mailchimp: mailchimp.com/resources
Marketing Week Magazine: www.marketingweek.com
Smart Insights: www.smartinsights.com
TED: www.ted.com/talks
The Drum: www.thedrum.com

Email marketing focused websites, inspiration and tools

Action Rocket: www.actionrocket.co
All Things Email: Allthingsemail.co.uk
Email on Acid: www.emailonacid.com
Hubspot: blog.hubspot.com
Kickbox: blog.kickbox.com

Kickdynamic: www.kickdynamic.com
Movable Ink: movableink.com
Only Influencers: www.onlyinfluencers.com
Phrasee: phrasee.co
Really Good Emails: reallygoodemails.com
SparkPost: www.sparkpost.com
Webbula: webbula.com

Social media blogs for the latest tips, guides and news

Brandwatch: www.brandwatch.com/blog/
Buffer: buffer.com/resources/
Copyblogger: copyblogger.com/copywriting-101/
Social Fresh: www.socialfresh.com
Social Media Examiner: www.socialmediaexaminer.com
Social Media Explorer: socialmediaexplorer.com
Socialmention: www.socialmention.com
Sprout Social: sproutsocial.com/insights/

Search resources and tools

Ahrefs: ahrefs.com
BuzzStream: www.buzzstream.com
Marie Hayes: www.mariehaynes.com/blog/
Moz: moz.com/blog
Search Engine Journal: www.searchenginejournal.com
Search Engine Land: searchengineland.com
Seer Interactive: www.seerinteractive.com/blog/
SEMrush: www.semrush.com
Yoast: yoast.com/seo-blog/

Research resources

Alexa: try.alexa.com/marketing-stack/audience-overlap-tool
Forrester's website: go.forrester.com/
Gartner's website: www.gartner.com/en
Global Digital Report: digitalreport.wearesocial.com/download
GlobalWebIndex: www.globalwebindex.com
Google Trends: trends.google.com/trends/
MarketResearch.com: www.marketresearch.com/

Mintel: www.mintel.com
Ofcom: Adult Media Consumption and Behaviour Reports: www.ofcom.org.uk
Statista: www.statista.com
Pew Research Center: www.pewresearch.org
Profound: www.profound.com/
The Market Research Society: www.mrs.org.uk
UK Office for National Statistics (ONS): www.gov.uk/search/research-and-statistics
US Census Bureau: www.census.gov/data/data-tools.html
World Advertising Research Centre (WARC): www.warc.com/

Books

Atherton, J (2020) *Social Media Strategy: A practical guide to social media marketing and customer engagement*, Kogan Page, London – Social media

Blanks, K and Jesson, B (2017) *Making Websites Win: Apply the customer-centric methodology that has doubled the sales of many leading websites*, Publishing in a Box – Conversion rate experts, for optimizing your website

Dunford, A (2019) *Obviously Awesome: How to nail product positioning so customers get it, buy it, love it,* Ambient Press, Swadlingcote – All things about positioning effectively

Godin, S (2012) *All Marketers are Liars: The underground classic that explains how marketing really works – and why authenticity is the best marketing of all,* reprint edn, Portfolio, New York – The art of storytelling

Handley, A (2014) *Everybody Writes: Your go-to guide to creating ridiculously good content*, Wiley, Hoboken, NJ – Perfect for content writing inspiration, tips and guidance

Nahai, N (2017) *Webs of Influence: The psychology of online persuasion*, 2nd edn, Pearson, London – Business consumer psychology

Newton, R (2016) *Project Management Step by Step: How to plan and manage a highly successful project*, 2nd edn, Pearson, London – Project Management

O'Neil, K (2016) *Pixels and Place: Connecting human experience across physical and digital spaces,* KO Insights New York – Focusing on creating a connected customer experience

Perkin, N and Abraham, P (2017) Building the Agile business through digital transformation, Kogan Page, London – Digital transformation

Perreault Jr, WD (2004) *Basic Marketing*, McGraw-Hill Higher Education, New York – To dig deeper into the 4Ps of marketing

Sleight, S (2000) *Managing Budgets (Essential Managers)*, DK, London

White, C (2017) *Email Marketing Rules: Checklists, Frameworks, and 150 Best Practices for Business Success*, 3rd edn, CreateSpace Independent Publishing Platform, Seattle – Email marketing

Twitter feeds to follow

Ann Handley: twitter.com/MarketingProfs
April Dunford: twitter.com/aprildunford
Campaign: Brands: www.twitter.com/CampaignBrands
CIM: www.twitter.com/CIMinfo
DMA: twitter.com/DMA_UK
Kate O'Neil: twitter.com/kateo
Marketing Week: www.twitter.com/MarketingWeekEd
Rand Fishkin: twitter.com/randfish
The Drum: www.twitter.com/TheDrum

INDEX

ACKNOWLEDGEMENTS

A huge thank you to everyone that has taken time out to review and contribute to this book: Dan Barker, Mark Ritson, Kevin Dunckley, Steve Kemish, James Delves, Robert Hancock, Catherine Loftus, Tim Bond, Michele Gettins, Henk-Frits Verkerk, Neil Hopkins, Victoria Peppiatt, Jono Alderson, Sara Meikle, Ade Lewis, Alicia Farrell, Heather Sheppard, Laura Whiting, Charlie Gibson, Tim Watson, Dr Dave Chaffey. I couldn't have done without your personal input and support.

Thank you to the team at Kogan Page for your expertise in getting the book on shelves and in online bookstores globally.

And a special thanks to my husband, Dan, who is always there to support me in everything I do, from my initial idea three years ago to helping me proofread the final pages in the early hours before printing. Constantly encouraging me that anything is possible with our two crazy pups Archie and Hugo. I dedicate this book to our soon-to-be new edition to our family, who was part of this journey right to the end!

CPSIA information can be obtained
at www.ICGtesting.com
Printed in the USA
JSHW062348070922
30224JS00008B/523